essential

ORGANIZE YOUR HOME

essential

ORGANIZE YOUR HOME

Everything You Need to Make Over Your
Living Space—Room by Room

Jason Rich

Adams Media
Avon, Massachusetts

To Emily Bendremer

Published by Adams Media, an F+W Publications Company
57 Littlefield Street, Avon, MA 02322. U.S.A
www.adamsmedia.com

ISBN: 1-59869-073-6
Printed by KHL Printing Co Pte Ltd, in Singapore.

J I H G F E D C B A

Illustrations by Barry Littmann.

Previously published as The Everything® Organize Your Home Book
Copyright ©2002, F+W Publications, Inc.

Acknowledgments

Thanks to Bob Adams, Pam Liflander, Allison Carpenter, and everyone at Adams Media. Thanks also to friends Mark Giordani, Ellen Bendremer, and Ferras AlQaisi, and a special thanks to my family.

Contents

Introduction

Do you find yourself surrounded by piles and piles of clutter? Does your home suffer from a lack of adequate storage space for all of your belongings? Do you feel like you're always disorganized, unable to find what you're looking for? Are areas of your home outdated and in need of renovation in order to make your living space more functional? Whether you're a full-time student, a homemaker, a full-time worker, or a retiree, chances are that by the time you're done meeting all of your personal and professional obligations, you have little time and energy left to focus on creating a more comfortable, well-organized living environment for yourself. You're not alone in the predicament, but many people have discovered that by taking an assertive approach to becoming more organized, the day-to-day stress in their lives is greatly reduced. They ultimately have more free time, and their overall productivity is greatly enhanced.

So, what does it take to become a well-organized individual? For starters, it takes internal desire, dedication, and commitment on your part. This book walks you through strategies and tips for becoming more organized and creating a better living environment for yourself. The purpose of this book is to help you take charge of various aspects of your life, creating a comfortable, well-organized home for yourself and the people you live with. Whether you live in a single-family home, studio apartment, condominium, or yacht or RV, the organizational strategies in this book will help you evaluate your living space, determine your needs, organize your belongings, and create a more comfortable and functional home for yourself.

Each chapter of this book focuses on a different room or area of your home. This book offers design and remodeling tips, tips for organizing each room or area, and strategies for making your living space more functional. Perhaps best of all, this book also suggests specific steps you can take and products you can use, no matter what type of budget you're on. For example, you can easily spend $3,000 or more to hire a professional closet/home organizer to design and custom-build a closet organizer for you. But you can also take a trip to your local home improvement or hardware store and achieve similar results for anywhere between $50 and $500 per closet.

Being an organized person isn't necessarily a skill you're born with, but you can learn it. Likewise, whether or not you consider yourself to be a neat freak, by reading this book, you'll discover quick and easy strategies for keeping your home clean and comfortable. While this book isn't meant to be about interior design or decorating, some of the chapters offer detailed tips for buying furniture and appliances. To develop a truly organized home, you want to ensure that the furniture and appliances you choose properly utilize the space they take up and that you get the maximum amount of function (in addition to visual appeal and comfort) from each item. For example, if you're going to invest money in a new couch for the living area, should you consider purchasing a sofa bed so that your living area can double as a guest room when you have guests? This is the type of question this book helps you answer as you embark on organizing your home.

Virtually everyone is surrounded by clutter. Clutter can take on many different forms and manifest itself in an abundance of ways within your home. One of the goals of this book is to help you greatly reduce or totally eliminate the clutter in your home and show you how to avoid creating new clutter. After all, if you invest a lot of time and money to redesign and reorganize your home without modifying your personal living habits, you'll create new clutter and will soon be in the same disorganized, clutter-filled situation you're in now.

Utilizing the organizational tools and strategies in this book may take some discipline at first. Pretty soon, however, you'll get into the habit of organizing and keeping clutter to a minimum without even thinking about it.

CHAPTER 1

Clearing Out Clutter

This chapter helps you figure out how to start organizing your home. You begin by taking inventory of the clutter in your home, and then break your home down into small areas that you can tackle in a few hours or a day. Finally, you begin to clear out the clutter in each area of your home. (To clear out clutter, you must throw out, sell, or donate anything you no longer want or need.)

Evaluating Your Living Space

Before you begin exploring each area of your home to develop a plan to redesign or reorganize it, spend a few minutes evaluating your living space as it is right now. As you do this, complete the following questionnaire:

What do you like the most about your current living space?

_____

_____

_____

_____

How would you rate the cleanliness of your living space? (Choose one.)

❑ Disgustingly dirty and unsanitary
❑ Totally unorganized and filled with clutter
❑ Sanitary and comfortable, but needs improvement
❑ Totally organized, highly functional, and comfortable

In terms of physical space, how would you rate your home currently? (Check all that apply.)

❑ Way too small and cluttered
❑ A decent size, but cluttered
❑ Just the right size for my needs
❑ In need of an overhaul
❑ Lacking storage space
❑ Too dirty
❑ Highly impractical and uncomfortable
❑ Outdated
❑ Too large

What do you like the least about your living space?

_____

_____

_____

_____

What improvements would you like to make to your home? Do certain areas need to be repaired, updated, renovated, or remodeled?

_____

_____

_____

_____

Based on the physical space available in your home, does your furniture and décor provide you with the maximum level of functionality and comfort? How could you better utilize the space within your home?

_____

_____

_____

_____

What are your living habits in each room of your home? Take a tour of your home, one room at a time, and create a list of the primary activities you do in each of the rooms/areas (using **TABLE 1-1**). For example, your kitchen may be a place for cooking, eating, reading, paying bills, using the computer, talking on the telephone, and/or watching television. Make sure you consider how other members of your household use each room or area as well.

TABLE 1-1

PRIMARY USES OF EACH ROOM IN YOUR HOUSE	
ROOM	PRIMARY ACTIVITIES AND USES FOR ROOM/AREA
Kitchen	
Dining area	
Living area	
Family room	
Master bathroom	
Other bathroom(s)	
Master bedroom	
Guest bedroom	
Children's bedroom	
Children's playroom	

PRIMARY USES OF EACH ROOM IN YOUR HOUSE (continued)	
ROOM	PRIMARY ACTIVITIES AND USES FOR ROOM/AREA
Home office	
Laundry area	
Closets	
Basement	
Attic	
Garage	
Backyard/shed	

As you walk through your home, pinpoint the areas that contain the most disorganization and clutter (using **TABLE 1-2**). On a scale of one to five, with five being the most disorganized and filled with clutter, rate each room or area of your home:

TABLE 1-2

AREAS OF DISORGANIZATION AND CLUTTER				
ROOM	BEST ORGANIZED			MOST CLUTTER
Kitchen	1	2	3	4	5
Dining area	1	2	3	4	5
Living area	1	2	3	4	5
Family room	1	2	3	4	5
Master bathroom	1	2	3	4	5
Other bathroom(s)	1	2	3	4	5
Master bedroom	1	2	3	4	5
Guest bedroom	1	2	3	4	5
Children's bedroom	1	2	3	4	5
Children's playroom	1	2	3	4	5
Home office	1	2	3	4	5
Laundry area	1	2	3	4	5
Closets	1	2	3	4	5
Basement	1	2	3	4	5
Attic	1	2	3	4	5
Garage	1	2	3	4	5
Backyard/shed	1	2	3	4	5

Now go through each room of your home and pinpoint the three biggest problems with the room itself, in terms of its design, layout, functionality, space limitations, and so on (using **TABLE 1-3**). Consider the following: Is the room too cluttered? Does the layout of the furniture limit the room's functionality? Could furniture be added or removed to improve the overall functionality and comfort of the room? Does the room lack adequate storage? Could the storage space within the room be put to better use? Is the lighting or climate suitable for what the room is used for?

TABLE 1-3

IDENTIFYING PROBLEM AREAS			
ROOM	PROBLEM #1	PROBLEM #2	PROBLEM #3
Kitchen			
Dining area			
Living area			
Family room			
Master bathroom			
Other bathroom(s)			
Master bedroom			
Guest bedroom			
Children's bedroom			
Children's playroom			
Home office			
Laundry area			
Closets			
Basement			
Attic			
Garage			
Backyard/shed			

Finally, take a few minutes to write down and describe everything you could do to your home—starting immediately—to create the perfect living environment (using **TABLE 1-4**). This list could include major tasks, like completely renovating the kitchen, or smaller tasks, like replacing the linens on your bed with more comfortable sheets. If your bedroom is cluttered with piles of dirty clothes on the floor, for example, list this as an issue that needs to be addressed.

TABLE 1-4

CREATING THE PERFECT LIVING ENVIRONMENT	
ROOM	**WHAT NEEDS TO BE DONE**
Kitchen	
Dining area	
Living area	
Family room	
Master bathroom	
Other bathroom(s)	
Master bedroom	
Guest bedroom	
Children's bedroom	
Children's playroom	
Home office	
Laundry area	
Closets	
Basement	
Attic	
Garage	
Backyard/shed	

Now that you have an idea of the problem areas in your home, keep a running list of tasks you can start immediately to begin transforming your home as it is now into your ultimate dream home.

Breaking Organization Down into Manageable Tasks

Instead of taking on your entire home right away, divide up this task into a series of smaller, more achievable tasks. Don't attempt to reorganize or redesign every room or area of your home all at once; instead, take on one project at a time. If you've determined that your bedroom closets are the biggest disaster in your home, that's a perfect place to start your organizational efforts. Trying to accomplish too much at once can easily become overwhelming and frustrating.

Always think in terms of your personal living habits (and the habits of the people you live with) as you begin to create a more organized living space for yourself. Consider which areas of your home you spend the most time in, and then determine ways you can make those areas more comfortable and more functional. Throughout the process, however, always be conscious of clutter. Answer the following questions:

- Does the room or area suffer from too much clutter?
- What can be done to eliminate the clutter? (Is this clutter that needs to be reorganized, put into storage, or discarded?)
- What type of clutter are you dealing with?
- What is the primary cause of the clutter? (Too much stuff, not enough storage space, laziness, and so on?)
- What will you do in the future to stop creating more clutter in each specific area of your home?

Suppose you choose your bedroom, for example. You may be in the habit of putting dirty clothes on the floor instead of in the laundry hamper. Perhaps you need to take more frequent trips to the dry cleaner, or you need to get into the habit of putting your shoes on a shoe rack in the closet, instead of scattering them around the bedroom floor. You may need storage shelves or a more efficient dresser.

After you decide on an area and have an idea of why the area is so cluttered, list the specific steps you need to take to organize the project (for example, you may need to buy shelves and a shoe rack, discard all the clothes you haven't worn in the last year, and so on). Also create a time frame (a deadline) for completing this project. Decide on a budget, too, and list any tools or other items you need to purchase or borrow to complete this project. Finally, consider whether you need assistance from an organizational expert, electrician, plumber, contractor, architect, and so on.

Make sure that you take on only one project at a time. After each project is complete, move on to the next. To ensure success, begin with smaller objectives. If you choose to begin by reorganizing your bedroom, for example, consider the bedroom itself to be a separate project from organizing your bedroom closet(s) or dresser(s), but connect these projects together so that one gets done immediately after the other in a timely and organized manner.

Getting Rid of Your Clutter

After pinpointing the area of your home you want to start with, take several trash bags or large boxes with you into the area and begin clearing out. Empty out closets, cupboards, drawers, shelves, and boxes, and place them into piles: one for items to keep in a handy spot, one for items to keep in storage, one for items to sell or give away, and one for items to throw away. If you're unsure about whether you can part with an item, consider storing it in your attic or basement for one year—if you haven't missed it during that year, you can discard it without fear that you'll miss it. Chapter 2 covers in depth how to clear out an area.

If you believe your unwanted items will be of value to someone else, you have two main options—sell them or donate them. This section focuses on tips for selling your items by holding a garage sale or yard sale, utilizing an online auction service (such as eBay or Yahoo! Auctions), selling your items to an antique store or consignment store, and donating them to charitable organizations.

Organizing a Yard Sale

One way to earn a bit of extra cash for getting rid of your unwanted stuff is to hold a yard sale or garage sale. Before embarking on this type of project, know what you're getting into and plan accordingly. A yard sale is an excellent opportunity to sell unwanted furniture, knickknacks, clothing, used sports equipment, jewelry, collectibles, and other personal and/or household items. Keep in mind, however, that at best, you'll probably receive only a fraction of what you originally paid for the items you're selling. People who attend yard sales do so in search of bargains. If they find something they want, they try negotiating for the lowest possible price.

After sorting through all of the rooms in your home, determine whether you have enough stuff to sell to make organizing, promoting, and actually holding a yard sale worthwhile. You may consider asking a few of your neighbors and friends to participate and sell some of their unwanted belongings, also.

Take inventory of the items you plan to sell. Make a point to clean up items so that they look like they're in the best condition possible. Then, set prices for the items you plan to sell, knowing that the price you set will likely be a starting point for a negotiation.

If you're selling clothing, for example, price the items at about 15 percent of what you originally paid for them. If you're selling collectibles, consider a price that's about half of what the book value is. For other types of items, set prices you think are fair, based on value and condition. You can always lower your prices during the actual sale. One way to ensure that your prices are fair is to attend several other yard sales in your community and see for how much other people are selling their stuff. Make sure you stick price tags on all of your items. You may also want to post signs stating that you're willing to negotiate. It's also an excellent strategy to offer a "buy two, get one free" offer on items like books, videos, CDs, video games, and some types of collectibles (like trading cards).

After you decide on which inventory to sell, set a date and time for your yard sale. You'll experience the most success if your event is held on a weekend. Keep in mind, there are many people who spend their weekends going from yard sale to yard sale in search of bargains. No matter what time you post as the start time for your sale, people will show up early, so be ready for them. You'll probably find that the largest crowd will appear during the first two or three hours of the sale.

It's common sense that your yard sale will attract the largest crowds if the weather is nice and you promote your event properly. Advertising is critical for drawing a crowd. Send out a notice to local newspapers stating the date, time, location, and types of items to be sold. Most community newspapers have a local calendar or events section in which yard sales are listed, sometimes free of charge. You can also take advantage of paid classified advertising.

As for other forms of advertising, nothing is more important that plastering your community with signs. Several days before the event, post signs in your community—on lampposts, in store windows (with permission), on community bulletin boards, and within supermarkets, for example. If you'll be selling some sort of special items, such as a rare coin collection or children's clothes, highlight this information on your signs. You also want to clearly display the date, time, and location of your event. If possible, create signs that are waterproof. (Most hardware stores sell plastic "Yard Sale" or "Garage Sale" signs; you can use a permanent marker to write in the important details.) It's also helpful to announce the reason for the sale. For example, your sign may say "Moving Sale."

Post your signs in high-traffic areas within a two-mile radius of your home. Your signs should answer these basic questions (but not necessarily in this order): who, what, where, when, and why. Remember to make the largest signs possible and make them easy to read. Make sure someone looking at your signs will learn the most important facts within a few short seconds. Sample yard sale sign may be as detailed as the following:

YARD SALE

Antiques, coin collection, bedroom and
living room furniture, and children's clothing.

Saturday, May 30th — 8:00 A.M. to 3:00 P.M. (rain or shine).
Location: #14 Main Street, Anywhere, USA

A yard sale sign can also be simple, as follows:

YARD SALE TODAY

Time: 8:00 A.M. to 4:00 P.M.
Location: 123 Main Street

Don't overlook the power of the Internet to promote your event. Local chat rooms and message forums are an ideal place to share information about your upcoming yard sale. You can also use the Internet for information about putting together a sale. For detailed tips on running a successful yard sale, visit the Bargain Bunny Web site at ✍ *www.bargainbunny.com.* There you'll find a series of articles that will walk you through the entire process, from preplanning to earning the most money possible during the actual event.

ALERT!

During the sale, station yourself in a location where you can oversee your entire event. Make sure your house is locked and have a cordless telephone handy. Keep all of your incoming (earned) cash in your pocket, not in a cash box that could be stolen.

On the day of the sale, hang balloons in front of your home and at the end of your street (if possible) to the attention of customers. As you begin to display your items, consider setting up a large bin or table and offering a few items for free. Select items that you want to get rid of, but that you don't think people will pay money for. Not only is offering a few items for free a nice gesture, it also helps create a buyer-friendly atmosphere and will help reduce shoplifting.

Whenever possible, display your items on tables or on portable clothing racks. Try to keep the items organized and readily accessible. Don't make people dig through piles of stuff to find what they're looking for. Also, divide up your items into categories. For example, set aside separate areas for used sports equipment, kitchen items, clothing, CDs and videos, furniture, collectibles, books, and so on.

Planning a successful yard sale takes preplanning and organization. While it requires a commitment of time, the benefit is you'll potentially earn extra cash.

FACT

If you decide to accept checks, make sure you can trust the check writer. Otherwise, accept cash only. Be able to direct people to the nearest ATM and be willing to hold an item for an hour or two if someone wants to come back in order to make a purchase. If you decide to hold an item, you may want to ask for a small down payment or deposit to ensure they'll return.

Selling Your Items Online

If you have a few expensive items to sell, such as furniture or collectibles, consider selling those items online, using an online auction service, such as eBay (✑ *www.eBay.com*) or Yahoo! Auctions (✑ *http://auctions.yahoo.com*).

An online auction is just like a live auction: People bid on an object, which is sold to the highest bidder. A potential buyer participates by bidding on an item that a seller has listed. The person who has offered the highest bid at close of auction wins the right to purchase the item at that price.

Make sure you list your items under the appropriate category within the online auction site. eBay, for example, offers a variety of main categories and subcategories, such as antiques and art, clothing and accessories, dolls and bears, jewelry, and so on.

When preparing a listing, have the following information available. It's an excellent strategy to post a digital photo of the item being sold, so that potential customers (Web surfers) can see exactly what they're bidding on. The operators of Yahoo! Auctions recommend that for each item to be sold, you list the information discussed in the following sections.

Title

Include a brief, thoughtful title that accurately describes the item you are selling. A title that's easy to understand will make your item easier for bidders to find.

Description

Describe the product in detail. The more detail you provide, the more confidence you'll inspire among the bidders.

Sales Policies

Select the types of payment you're willing to accept. These could include cashier's checks, money orders, cash, personal checks, credit cards, or an online payment option.

Shipping Options

Decide whether you or the buyer pays the shipping costs. Decide when the item will ship, either upon receipt of payment or immediately after the auction closes. Indicate whether you're willing and able to ship outside of the United States.

Quantity of Item

If you have more than one of the same item, and you would like to sell each one individually (in this case there may be several buyers), enter the quantity to be sold.

Starting Price

Enter the price that will be used to start the auction.

Length of Auction

Determine how many days the auction will last.

Selling Your Items to an Antique Store or Consignment Shop

If you only have a few items you're interested in selling, and these items (such as antiques, jewelry, furniture or collectibles) have significant value, consider working directly with an antique store or consignment shop to sell them. These shops may pay you a negotiated price upfront, or you may have to wait until the consignment shop sells your items before you receive your money. Either way, you can potentially earn cash for your unwanted items. Check the Yellow Pages for a list of consignment shops and/or antique dealers in your area.

Assuming you know that the items you're hoping to sell are valuable, get them appraised independently so you know exactly what they're worth before negotiating a sale price.

You'll likely find a variety of consignment shop agreements. Some charge a straight commission (as much as 50 percent of the purchase price on items sold). Other shops charge space rental plus a commission, while still others charge a flat space rental fee. For items that don't sell quickly, some shops require that you remove the merchandise or mark it down within a specified time. Be sure to ask what the policy is for the consignment shop you are considering. Also, make sure to get the terms in writing.

Donating Your Items to Charity

No matter what items you have to get rid of, consider making a donation to a local charity. Depending on the charity, you can donate used clothing, furniture, appliances, vehicles, canned (or prepackaged) food items, old sports equipment, eyeglasses, and just about anything else that someone who is less fortunate than you may be able to use.

While you won't receive cash for making a donation to a charity, you can take a tax deduction if the charity you donate your stuff to is legitimate and provides you with a receipt.

ALERT!

Charitable donations are usually tax deductible; however, there are specific guidelines you'll want to adhere to. For information on how to claim a tax deduction for a donation, contact your accountant or financial advisor. You can also visit the IRS's informative Web site at ✍ *www.irs.gov.*

The Woman's Alliance

The Women's Alliance (✆ 305-642-7600, ✍ *www.thewomensalliance.org*) is a national not-for-profit membership alliance of independent community-based groups that increase the employability of low-income women by providing professional attire, career skills training, and a range of support services from dental care to health and wellness programs.

Dress for Success

This not-for-profit organization (☎212-545-DSNY, ✎*www.dressforsuccess.org*) helps low-income women make tailored transitions into the workforce. Each Dress for Success client receives one suit when she has an interview and a second suit when she gets the job. Women are referred to Dress for Success by a continually expanding number of diverse, not-for-profit member organizations that include homeless shelters, domestic violence shelters, job training programs, and English-as-a-second-language programs.

The Salvation Army

The Salvation Army (☎845-620-7200, ✎*www.salvationarmy.org*), an international movement, is an evangelical part of the universal Christian Church. Its message is based on the Bible, and its ministry is motivated by the love of God.

> To find a charity in your area, contact your local town hall, city hall, or the telephone book. You can also visit the Helping.org Web site (✎*www.helping.org*) for an extensive listing of over 700,000 charities and not-for-profit organizations throughout America that accept all kinds of donations—including cash.

Volunteers of America

Volunteers of America (☎800-899-0089, ✎*www.volunteersofamerica.org*) is a national, not-for-profit, spiritually-based organization providing local human service programs and the opportunity for individual and community involvement. Volunteers of America programs serve individuals and families in some 300 communities across the country, and volunteers have an important role in the success of these programs. Volunteers actively engage in many of the services, delivering meals to the elderly in their homes, reading mail to residents of nursing homes, and providing other services that make a real difference in people's lives.

Goodwill

Goodwill Industries (✆ 800-664-6577, ✉ *www.goodwill.org*) provides people with the tools they need to succeed. It is one of the world's largest not-for-profit providers of employment and training services for people with disabilities and other disadvantaging conditions, such as welfare dependency, illiteracy, criminal history, and homelessness. Each year, Goodwill employees process millions of donations—clothes, appliances, and furniture—that become bargains for smart shoppers. While each of Goodwill's 1,700 stores is different, all offer certain basic items that guarantee great values.

FACT

Prior to making a donation, Goodwill asks that people wash or dry-clean clothing, test electrical equipment and battery-operated items, and check to make sure all pieces and parts to children's games and toys are included. If you're planning to donate a computer or used vehicle, check with your local Goodwill Industries to determine standards for those donations. In addition, don't donate items that have been recalled, banned, or don't meet current safety standards.

Career Gear

Career Gear (✆ 212-273-1194, ✉ *www.careergear.com*) is a grass-roots organization founded in New York City with one goal: to provide business-appropriate attire to men seeking employment. Thanks to the success of this program and due to incredible demand, Career Gear expanded its services to include career counseling, motivation, and job retention. In 1999, the organization opened its first Career Gear Affiliate Program in Miami, Florida. Additional affiliate programs will open around the country over the next several years. Career Gear has helped hundreds of men successfully re-enter the workforce.

Keeping Your Home Clutter-Free

As you begin to reorganize, redesign, or otherwise clean up and overhaul your home, make sure your hard work, as well as your time and financial investment, pay off. Unless you make an ongoing effort to keep your home clean and organized, you'll quickly discover that it won't stay that way for long. Clutter will start to build up, and before you know it, you'll be back to where you started. Think carefully, therefore, about your daily habits and behaviors. Determine what needs to change to ensure that after your home is clean and organized, it stays this way.

If you live with roommates, a spouse, or an entire family, don't take on organizing and cleaning your home as an ongoing personal crusade. Solicit the help of the people you live with and insist on their support to maintain your efforts. Teach the people you live with to clean up after themselves, sort out (and even do) their own laundry, and put items back in their proper place when they're done using them.

CHAPTER 2

Creating Closet and Storage Solutions

Whether you live in a house, apartment, or condo, chances are your living space is equipped with closets. To create a truly organized household, you want to carefully organize your closets to create additional storage space, more easily find your belongings, and take better care of what you're storing in your closets.

Exploring the Closets in Your Home

After you decide that your closets are in need of reorganization, the easiest approach is to focus on one closet at a time or one room at a time. You may, for example, consider reorganizing all of your bedroom clothing closets at the same time to ensure your various garments are stored in the proper locations.

FACT

Before closets were actually built into homes and apartments, people stored their clothing in armoires, which were popular when people were charged taxes for every room in their houses, including closets. Later, in the United States, it became a popular trend to store clothing in chests and trunks. Today, closets are the most popular way people store their wardrobe and other belongings. In fact, closet organization has become a $1 billion per year business in the United States alone.

Clearing Out Your Closets

To begin the closet organization process, choose a closet or a room and follow the basic steps in this section. If you choose to hire a professional closet designer, the person you hire will come to your home and do many of these steps for you. The following steps for clearing out your closets use the example of clothing closets, but the same basic rules apply for any type of storage closet.

Before beginning, determine what specific purpose the newly organized closet will have. Will you use this closet to store your everyday wardrobe, coats, or linens?

1. Empty your closet.
2. To inventory all items in your closet, neatly lay out the contents on a nearby floor or open area.

3. Decide which items taken out of the unorganized closet actually belong there and which items should be stored elsewhere.
4. Eliminate or discard anything that's damaged, outdated, not your style, or the wrong size.

Planning Your Closet's Uses

After you discard what you no longer need from your closets, consider whether you'll eventually replace those items. For example, if you discard clothing that's no longer in style or that no longer fits, will you buy new clothing in the near future to replace it? If so, make sure you allocate room in your closet for these new purchases.

When buying new clothes, avoid purchasing items you don't need. A sale item is a bargain only if it's in style, looks good on you, and goes with an article of clothing you already own. Before going shopping, examine your wardrobe and identify (in writing) the items you really need.

Evaluate the contents of the closet and determine the best way to actually store these belongings. For example, would installing additional shelves, rods, or drawers provide additional space? Most basic closets are equipped with a single rod for hanging clothing. The height of most closets, however, allows for at least two rods, which in essence doubles the amount of space you can use to hang garments. In addition, you can use specially designed hangers to increase the number of garments you can hang in a limited amount of space.

When organizing a clothing closet, keep your most-used items visible and easily accessible. According to Mary Lou Andre, the president of Organization By Design (✆ 800-578-3770, ✍ *www.dressingwell.com*), "We wear twenty percent of our wardrobes eighty percent of the time." To utilize the wardrobe pieces you have, she recommends assembling complete outfits, including accessories, and storing them on a single hanger.

Plan to sort your hanging items by type or category. For example, divide up suits so that all jackets are together, all skirts are together, and so on. Sort within each category by color and/or fabric type. Doing this should help you to create new outfit combinations by mixing and matching garments. You can divide your wardrobe into further categories, like shirts, skirts, pants, jackets, suits, turtlenecks, sweaters, athletic apparel, T-shirts, jeans, and so on. You can also sort your clothing by season.

To determine how much room you have for closet organizers (discussed in the following section), carefully measure the empty closet. Round each measurement to the nearest $\frac{1}{8}$th of an inch, taking the time to be as accurate as possible. Be sure to write the measurements down as you take them (see **TABLES 2-1** and **2-2**), and check your work at least twice. When measuring a reach-in closet, determine the width of the closet by measuring the inside space between the two sidewalls, determine the height by measuring from the floor to the ceiling, and determine the depth by measuring the distance between the inside surface of the face wall or door and the back wall (see **FIGURE 2-1**). To measure a walk-in closet measure the width of each wall, determine the closet's height by measuring from floor to ceiling, determine the width of the doorway by measuring the distance from frame to frame, and measure the height of the doorway, too (see **FIGURE 2-2**).

When cleaning and organizing your clothing closet, plan to store off-season clothing (laundered or dry-cleaned) elsewhere, such as in another closet, in boxes under the bed, or in your luggage. Include a cedar block in any box that contains wool garments.

TABLE 2-1

REACH-IN CLOSET MEASUREMENT WORKSHEET			
MEASUREMENT	CLOSET #1	CLOSET #2	CLOSET #3
Width			
Height			
Depth			
Doorway width			
Doorway height			
Door type*			
Built-in fixtures**			

*Bi-fold, hinge, sliding, and so on
**Windows, vents, lights, switches, and so on

FIGURE 2-1:
Measuring a
reach-in
closet

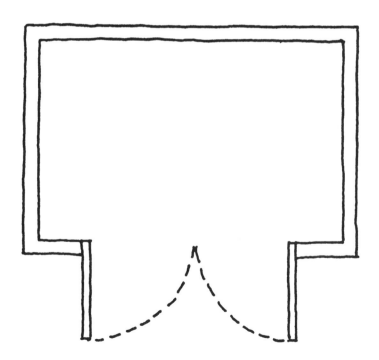

TABLE 2-2

WALK-IN CLOSET MEASUREMENT WORKSHEET			
MEASUREMENT	CLOSET #1	CLOSET #2	CLOSET #3
Wall #1			
Wall #2			
Wall #3			
Height			
Doorway width			
Door type*			
Built-in fixtures**			

*Bi-fold, hinge, sliding, and so on
**Windows, vents, lights, switches, and so on

FIGURE 2-2:
Measuring a
walk-in closet

Considering Closet Organizers

Closet organizers and specialized hangers are inexpensive items that make organizing your closets a snap. Several types of organizers fit easily into any closet.

General Organizers

Visit any linen superstore or check out almost any catalog or Web site that features closet organizational products and you'll find a wide selection of closet organizers. These component-based storage systems allow you to customize the inside of your closets, without the high cost of hiring a professional closet-organization company. After you've measured your available closet space and know exactly what you want to store in your closet, you can design a closet-storage system by mixing and matching modules. For example, the Hold Everything Catalog (✆ 800-421-2264) offers stacking wooden drawers, cubes, and shelves that you can mix and match. This system can be combined with a closet's existing rod for hanging garments.

Shelves and Shelf Dividers

Shelves provide you with a place to put all the things that would otherwise go on the floor or in a dresser drawer. Consider using preassembled stackable shelves. They're available in a variety of sizes and can be customized to fit the dimensions of your closet. You can purchase closet shelving at most home improvement or hardware stores.

Shelf dividers separate your shelf into small sections that you use for a stack of sweaters or a stash of purses, without having them tumble over or get creased or scratched. Other divider systems organize socks, hosiery, jewelry, and folded linens.

Baskets

Ventilated baskets serve practically any purpose you can name. Removable laundry baskets in closets serve as portable hampers. Baskets in kids' closets double as portable toy bins. Mudroom baskets provide ample storage for gloves, hats, and sports gear, letting damp outerwear breathe and dry.

Canvas Wardrobe Storage

For storing off-season clothing, canvas wardrobe storage systems offer an ideal solution. Hanging garment bags, hanging canvas shelves for sweaters, hanging folding drawers for small items, such as scarves or socks, bedding bags for storing blankets and other large items, and shoe holders are all available. You can mix and match pieces to create a customized and organized closet. An alternative is to purchase nylon clothing protectors that offer clear heavy gauge vinyl windows.

Shoe Racks

To improve the organization of your clothing closet, invest in a sturdy shoe rack. If you're stuck with a small closet, purchase a hanging shoe rack that you can attach to the back of the closet door, for example. Most stores also sell shoe bags with pouches that you can attach to the wall of your closet. Keep in mind that the pouches built into some show racks are also ideal for storing scarves or belts. Make sure the pouches are transparent so that you can see exactly what's stored inside them.

The Hold Everything catalog (✆ 800-421-2264) features a wide selection of shoe storage systems, including an Over-Door Storage System that allows you to free up floor and drawer space, yet store and display your entire shoe collection. The catalog also features a selection of stackable wooden and metal shoe racks and shoe cabinets.

When storing expensive shoes, consider investing in shoetrees: devices that you place within each shoe in order to preserve the shape of it. Cedar shoetrees also absorb moisture and odors.

Tie and Belt Racks

Although ties and belts are loose items, you can still organize and display them in your closet. Special holders/storage tacks for neck ties and belts can be attached to a closet wall or door, or in some cases can be hung from the closet's rod. Some racks also slide out when you need them and tuck away when you don't. Be sure to store tie racks close to dress shirts so that coordinating outfits is easy. Pegs with nubbed tips keep ties in place and prevent wrinkling.

Jewelry Organizers

Jewelry organizers, which are often felt-lined, keep your valuable and delicate possessions cushioned and protected. In some cases, a top tray slides and lifts out, giving you two layers of storage in a single drawer. Combinations of large and small compartments work for different types and styles of jewelry and accessories.

Specialty Clothes Hangers

When organizing any clothing closet, you want to purchase a variety of clothes hanger styles. Before you decide which types of hangers are best for you, get rid of all the bent and out-of-shape metal hangers typically provided by dry cleaners. You can find hangers that are designed to hold specific types of garments. Traditionally shaped wooden or plastic hangers are excellent for preserving virtually all of your hanging clothing. Suit hangers are designed with a special pant rod, so a single hanger neatly holds both pants and a jacket. Cedar hangers have all the benefits of traditional wooden hangers, but also absorb moisture and discourage pests (such as moths) from damaging your clothing. Collapsible, multi-tiered hangers save space by allowing you to hang multiple garments in one small area.

A Better Hanger Company

A Better Hanger Company's products (✐ *www.abetterhanger.com*) represent a new way people care for their clothes. The company offers two types of hangers: the Folding Hanger and the Travel/Tie Hanger.

Both are constructed from high-strength plastic. The Folding Hanger has a patented folding action that you can insert into neck openings without stretching the garment or having to unbutton it. The patented design also includes a flared shoulder edge (which eliminates shoulder puckers), a swivel hook (allowing hangers to be linked vertically to maximize closet space), and a unique locking mechanism (enabling users to take clothes off a hanger without removing the hanger from the clothes bar). The Travel/Tie Hanger features a center capture bar, which creates a gentle tension to hold clothes or ties in place. Because the bar is covered with the soft side of Velcro, it also eliminates creases as well as the white line that's sometimes created when wire hangers oxidize.

Hanger Handler

Hanger Handler, from Axiomatic Products Corporation (available at ✆ 888-266-8246 or ✑ *www.hangerhandler.com*), is a new, multifunctional tool designed to make handling clothes hangers—either wire and plastic—easier and more comfortable. The product easily holds up to thirty hangers and sustains fifty pounds or more of garments. By shielding hands from hanger tips, Hanger Handler keeps hanger tips from pressing into the palm of your hand while transporting multiple clothes hangers. The uses of this product include carrying dry-cleaning, traveling (with or without garment bags), moving, reorganizing closets, and shopping. Hanger Handler, which can be held like a suitcase handle or over the shoulder, is also designed to hang on interior handles or hooks in the car and on closet rods, on coat hooks, and over doors at home. Loading and unloading is easy by simply sliding the Hanger Handler over hanger hooks. It's available for under $10 at The Container Store (✆ 800-733-3532, ✑ *www.containerstore.com*), selected Bag 'n' Baggage retail stores, and Travel 2000 stores.

Hangco

Hangco (✑ *www.trendmarketing.net*) is an innovative new clothing hanger designed to preserve the original shape and body of your favorite garments, including blouses, blazers, suits, sweaters, furs, and fine washables. Unlike traditional wire hangers, Hangco allows your clothing to rest naturally, without leaving marks or indentations or distorting the shape. Hangco hangers allow wet garments to dry evenly and quickly. These hangers are ideal for everyday use and for long-term storage of your off-season wardrobe.

Jam-It Slack Rack

The Jam-It Natural Wood Valet (✐ *www.organize-everything.com* and ✐*jamitslackrack.html*) maximizes space on any doorjamb. Use it for clothes or towels. It's easy to install and mounts right on a doorjamb.

Hinge-It

The Hinge-It valet (available at ✐*www.organize-everything.com/hinitinval1.html*) maximizes space behind any door. Use it for clothes or towels. It's easy to install and mounts right on any door hinge.

Double Hang

Double Hang (✐*www.organize-everything.com/doublehang.html*) doubles the clothing hanging space in your closet. The heavy, natural wood bar (which is the size of a closet rod) hangs on chrome-plated steel posts to provide extra room for blouses, shirts, and pants. The size is 29.5" wide × 33.5" long, and it hangs 32".

Round-A-Belt Organizer

The Round-A-Belt Organizer (✐*www.netwurx.net/~organize*) holds up to forty belts. It's a patented, space-saving system for organizing your belts into five different sections to suit your personal style. You can easily remove belts individually.

Clothes Hangers Online

Clothes Hangers Online (✆ 800-600-9817, ✐*http://hangersonline.store.yahoo.com*) offers the Six Tier Shirt/Blouse Hanger, a chrome hanger with a unique design that holds six shirts or blouses. The company also offers Hook 'n' Hang hangers, which can hold up to twenty shirts, belts, and/or accessories. They're manufactured from heavy-duty molded plastic. The hanger arms fold up and lock into place, creating more space in your closet.

The Closet Carousel

The Closet Carousel system (✆ 800-896-0902, ✍ *http://closets.net//frm2.htm*) works much the same way as the clothing carousels you see at many dry-cleaning establishments, only this elaborate closet organization product is designed for the home. The system operates using standard household electricity and can be customized to fit in most standard-size closets. The company's Web site offers over twenty different closet layouts to consider. With the push of a button, the Closet Carousel showcases your entire wardrobe and provides extra storage space. If you have a minimum closet size of 4'6" × 6', the Closet Carousel can make your existing closet space more efficient and your new closet space both practical and luxurious. It comes with easily adjustable single- or double-tier hanging; adjustable baskets for storing folded garments, handbags, and other accessories; and specially designed adjustable shoe racks. The company makes ten standard models.

Quiet Power Automatic Tie Rack

Using a carousel-like design (scaled down considerably from what you'd find at a dry-cleaning establishment), the Quiet Power Automatic Tie Rack from the Sharper Image (✆ 800-344-4444, ✍ *www.sharperimage.com*) showcases and organizes your neckties as they glide quietly past you for easy selection. Touch the control bar to rotate left or right in one full revolution or press the Stop button when you've reached your selection. A bright light helps you see true colors, and then switches off after rotation stops. The oval track holds seventy-two ties in a $5\frac{1}{4}$" section of your closet rod. Four double hooks underneath hold belts and scarves, increasing the hanging spaces to eighty. This unit comes with hardware for easy mounting to wood shelving, closet rods, or metal closet systems. This unit requires four C-sized batteries or plugs into any standard wall outlet using the AC adapter.

Space Bags

If you watch television infomercials, you've probably seen ads for Space Bags (✆ 800-469-9044, ✍ *www.spacebag.com*). After you fill these large, heavy-duty plastic bags, you use a standard vacuum cleaner to suck out all of the remaining air within the plastic bag and dramatically decrease the size of what you'll be storing. The Space Bag storage system protects your valuable belongings by vacuum-sealing them in polyethylene and nylon. The system incorporates three sophisticated technologies to create the airtight seal and lock out water, moisture, mildew, dirt, bugs, and allergens. It also retards oxidation, which damages natural fibers and many synthetics. Items stored in a Space Bag can be stored in your garage, attic, or basement, freeing up precious closet space in your primary living area. They come in sizes as large as 36" × 48" and as small as 14" × 20".

Custom Building Closets Yourself

After you've taken inventory of what will be stored in your closet and carefully measured the closet space you have available, you can choose to purchase prefabricated closet organizers, shelves, drawers, rods, and other organizational accessories. Most of these accessories are designed to fit standard-sized closet spaces. The trick, however, is determining in advance what closet organizing accessories you want to implement into your closet. This means deciding what types of shelves, drawers, shoe racks, hooks, specialty hangers, and lighting you require (see the preceding section).

If you're handy with tools, you can opt to build your own closet organizers from scratch. This means you'll build your organizer directly into the closet space and attached to the floor, walls, and/or ceiling. It will be custom-built to fit the exact dimensions of your closet. Opting to custom-design a closet yourself is a time-consuming project. If you're making the decision to embark on this project, you want to ensure that the end result is functional and creates the exact storage environment you need. As you begin planning what your closet will look like and how you will organize it, answer the following questions:

- Based on the appearance and organization of your closet now, what can you change to make it more organized and functional?
- Is the space currently being used efficiently?
- Is there enough room to install drawers and/or cabinets with doors that open and close?

- Do you need more shelf space, hanging space, and/or drawers in the closet? If so, how will you utilize this space?
- Can you get by using specialty hangers as opposed to doing construction and installing a customized closet organizer?
- Is the floor space and door space being utilized right now or are shoes and other items stored inefficiently?

Hardware superstores sell do-it-yourself closet organizers, which include most of the materials you'll need to customize your closet. Just be sure that the kit you buy fits the closet you have in mind. In addition, some of the tools you'll need to install prefabricated closet organizers include a Phillips head screwdriver (a power screwdriver is even better), hammer, stud finder, level, tape measure, circular saw or fine-tooth saw, and pipe cutter or hacksaw.

FACT

If your closet is poorly lit, consider purchasing an inexpensive battery-operated light from your hardware store. Most mount easily to the wall with tape or small screws, but you'll have to change the batteries from time to time. You can also hire an electrician to install additional lighting controlled by a simple pull chain, wall switch, or an automatic door switch. For information about several closet lighting options, visit the eLights Web site at ✍ www.elights.com/closet.html.

Hiring a Closet Organizer

A far more costly alternative for achieving this objective is to hire a professional closet organizer. Many companies, such as Closet Factory (✆ 800-692-5673, ✍ www.closet-factory.com), Techline (✆ 800-356-8400, ✍ www.techlineusa.com), and California Closets (✆ 888-336-9709, ✍ www.calclosets.com), specialize in custom-designing closets for any purpose. When you hire one of these companies, an organizational/ closet-design specialist arrives at your home to inventory what you'll be storing in your closet(s) and take measurements. He or she then designs a customized closet to meet your needs.

Custom rods, shelves, drawers, hooks, lighting, and other in-closet accessories are built specifically to fit your closet and needs. Many of closet-design companies guarantee that by using their services, your available closet space will double. In almost every case, this is true; however, hiring one of these closet organization companies tends to be expensive.

All of the professional closet-design companies offer free in-home consultations and provide free price quotes in conjunction with a personalized needs evaluation. Obtain multiple quotes from different companies and determine what each is offering. In addition, you'll be able to obtain ideas from multiple experts, free of charge, which you can implement with whomever you hire to design your closet space.

If you have access to the Web, a company called Storage By Design (✆ 877-7720-2313, ✑ *www.customclosets.com*) offers an interactive closet-design tool. While this design tool focuses on the company's closet organization products, you can also use it to generate design ideas for virtually any type of closet.

Using Alternative Storage Areas

When storing items like clothing, closets are a popular solution. But if you have limited closet space, you're forced to come up with alterative solutions for storing all of your stuff. When figuring out alternative solutions, be extremely conscious of what you're storing and what type of special precautions you need to take to ensure the safety of what's being stored. For example, never store clothing in cardboard boxes in an attic or basement (or anyplace else that isn't climate controlled). You also have to consider whether pests (such as moths) pose a threat to what you're storing. Before storing anything figure out what items you need to store, how much non-closet storage space is available, and what special precautions you need to take. After you've answered these questions, you should be able to identify the types of containers required to store your items.

Looking around your home, you'll probably find several ideal places for storing out-of-season clothing, linens, towels, bedding, and other items. For example, you may consider purchasing an armoire for out-of-season items or even as an ideal alternative to a closet. Most high-end furniture stores sell various styles of armoires. On the Web, you can point your browser to the Armoires & More Web site (✍ *www.armoirestore.com*) or call ✆ 800-5-FURNISH to see a catalog with a broad range of armoire styles.

Under your bed is an excellent and often underused storage space. You can place items, such as out-of-season clothing, in plastic containers, within Space Bags (described earlier in this chapter), or in suitcases, and store them beneath your bed.

Air-tight plastic containers, which are sold at mass-market retailers (such as Wal-Mart), hardware stores (such as Home Depot), or at retailers (like Hold Everything, Bed, Bath & Beyond, the Container Store, and Lillian Vernon); all provide a safe way to store most types of clothing in untraditional places, such as an attic, basement, or garage. Rubbermaid (✍ *www.rubbermaid.com*) is just one popular manufacturer of large plastic storage containers that you can use for storing clothing and other items. Plastic containers come in a wide range of sizes, shapes, and colors (including clear).

For storing and displaying books and various other knickknacks, consider using bookcases and shelving. Bookcases come in a wide range of styles and designs, and you can use them in various rooms of your home, including bedrooms, living areas, dens, home offices, libraries, and playrooms. You can build a special shelf for cookbooks, for example, onto a wall in your kitchen. Be sure to visit several furniture store showrooms and office furniture stores when choosing bookcases. To save floor space, consider utilizing a narrower bookcase, for example, that towers upwards, placing your most commonly used items at eye-level and your least used items higher up. If you're handy with tools, you can custom-design and build your own bookcases or shelves.

Organize your books, CDs, DVDs, software packages, and videos on your shelves. Don't just place them haphazardly. Take the approach of bookstores and libraries and organize your books by author name, book title, or subject. Secure books on the shelves with bookends. As for your knickknacks, choose shelving that complements what you're trying to display and make sure ample lighting highlights these items. Organizing shelves is a creative effort, because in addition to functionality, you want the items on your shelves to be visually appealing.

ALERT!

Whether you're utilizing bookcases or shelving, make sure what you're storing or displaying isn't too heavy for the shelves. Books can be extremely heavy. If the weight of your books is too much for the shelves or bookcase, the unit could collapse and create a dangerous situation. If shelving or bookcases are being affixed to walls, make sure you've done the installation properly. Many bookcases and shelves list the maximum weight allowances.

Maintaining Your Newly Organized Closet

Organizing your closets is important, but taking good care of your belongings, including your wardrobe, helps ensure their long life and protects your investment. This section focuses on specific tips and products that will help you maintain your closets and the items you store in them.

Having your more valuable or delicate garments dry-cleaned is always a good strategy, as is using the best possible laundry detergent when you're laundering your clothing. After all, if you wear one of your favorite suits or dresses to a smoke-filled night club, and then return home and hang up that article of clothing in your closet, the smell of smoke that's ingrained in the fabric will spread to nearby clothing. Likewise, smells from laundry detergents and perfumes also spread among clothing stored within a closet unless you take proper precautions.

Consider storing only clean clothing in your closet. To prevent smells, use an air freshener, a fabric-treatment solution (such as Febreze), an air purifier, or cedar wood blocks, depending on the type of odors you want to eliminate and what you want the end result to be. Using cedar blocks or cedar hangers, for example, helps to naturally eliminate mustiness and absorb moisture from a closet or drawers, plus they fight off insects, such as moths.

FACT

Febreze Fabric Spray (☎ 800-308-3279, ✐ *www.febreze.com*) is a cleaning solution from Procter & Gamble that's available in supermarkets. It neutralizes odors from virtually all types of fabrics and is designed for fabrics that can't easily be washed. You simply spray Febreze evenly onto the fabric until it becomes slightly damp. The Febreze molecules penetrate into the fabric, cleaning away odor-causing molecules as the fabric dries. While Febreze leaves a scent on the fabric for a while, this scent goes away with time.

Portable air purifiers are also ideal for keeping clothing stored within a closet smelling fresh. The Compact Ionic Dry Cleaner from the Sharper Image (☎ 800-344-4444, ✐ *www.sharperimage.com*) removes odors from clothes with sanitizing ozone. When this unit is used in a clothes closet, it allows you to wear fresh-smelling clothes all the time, without dry cleaning. (The unit doesn't actually clean clothing. It just removes odors.) It hangs in a closet and circulates natural ozone to reduce odors in all fabrics.

After your closets are cleared out and organized and you find yourself with newfound storage space, don't make the mistake of expanding your belongings to fill the newly available space. Focus on your needs and make a conscious effort to maintain the level of organization you have just worked so hard to achieve in your closets.

CHAPTER 3

Organizing Your Kitchen

This chapter explores a variety of ways to plan and organize your kitchen, allowing you to create an environment that's clean, healthy, and comfortable. Even if you're stuck in a kitchen that's outdated and poorly laid out, you can still take steps to keep it well organized and clean, storing items so that they're easy to find and readily available when you need them.

Designing a New Kitchen

If you're lucky enough to be able to design your kitchen from scratch, choose your own brand-new appliances, and decide where those appliances will be positioned, consider yourself lucky—especially if you enjoy cooking and plan to spend a considerable amount of time in your kitchen. To save time and money, spend time preplanning.

Begin by drawing a layout of your current kitchen. Draw a rough sketch of the floor plan and note the measurements of the cabinets, appliances, and countertop space (see **FIGURE 3-1** for an example). You may be able to save time by requesting a floor plan or blueprint from your architect or builder. You can also use the Kitchen Measurements Guide available online at Kitchens.com (✆ 312-857-1600, ✎ *www.kitchens.com*).

FIGURE 3-1:
A typical kitchen layout

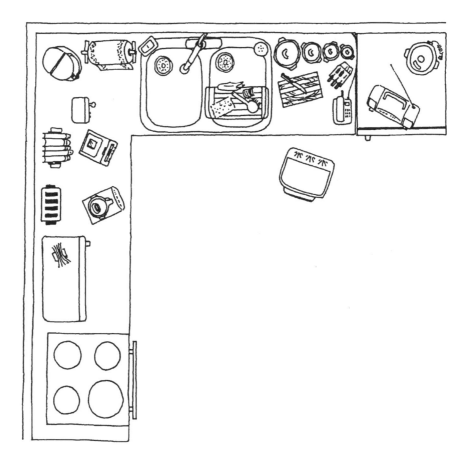

Unless you're incredibly handy with tools, in addition to being an electrician and plumber, it's an excellent strategy to enlist the help of a professional kitchen designer, architect, and/or contractor, not only to help you design your kitchen, but also to coordinate the various workers needed to make your new or remodeled kitchen a reality.

How can I save money as I remodel my kitchen?
Instead of rebuilding your kitchen from scratch, you can save a lot of money by refacing your cabinets and replacing the countertops. You can also replace a few, but not all, of the appliances to add more modern conveniences into your existing kitchen.

After you decide you're going to invest in a new kitchen, the Kitchens.com Web site recommends asking the following questions as a first step (see **TABLE 3-1**).

TABLE 3-1	INITIAL KITCHEN-LAYOUT QUESTIONS

Why do you want a new kitchen?

_____

_____

_____

What's on the wish lists of others who will be using your kitchen? (This may be as simple as your spouse wanting an ice and drinking water dispenser on the outside door of your new refrigerator.)

_____

_____

_____

Where can you incorporate current elements in the new kitchen? (Can you use existing appliances, cabinets, layout, and so on?)

_____

_____

_____

What do you like most and least about your current kitchen?

What specifically don't you like about how it looks?

Do you currently have enough countertop space to prepare meals and store appliances?

Is the kitchen sink large enough?

Do you have enough refrigerator and freezer space?

Do you need more storage space for food, pots/pans, flatware, dishes, and so on?

Do you have adequate shelf space?
Can you adjust your cabinet shelves?
Do your cabinet doors open easily?

Is there enough space in the kitchen for you to comfortably prepare meals?

Aside from cooking, what else do you do within this area of your home (eat, pay bills, do laundry, use the computer, watch TV, talk on the telephone, and so on)? What would you like to be able to do in this area that you can't do now?

Do you currently have enough electrical outlets?

Is your dishwasher easy to load and unload? Is it quiet? Does it offer the functionality and capacity you need?

Is fresh water easily accessible when you're cooking? Do you need an additional sink or faucet? What about a built-in water filter?

_____

_____

Is your kitchen easy to clean? _____

Do you have enough light? _____

What would be the ideal seating options within the kitchen? Based on available space, what's practical?

_____

_____

_____

What general kitchen style and décor do you like (contemporary, traditional, country, eclectic, and so on)? _____

What is the architectural style of your home? Do you want your new kitchen to reflect this style? _____

What are some of the styles and products that you like—those you've seen in a designer's showroom, on the Kitchens.com Web site, in publications, or elsewhere?

_____

_____

What do you like about your friends' kitchens?

_____

_____

_____

What color schemes do you like? Which ones do you dislike?

_____

_____

_____

Using a Kitchen Designer

A kitchen designer will typically visit your home to take measurements, create a design and draft a floor plan, develop a detailed budget and schedule, order products and materials, coordinate work with construction and contractors, and oversee the installation and placement of the cabinets and other design elements.

The designer may charge a fee of $50 to $150 per hour or a retainer of $300 to $5,000 per job. Often, the designer's payment will be taken off the total cost of the job if you end up buying your new kitchen components from him or her.

According to the National Kitchen and Bath Association, most firms require a down payment of 50 percent of the total cost of the job when you sign a contract. The designer will typically expect another 40-percent payment when the cabinets are delivered and the balance when the job is completed. The total cost of the job will largely depend on the type of materials you select.

To find a professional kitchen designer to work with, take advantage of a referral from someone you trust, such as a friend or relative. You can also obtain a referral from a professional organization, such as the National Kitchen and Bath Association, or from the local Chamber of Commerce in your community. If there's a home improvement center or kitchen appliance dealer/showroom in your community, ask the salespeople for a referral. Make sure you choose someone willing to work within your budget, who has experience designing kitchens for your type of home, and who understands your personal needs and taste.

Budget Issues

When planning a budget for remodeling your kitchen, the National Kitchen & Bath Association reports that the average cost of a new kitchen is $22,100. This, however, will vary greatly based on a wide range of factors, including the types of appliances you purchase and the actual building materials you use to construct your kitchen. The cost of new kitchen cabinets will eat up about 48 percent of the entire remodeling budget. Labor costs will account for about 16 percent of your overall budget (but this, too, will vary greatly based on the amount of electrical, plumbing, and general construction work that needs to be done). New countertops will represent about 13 percent of your remodeling budget. Appliances, fixtures, and fittings represent 12 percent of the budget. If you choose to hire a professional designer, expect to pay either a flat fee or a percentage (10 to 15 percent) of the total cost of goods purchased.

Based on these rather high figures, consider the primary reason you're remodeling your kitchen and determine whether the expense is worth the reason. Also consider whether you're planning to stay in this home for many years to come. Think about how significant of an investment you're willing to make financially to create the ultimate dream kitchen for yourself. Also consider your overall budget and how this budget should be divided between construction, purchasing appliances, and the installation of appliances.

Kitchen-Design Strategies

As you consider the design of your new kitchen, think specifically about who will be using it and all of the things it will be used for. Use **TABLE 3-2** to answer some basic design questions.

TABLE 3-2

KITCHEN DESIGN WORKSHEET
Who will be using the kitchen?
Will young children or elderly family members use the kitchen?
Does anyone using the kitchen have special needs?
Where do you plan to eat meals after the new kitchen is completed?
Do you require a kitchen table or a counter (island or peninsula) with stools (see **FIGURE 3-2** for an example)?

What other activities will take place in your new kitchen?

_____

_____

_____

Will you use the kitchen to entertain? How often?

_____

_____

What is your entertainment style (formal or informal)?

_____

_____

When you entertain, do you typically cook food yourself or have parties catered?

_____

_____

How many guests do you typically invite when you entertain? _____

Do your guests ever end up in the kitchen? _____

What are your storage requirements (think in terms of food, small appliances, pots/pans, dishes, flatware, cookbooks, paperwork, cleaning supplies, and so on)?

_____

_____

_____

What is your cooking style? _____

Who is the primary cook? _____

Is the primary cook left- or right-handed? _____

How tall is the primary cook? _____

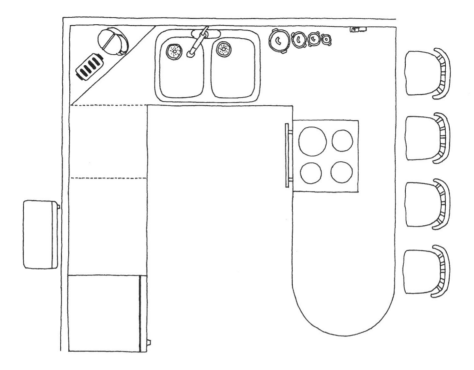

FIGURE 3-2:
A well-designed
kitchen

Also consider which storage improvements you would most like to see in your new kitchen. Inventory your current kitchen, looking at everything you have in there now. Where would you put it all in the newly designed kitchen? Would you like your new kitchen to have a special spot for storing trays, cookie sheets, and other flat items? What about building taller shelves for storing wine glasses and vases? Is a recycling center important to you?

Consider how you shop for groceries. Do you typically shop for the week or for each meal? Do you buy in bulk and freeze perishable items? Do you typically buy nonperishables in bulk (to save money), and need extra space to store these items? Write down every storage idea you have.

For each appliance you need, you'll be required to make a separate set of decisions. Always think in terms of what your needs are, the quality of the appliance, the warrantee that's being offered, and the price of the unit itself. In terms of your kitchen sink, its functionality and appearance are important, but you also have safety issues to consider. After all, your sink is what will be used to keep the rest of the kitchen clean and germ-free. When it comes time to choosing your kitchen sink, use **TABLE 3-3** to help you make the decision.

| TABLE 3-3 | KITCHEN SINK WORKSHEET |

Do you plan to wash or just rinse dishes in the sink? After each meal or cooking/baking project, approximately how many dishes will need to be rinsed or washed? _____

Do you prefer an easy-to-clean stainless steel sink or a colored sink?

_____

Will you want to set a cutting board across the sink for chopping vegetables?

_____

How often will you need to soak pots and pans? Will soaking these items for extended periods limit your ability to use the sink for other purposes? Do you need two sinks? _____

How will your countertop material affect your choice of sink material?

_____

Is the sink close to the dishwasher? _____

Is there ample room to store a dish rack next to the sink? What about dish rags, towels, and paper towels? Where will you keep the hand soap and dish soap container? _____

What type of faucet do you want? What special features are important to you? Do you want to incorporate a water filtration system into the sink/faucet?

_____

Within the kitchen, where would a sink (or sinks) be placed most conveniently for your cleaning, cooking ,and food preparation needs?

_____

Will you have a dishwasher, or is the sink the primary way your dishes, pots, and pans will be washed? _____

FACT

The National Kitchen & Bath Association (☎ 877-NKBA-PRO, ✍ *www.nkba.org*), has led the kitchen and bath industry for more than thirty-five years. NKBA helps consumers by acting as the ultimate resource for everything from finding a design professional in your area to informing you on industry trends, products, and services. Other useful Web sites include: iWANTaNewKITCHEN.com (✍ *www.iwantanewkitchen.com*), Kitchen Source (✍ *www.kitchensource.com*), Kitchen & Bath Design News (✍ *www.kbdn.net*), Gourmet Spot (✍ *www.gourmetspot.com/ kitchendesign.htm*), KitchenWeb (✍ *www.kitchenweb.com*), and Kitchen.net (✍ *www.kitchen-bath.com*).

Creating a Kitchen-Design Wish List

Compile a kitchen wish book or scrapbook. As you go through magazines, visit showrooms, and surf the Web, stuff a folder or scrapbook with photos, drawings, descriptions, and lists of what you want in your kitchen. Consider which features and appliances you want to incorporate into your newly designed kitchen. Use **TABLE 3-4** to create your wish list.

TABLE 3-4

KITCHEN WISH LIST		
KITCHEN ITEM	**YES**	**NO**
Additional counter space (that's easy to clean)	❑	❑
Adjustable shelving	❑	❑
Appliance garage (for small and mid-sized appliances)	❑	❑
Bookshelf for cookbooks	❑	❑
Breadbox	❑	❑
Built-in icemaker (with cubes and/or crushed ice) in the refrigerator	❑	❑
Computer work area	❑	❑
Cooking range or indoor grill	❑	❑
Cutlery storage area	❑	❑
Dishwasher	❑	❑
Divided silverware/flatware drawer	❑	❑
Divided tray storage	❑	❑
Extra refrigerator or freezer space	❑	❑

KITCHEN WISH LIST (continued)		
KITCHEN ITEM	**YES**	**NO**
Garbage disposal	❑	❑
Hot water dispenser	❑	❑
Lazy Susan storage (in cabinets)	❑	❑
Microwave	❑	❑
More drawer storage	❑	❑
More electrical outlets	❑	❑
More shelf storage	❑	❑
New or larger island area	❑	❑
Range hood	❑	❑
Recycling area	❑	❑
Refrigerator	❑	❑
Spice rack	❑	❑
Task lighting	❑	❑
Television or radio	❑	❑
Tilt-down drawer for sponges (in the sink cabinet)	❑	❑
Trash compactor	❑	❑
Under-cabinet lighting	❑	❑
Warming drawer	❑	❑
Wine chiller	❑	❑
Wine rack (freestanding or one that's built into a wall or cabinet)	❑	❑

Whether your dream kitchen is large or small, you'll need to organize and store your ideas, samples, floor plans, receipts, and contracts throughout the project. With these tasks in mind, the Personal Project Organizer System, available from iWANTaNewKITCHEN.com, was designed by kitchen professionals for easy access, transport, and storage. This organization package will help you keep track of every detail involved in your kitchen building/remodeling process. Ultimately, by taking a well-organized approach to this project, you'll save time and money and be happier with the final project after it's completed.

Creating Clutter-free Kitchen Countertops

Whether you have the budget to redesign your kitchen from scratch or simply give a facelift to your existing kitchen by refacing your cabinets and adding a few new appliances, creating clutter-free countertops will make a huge difference in how functional your kitchen actually is after the redesign work is done.

When choosing your countertops, Kitchens.com recommends asking yourself the questions in **TABLE 3-5**.

TABLE 3-5	COUNTERTOP WORKSHEET

Do you want a smooth or textured feel?

Do you want the ease of cleaning an integral sink?

Do you like a consistent color, one that's broken up by granules or veins, or one that's patterned?

Do you care whether the materials are natural or man-made?

Will you want to chop, slice, and dice on the countertops or use a cutting board?

Will you want to roll dough on the countertops?

Where will you place hot pots?

Are you concerned about staining the countertops as a result of spilling liquid substances, such as wine or juice?

You'll also need to determine exactly how much countertop space you'll have available, where the counters will be located (based on the proposed location of major appliances), and what (if anything) will be stored on the countertops. Take a look at your kitchen right now. What's on the counters? When you redesign your kitchen, will anything that's currently stored on your countertops be relocated into cabinets or onto shelves? What new small or medium-sized appliances will you purchase that will go on the counter? Are you considering the purchase of an indoor grill for the added convenience of being able to prepare a quick meal?

To free up counter space, consider using appliances (such as a microwave and/or television) that can be installed under your cabinets. Also, can you install a telephone on a nearby wall with an extra-long handset cord (or a cordless handset), so that you can travel around the entire kitchen area unimpeded by cords? Can you utilize a paper towel rack that hangs on a wall or on the side of your refrigerator so that it doesn't take up countertop space?

As you actually use your kitchen, don't allow items to pile up (especially dirty dishes, utensils, and cooking tools). After you're done using something, place it in the sink or dishwasher. If the item is clean, return it to its proper storage location in a drawer or cabinet. When not in use, can your toaster, waffle iron, can opener, mixer, food processor, juicer, or other small appliance be kept in a cabinet or drawer? Unless you use an appliance or kitchen tool regularly, keep it on your countertop only when it's needed. Otherwise, clean it off and put it away.

Next to most kitchen sinks, you'll find a dish rack. This is a common place for clutter (dishes, glasses, and silverware) to collect. To begin with, invest in a dish rack that's made of stainless steel or another easy-to-clean material. Also, look for a unit that can temporarily store dishes, bowls, glasses, pots, pans, silverware, and other items until they're ready to be placed back in their proper storage place or into the dishwasher after being rinsed off. The dish rack should not become a permanent storage place for your dishes after they've been rinsed off.

FACT

Williams-Sonoma (✆ 800-541-2233, ✎ *www.williams-sonoma.com*) sells a stainless-steel dish rack that's designed with separate compartments for silverware, plates, bowls, mugs/glasses, and stemware. The unit is a cinch to keep clean and drains easily to promote the quick drying of dishes. If you live alone and only use a few dishes at once, a smaller version of this dish rack is available. Both come with a draining mat/tray.

Organizing Your Kitchen Cabinets and Drawers

Within your kitchen, you probably own dozens or even hundreds of small kitchen tools, utensils, and other items that need to be separated, organized, and stored. In addition, you probably have plenty of nonperishable food items, pots and pans, dishes, glasses, small and medium-sized appliances, cookbooks, and cleaning products.

Just as you'll do with your closets (see Chapter 2), when you begin to organize your kitchen cabinets and drawers, empty everything out and take a complete inventory of what needs to be stored. Get rid of old items that are broken or that you no longer need. Next, put together all similar items (such as canned goods, silverware, wine glasses, and so on) and determine how much storage space each set of items will need. Consider how often each group of items will be needed. Keep items that will be used often, such as your everyday silverware, in a drawer that's easy to access and conveniently located. Less frequently used items can be placed in the back of cabinets that aren't as readily accessible.

Here's how you may want to divide up and categorize the items in your kitchen that require storage:

- Baking tools and items
- Cleaning products
- Everyday dishes
- Everyday glasses and mugs
- Everyday silverware and flatware
- Formal dishes and fine china
- Formal silverware
- Kitchen linens (tablecloths, dish rags, napkins, and so on)
- Kitchen tools
- Pots and pans
- Serving dishes
- Small and medium-sized appliances
- Specialty items used for entertaining (cheese board, ice bucket, serving platters and bowls, chip and dip plate, and so on)

- The pantry (non-perishable food items)
- Wine glasses and formal glasses
- Wines bottles (opened and unopened)

After your kitchen items are divided into categories, determine whether each group needs cabinet space, drawer space, or some other type of storage. Will all of these items be kept in the kitchen, or will some items, such as your fine china, be kept in the formal dining area? Measure all of your available cabinet space and make sure that the items you plan to store there will fit. For example, are your bread machine, mixer, slow cooker, blender, pasta machine, toaster, and waffle iron too tall or too wide to fit within your cabinets?

When storing your pots and pans, one strategy is to purchase a matching set of pots and pans that are designed to be stored together. In addition, iWANTaNewKITCHEN.com reports it is becoming more popular to incorporate drawers into base cabinets for large items, such as pots and pans. "These drawers allow you to see and reach items in one easy step. Overhead or wall-mounted pot/pan racks are also popular for storage and display. This saves valuable space and keeps pots and pans within easy reach. It also reduces wear and tear on cabinetry due to the heavy-duty nature of these items."

Arrange your cupboards so that things used most frequently, such as plastic ware, mugs, cups, saucers, and plates are in the easiest-to-reach places. Likewise, organize the pantry so that breakfast cereals, beverages, and other packaged foods are easiest to locate and make sure that bags, napkins, plastic wrap, and foil are also easy to find. In addition to using a spice rack for storing your spices, try alphabetizing the individual containers, so that you know that your chives are just inches away from your cinnamon.

Separate all of your kitchen tools and items from food and nonperishable items. Cleaning products, for example, can be kept under the sink, away from canned goods and your pots and pans. Store products for dishwashing, mopping, stove polishing, and countertop cleaning in one convenient place. If you choose to store them beneath the sink, use a safety lock to keep out curious toddlers. Mops, brooms, pails, and dustpans can be kept in the broom closet.

FACT

For the ultimate collection of kitchen organization tools, visit any Lechters retail store (✆ 800-605-4824) or visit the company's Web site. To find a Lechters retail store near you, point your Web browser to ✐ *www.lechtersonline.com/Explorer/locator.htm*. To find out about the many kitchen organizational tools available, visit ✐ *www.thinkkitchen.com*.

If you're building a house or remodeling your kitchen and get to choose your kitchen cabinets and drawers, answer the following questions:

- Do you prefer a traditional, antique, or modern look?
- Do you prefer doors with details, such as curves, panels, or beading, or those with flat, smooth surfaces?
- Do you prefer simple pulls and knobs or statement-making, decorative hardware?
- Do you prefer the look of stained wood, paint, plastic, stainless steel, or glass?
- What are your storage requirements?
- What general color would you like the cabinets to be?

If you're staying with your existing layout and your cabinet and drawer space is limited, consider using organizational tools, such as drawer organizers. In cabinets, you can easily add internal shelving to instantly create additional room. Within some of your kitchen drawers, utilize various types of drawer organizers. For your silverware drawer, for example, you can use a basic organizer for sorting knives, forks, spoons, and other utensils. These drawer dividers and organizers are typically constructed from plastic or metal. They're extremely cheap and make organizing those smaller items that get stored in drawers much easier. Kitchen, Etc. (✆ 800-232-4070, ✐ *www.kitchenetc.com*), for example, offers over twenty-eight different styles of drawer organizers for the kitchen. Figure out which items need to be stored within each drawer, and then determine the size of the individual compartments or sections you want to divide the drawer into. This helps you choose the best divider/organizer to meet your needs for each specific drawer. Some items, such as knives and cutlery, require special storage to keep them from getting dull or damaged. A hardwood knife block (stored on a countertop) or a magnetic wall-mounted knife rack/utensil holder may be more suitable for your fancy knifes and cutlery than a drawer.

Organizing Your Refrigerator and Freezer

The first step to organizing your refrigerator and freezer is to empty it out and clean the appliance itself. Remove all of the shelves and clean them thoroughly. Start on the top shelf. Decide what will be kept, and then throw away old leftovers, anything that has acquired mold, and anything you know you'll never eat. Open all containers and check what's inside. Check the dates on all applicable items. Throw out anything that's out of date or questionable.

Next, inventory the items that belong in your refrigerator and decide how you'll organize them. Take full advantage of the drawers, shelves, and refrigerator door. Keep similar items, such as drinks, together. Store small loose items and leftovers in clear plastic containers (so that you can see what's inside).

During this clean-up and organization process, create a shopping list of items you need to purchase. As you decide which items belong in your refrigerator or freezer, consider the tips from the Home & Garden Television Web site (*www.hgtv.com*) in the following sections.

Items for the Refrigerator

Place meats in the refrigerator's meat or deli drawer. This area is colder than the rest of the refrigerator. Keep hamburger in the freezer if it won't be cooked within three days. Store fish overnight in a strainer that's piled high with ice and placed in a bowl. You're better off, however, eating fish when it is fresh.

Never keep eggs in the refrigerator door. This will expose them to air each time the door is opened and closed. Instead, keep them in the carton on an upper shelf in the refrigerator.

Crisper drawers are good for vegetables, such as peppers. These drawers typically have humidity control designed to help prevent vegetables from losing moisture. (The drawers seal tightly, which limits oxygen intake. The more oxygen intake, the quicker a food will deteriorate and spoil.) Keep lettuce fresher by storing it in a heavy-duty zipper bag. Discard the outer leaves that contain excess moisture. Wrap the lettuce in a paper towel, insert it in the plastic bag, squeeze as much air out of the bag as possible, and seal the bag.

Items for the Freezer

Store perishable spices in the freezer door within a plastic bag. In addition, store whole-wheat flour in the freezer. (White flour, however, can be stored at room temperature.) Freeze meats that you don't plan to use within three days of purchase.

Room-Temperature Items

Don't store potatoes in the refrigerator. The starch breaks down quickly, which leaves the potato mushy if baked. In the same way, tomatoes and cucumbers should be stored at room temperature. If you want these items cold in a salad, chill them before serving.

Hang bananas from a small rack or place them in a basket. Don't store them in a refrigerator. Citrus fruits are also good at room temperature because they have a waxed surface that keeps moisture from escaping.

Storing Pantry Items

Storing food items and keeping them organized is a challenge onto itself. Plastic containers, such as Tupperware (*www.tupperware.com*) or Gladware (*www.gladware.com*) are ideal for storage, because these containers are airtight and can be stored in the refrigerator or freezer, placed in a microwave, and then cleaned in a dishwasher and reused later. In addition to keeping items organized, they're also designed to maintain freshness. These containers are also easily stackable to maximize storage space, plus they're inexpensive.

In addition to plastic containers, plastic food-storage bags (such as Glad-Lock Zipper Storage Bags and ZipLoc Freezer Bags) come in a variety of different sizes and can be used for properly storing foods and other kitchen-related items. These bags can hold just about anything, including fruits, snacks, cereals, and meats. Because food should never be left uncovered in the refrigerator or on a countertop, plastic wrap (such as GladWrap) should be used to cover your plates, bowls, and foods. Both plastic storage bags and plastic wrap are clear, helping you see what's being stored or covered.

Store each type of food correctly in order to prevent spoilage. Always wrap food tightly and neatly in enough plastic wrap so that air doesn't seep in. This prevents mold from growing. In addition, separate raw meat, poultry, and seafood and put each into its own airtight plastic food-storage bag. This way, you eliminate the possibility of these raw meats cross-contaminating other raw food.

Avoiding Bacterial Contamination

Not only is keeping your kitchen clean an absolute must for maintaining an organized environment, it's also critical for maintaining your health. If not kept clean, bacteria and mold can spread throughout your kitchen and into your food, which could result in serious illness. Whether you're storing perishable foods, cooking, or cleaning, there are all kinds of safety measures you should take within your kitchen. The Partnership for Food Safety Education sponsors the Fight Bac! Web site (✍ *www.fightbac.org*), which offers an abundance of information about keeping your food safe from dangerous bacteria.

If not kept under control, bacteria can grow on food products (particularly meat, fish, and poultry), on kitchen surfaces (countertops and cutting boards), on knives and other utensils, and even in the kitchen sink or in the refrigerator itself. To prevent bacteria from taking over your kitchen, the Partnership for Food Safety Education recommends taking four primary precautions, covered in the following sections.

Clean

When working in the kitchen, wash your hands, utensils, and kitchen surfaces often. After a knife or plate touches raw meat, for example, wash it immediately. Wash your hands, using warm and soapy water, before and after you handle raw foods. Wash your cutting board, dishes, utensils, and countertops after each use (especially after handling raw meat, poultry, or fish). Use separate cutting boards for raw meats and vegetables, for example.

Separate

Don't cross-contaminate foods. Store meats, poultry, and fish away from other foods. Wrap or package each separately. Ask your local butcher for information on how to properly store specific types of meat, fish, and poultry for short (one to three days) or long periods of time.

Cook

When cooking your meat (poultry or fish), use the proper cooking temperature and cook for the appropriate amount of time. As you cook meat, use a clean thermometer to measure the internal temperature to determine when it's done.

Chill

Refrigerate and store your food properly.

ALERT!

When storing and preparing meat, poultry, and fish, never take any chances. If you have questions, ask the butcher at your local supermarket or call the USDA's Meat and Poultry Hotline at ✆ 800-535-4555. For seafood-related questions, call the FDA's Food Information and Seafood Hotline at ✆ 800-332-4010.

Managing Coupons

How would you like to save $5, $10, or even $50 every time you shop at the supermarket? If this sounds appealing, coupon clipping may be the answer! Searching for and clipping coupons from the newspaper or from advertising circulars can be a time-consuming task, but many people find this to be a relaxing rainy day or Sunday afternoon activity.

Many people use a portable binder with clear pockets to sort, categorize and store their coupons. For example, you may have a categories called "Cleaning Products" and "Pet-Care Products," and you simply place all related coupons in that category within the same pocket.

An alternative is to use a small file box and store your coupons alphabetically, either by product name or brand name. For example, Ivory soap could be filed under "I" for Ivory or "S" for soap, depending on your coupon filing system.

Another alternative is to use a batch of small envelopes, each marked with a separate coupon category. The disadvantage to this method is that you have to carry around a handful of envelopes and sort through them when you go to the supermarket.

FACT

Do you hear the sound of money going down the drain? It might be from all the unused coupons! Recent statistics reveal that more than 3,000 manufacturers offer consumers nearly 330 billion coupons every year. These coupons are worth an estimated $280 billion in potential savings. However, only about eight billion coupons, representing $4.7 billion, are actually used by consumers to save on grocery bills.

Using coupons can be a fun way to save money, if you're willing to invest the time needed to clip the coupons, bring them to the store, find the right product, and redeem the coupon. As a general rule, clip and store coupons for only those products you already use (or definitely want to try). If you're not careful, your coupon file could easily get cluttered with coupons you have no intention of using.

As you clip your coupons, pay attention to the expiration date and the fine print. If the coupon is clipped on Sunday, but you won't be food shopping for at least a full week and the coupon will expire before you get to use it, don't bother saving it. Likewise, to redeem the coupon, determine what exactly you need to purchase. If you're required to purchase an extra large container of laundry detergent, but you need only a small container, do the math and find out how much the savings will be if you purchase the larger container using the coupon.

After you clip your coupons, create a written shopping list for yourself. On the list, place a star or some other notation next to the items you have a coupon for. Next to that item, list the specific name brand and size you need to purchase in order to redeem the coupon.

So, where can the best coupons be found? For starters, try the Sunday newspaper and look for inserts and circulars. Look also in the newspaper's weekly food section, which typically appears on Wednesdays. You can also find coupons in general-interest magazines and in women's magazines.

Many supermarkets and libraries offer coupon swap-boxes for consumers. Drop off your unused coupons and grab a few you'll actually use in order to save money. Many supermarkets also have in-store displays that dispense coupons that you can use at checkout.

If you have access to the Web, visit the Web site of the supermarket where you typically shop. Online coupons (which you can print out and redeem) may be offered. There are also Web sites dedicated specifically to distributing coupons to consumers online. Check out *www.CentsOff.com*, ValuPage (*www.supermarkets.com*), eCoupons (*www.eCoupons.com*), Refund Sweepers (*www.refundsweepers.com/foodstores.shtml*), and SmartSource (*www.smartsource.com*) for starters.

Seek out supermarkets that will double or even triple the face value of manufacturers' coupons. Some supermarkets do this only on certain days of the week, so plan your shopping accordingly. Likewise, to obtain additional savings, be sure to join the shopper's advantage club (which gives you a card or key chain tag that gives you additional savings) now offered by many supermarkets. Membership to these clubs is usually free.

Organizing Recipes

If you enjoy cooking, chances are over time you'll acquire many recipes—from cookbooks, magazines, friends, relatives and/or the Internet. One way of storing these recipes is to purchase a three-ring binder with dividers, along with a handful of clear protective sheets that you can insert papers into. Divide the binder up into sections, such as "Appetizers," "Desserts," "Chicken Dishes," and so on, and then file your recipes within the binder. Keep this binder with your cookbooks, on a shelf in the kitchen.

An alternative is to file your recipes in a file cabinet or even on the computer. You can find several off-the-shelf electronic cookbook computer software packages on the market. In addition, you can use a database management program to enter and file your own recipes.

A personal digital assistant, such as the Handspring Visor (✐ *www.handspring.com*) or Palm (✐ *www.palm.com*), can also be used as a handheld electronic recipe storage system. Using any Palm PDA, a program called CookBook (✐ *www.dovcom.com/cookbook.html*) is an easy-to-use database that allows you to store your favorite recipes on the Palm PDA device for quick reference in the kitchen. Store recipes in any of fifteen user-defined categories. The program supports basic editing features (cut, copy, paste, and so on) and the Palm system's Find feature.

FACT

If you have a PDA capable of wireless communications, you'll be able to impress your friends with Cocktail Wireless. Use this service to obtain cocktail and drink recipes with the click of a pen. Access over 6,000 recipes, from traditional to trendy. Cocktails, punches, hot drinks, shooters, and non-alcoholic beverages are available from this online database maintained by the Rovenet Wireless Internet Portal (✐ *http://165.254.148.22/cocktails.htm*).

You can also use your PDA to create and maintain your grocery shopping list. Because a PDA is totally portable, you can carry it around throughout the day and take it to the supermarket. MyShoppingCart

(✎*www.palmsoftnet.com/myshopc/index.htm*), from PalmSoftNet.com, is a Palm PDA program designed with "simple to use" in mind. Basically, it is your daily groceries shopping list in a digital format. The program helps you to prepare and remember what you have to buy when you're in the store or supermarket.

Dealing with Trash and Recyclables

Out of all the rooms in your home, the kitchen is probably where the majority of your trash is created and collected. The trash created in the kitchen will most likely include food scraps and other perishables, which, if not disposed of properly, will start to smell and could attract bugs or rodents.

Within your kitchen, utilize a large, airtight garbage can (made from plastic or metal) in conjunction with durable, plastic garbage bags. A stainless steel garbage can in the kitchen will be the easiest to keep clean and will last for many years. Choosing a model that has a foot-lever to open the garbage can's lid without touching it with your hands offers both added convenience and makes handling garbage more sanitary.

After a garbage bag is full, seal and dispose of it as quickly as possible. If you're tossing away food scraps, place these scraps within a small plastic bag that can be sealed and toss that into the larger garbage bag. This will reduce bad smells.

To maintain a clean environment, you'll also want to spray your garbage can with disinfectant spray (that also removes odor) and clean the garbage can itself on a regular basis.

When you visit a supermarket, you'll quickly discover that plastic garbage bags come in a wide range of shapes and sizes. Glad (✎*www.glad.com/products/index.htm*), for example, offers over ten different styles of garbage bags designed for household use.

If you live in a community that encourages recycling, you'll want to separate newspapers, glass bottles, and cans from your regular garbage and store these items in containers until they can be picked up or brought to a recycling facility. To keep away bugs, make sure you wash all bottles and cans before storing them.

The following recycling tips come from the Glad Products Company:

- If your recyclables aren't organized, they can make a mess out of your kitchen. Small bins lined with wastebasket bags can separate recyclables like aluminum, plastic, newspaper, and glass. This can help keep kitchen clutter to a minimum.
- Unless you want to invite ants into your kitchen, always rinse out recyclable cans and bottles. Unrinsed, they can create a sticky, smelly residue.
- Don't bother removing labels for recycling. To save water, clean only enough to prevent odors. The high temperature used in processing recyclable metal and glass deals easily with contamination.
- Steel, glass, and aluminum are easy to recognize and recycle. Be sure not to mix glass bottles with other types of glass, such as mirrors, glass tableware, or other items.
- Most paper products can be recycled—newspapers have been for decades. Recently, other types of paper have been included, too. Collect large quantities of clean, well-sorted, dry, and uncontaminated paper such as magazines, posters, and catalogs.

Creating a Family Message Center

If you live in a household with other people, chances are you all have very different schedules, so communicating may be a challenge. Thus, you may want to create a family message center in the kitchen (such as on a refrigerator door). This message center may include a large corkboard or dry erase board (for posting messages) and/or several bins for sorting each individual's mail. On this message board, you can maintain a food-shopping list that all members of the family can contribute or add to based on their needs. For example, if someone drinks that last of the orange juice, it would be his or her job to add orange juice to the shopping list.

CHAPTER 4

Arranging a Spacious Dining Area

Y our home's dining area may be where your family gather to dine every morning for breakfast or each evening for dinner. This chapter offers strategies for organizing your dining area; choosing the right furniture to meet your needs; storing your fine table linens, china, and silverware; and hosting a well-organized social gathering in your dining area.

Determining Your Needs

As with each room in your home that you want to redesign or organize, the first step involves determining what your needs are. Answer the following questions:

- What will the primary use of this room be? (Casual dining with your family? Formal dining with friends, family, and/or business associates? Storage? Will this room double as a place for you to do work or your kids to do homework?)
- How often will you use the dining area for dining? (Nightly, weekly, monthly, once a year? Only for holidays?)
- How often will the dining area be used for activities other than dining?
- How many people will you typically need to accommodate? While you may have all of your relatives over each year for Thanksgiving dinner, for example, during the rest of the year, will you typically only have four or six people dining in this room?

Flooring Options

The décor and functionality of the room will, in part, be dictated by the type of flooring you choose. Lush carpeting, hardwood floors, linoleum, tile or area rugs all set different moods and impact how easily the room can be cleaned. If you choose to utilize an area rug or Oriental rug in your dining area, avoid putting your dining room table and chairs on the rug unless it's large enough so the chairs can be moved in and out without catching on the edge of the rug.

Furniture and Storage Options

The primary furniture in most dining areas consists of a table (which is often expandable using leafs) and chairs. Based on your needs, how large does the dining room table need to be? When expanded (using the leafs), how many people can it accommodate?

If you'll be purchasing new dining room furniture, instead of making your buying decisions based on knowing, for example, that the only time you'll have more than six people dining at the table is when the entire family visits for Thanksgiving, focus on what your year-round needs are. You can always add a folding table and folding chairs to accommodate the additional relatives for that one gathering each year. There's usually no need to spend extra money or use up too much space by purchasing a dining room furniture set that's too big to meet your needs.

In addition to the dining room table and chairs, think about what you'll be storing in your dining area. Do you require shelves or glass cabinets to display knickknacks or fine china? Are drawers more important for storing your table linens, fine flatware, and those larger serving dishes that don't fit in your kitchen cabinets? When choosing a china cabinet, hutch, buffet, sideboard, vitrine, and/or credenza, think first about exactly what you'll be storing and displaying. Take an inventory of your china, formal flatware, large serving pieces, and table linens to determine how much drawer space, shelf space, and cabinet space you'll actually need. Will your wine collection also be stored here? What about items from other rooms or your holiday decorations? You'll ultimately want to store similar items together using proper storage materials. For example, for your expensive formal flatware, you'll probably want to store it in a multi-compartment flatware tray, flatware chest, or storage box (with an anti-tarnish lining). Your first consideration should be functionality. After you find items that meet your storage needs, focus on style and how the item fits into the overall décor of the room. The Western Silver Company (✆ 800-850-3579, ✒ *www.westernsilver.com/flatware_guide.html*) offers detailed information on purchasing and storing silverware.

Create a detailed list of what new furniture, if any, you'll need in your dining area, and then measure the room carefully and sketch out a room design in graph paper. You'll, of course, want to ensure that all of the furniture you plan to add into the room will fit properly. When taking measurements, don't forget to consider the size of the dining room table when it's fully expanded. Also make sure you leave room for people to pull out their dining room chairs in order to sit up or sit down. You'll also need ample room to walk around.

Use **TABLE 4-1** for a detailed furniture list and measurements for your dining area.

TABLE 4-1	DINING AREA FURNITURE MEASUREMENTS	
FURNITURE		**MEASUREMENTS**
Dining room table (without leafs)		
Dining room table (with leafs installed)		
Dining room chairs		
Wine rack/liquor cabinet		
China cabinet		
Hutch/buffet/vitrine		
Credenza		

If your living space simply doesn't have room for a full-sized dining room set, yet you still occasionally want to create a formal dining experience in your home, consider transforming a standard folding card table into an eight person dining table using a sturdy padded table topper, such as the one offered in the Solutions catalog (✆ 800-342-9988, ✍ *www.solutionscatalog.com*). The 48" Round Card Table Extender (item #63586) or the 54" Round Card Table Extender (item #63587) are sturdy padded toppers that get placed on a standard folding card table. The deluxe $^5/_8$"-thick padding features a vinyl top and woven polyester bottom that won't scratch your table. Special side straps secure this table top to the table legs to prevent slipping. This particular item folds flat for storage and is priced under $90. Simply add a formal tablecloth, fine china, and some candles, and you've instantly created a formal dining experience.

FACT

One common term used by furniture stores when referring to a dining room set is "nine-piece suite." The nine pieces include the table, four side chairs, two armchairs, a buffet, and a hutch. In some cases, however, a nine-piece suite includes the leaves (which lengthen the table) as pieces but doesn't include the buffet and hutch. When shopping for furniture, make sure you understand exactly which pieces you're getting when quoted a price for a dining room set.

Dining room tables come in many sizes and shapes. The most common are rectangular-shaped tables in lengths of six or eight feet with a width of forty-two inches. These tables may be expandable to accommodate additional guests. When choosing your table, in addition to measuring the length to ensure a proper fit within the room, also consider the width. In smaller dining areas, consider utilizing a round table, which may also come with leaves.

When not in use, keep the leaves from your dining room table out of the way, against the back wall of a nearby closet, for example. To keep them from getting damaged, wrap a towel around each leaf as you place it against the closet wall (out of the way, behind your coats and jackets).

As for your dining room chairs, you also have many options. In terms of sizing, most interior design experts suggest leaving at least twelve to eighteen inches of space between each chair. This gives the people sitting down ample elbow room. No matter what its style, a typical dining room chair measures around twenty-two inches wide. Also, when considering your available space, try to leave at least twenty to thirty inches between the back of each chair and the nearest wall or door. This provides plenty of room for people to move around.

FACT

If you're buying a hardwood dining room furniture set, purchase your wood dining chairs at the same time as the table (especially if they're made from the same type of wood and designed to match perfectly). Over time, wood oxidizes, and the color of your furniture will become richer and deeper. Ideally, you want your table and chairs to oxidize at the same rate so it does not appear that your chairs are lighter in color than your table.

As you choose a style for your dining area, go for something simplistic. Interior decorators call this approach "casual elegance." When you're hosting a formal dinner gathering, for example, you can enhance the overall décor of the room using fine table linens, fine china, and mood lighting. Think in terms of the overall functionality of the room. If the dining area will also be used as a place for doing paperwork or casual dining, it should provide a comfortable environment for these uses.

Another consideration when choosing your dining room furniture is to ensure that its style (as well as its quality and craftsmanship) will stand the test of time. When guests come into your home ten years from now, you don't want their reaction to be, "Wow, I remember when this used to be popular." While the dining room furniture will most likely be an investment that lasts for decades, you can update the look of your dining area using new wallpaper, changing the flooring, painting, changing the lighting, reupholstering the chairs, or using different styles (or colors) of table linens.

To protect your table top, contact the Factory Direct Table Pad Co. (✆ 800-737-4194, ✐ *www.tablepads.com*) for a high quality table pad. The pad, which won't scratch your table, protects from sweating glasses, nicks and scratches, and dropped dishes. Each pad is tailored to fit your table top.

Chandelier and Lighting Options

For dining areas, in order to ensure comfortable lighting across the entire table and throughout the room, mount an overhead chandelier from the ceiling, over the dining room table. Additional floor lamps, lighting mounted to the walls, or table lamps, for example, can be added to add accent lighting. To see a wide selection of dining area lighting options without leaving your home, point your Web browser to ✐ *www.elights.com*.

As a general rule, you'll probably wind up centering your dining room table directly under your chandelier (or other hanging lighting fixture). In an attempt to redesign the room on a budget, consider angling the table diagonally in the room, for example, to create a totally different effect.

Typically, when you're hosting a formal or romantic dinner, you'll want mood lighting. Consider installing a lighting fixture with lights that can be dimmed. You may also want to incorporate decorative candleholders on the dining room table and walls, if you choose to use candlelight.

When choosing lighting for your dining area, you have many options. A simple lighting fixture may cost under $50, while a fancy chandelier could cost anywhere from $100 to several thousand dollars.

Chandeliers that accommodate 200 to 400 watts provide an abundance of overall illumination. Install the fixture thirty inches above the table to allow for ample headroom when standing. The diameter of the fixture should be twelve inches less than the overall width of the table. Matching wall mounts or recessed downlights can also be used to add accent and sparkle. Consider installing the chandelier using a dimmer light switch.

You can easily enhance the appearance of many formal lighting fixtures by using flame-shaped bulbs in traditionally designed lighting fixtures or using globes or tubular bulbs in contemporary lighting fixtures. Consider using clear bulbs with crystal, clear or other transparent fixtures, and glass shades. Frosted or coated bulbs work the best with opal, etched, and other translucent glass shades or diffusers.

If you have artwork to showcase in your dining area, or you want to proudly display your fine china (or statues, for example) that are enclosed in a display case or positioned on a shelf, you can add drama to walls or interest to a fireplace through the use of accent lighting. Direct more intense light levels onto artwork or sculptures with directional wall, ceiling, or recessed fixtures.

For help in choosing the appropriate lighting for your dining area, visit any lighting specialty store, hardware store, or home improvement store. You can also solicit the services of an interior decorator.

Storing and Cleaning Linens

Consider the table linen you showcase in your home to be the backdrop for your fine china, crystal, and silver. Real table linen can be expensive, but like your dining area furniture, should be considered an investment. Before you purchase table linen, be sure to know the exact measurements of your table. A formal tablecloth should hang down from the edge of the tabletop approximately eighteen inches.

Refrain from storing fine table linen in the original plastic packaging it may have been sold in. A plastic container or bag will trap moisture and bacteria, which could eventually cause discoloration. Also, don't store your table linens so tightly folded that they crease. Keeping a tightly folded tablecloth in an overcrowded drawer, for example, will damage the fabric over time.

If you're about to invest in an expensive tablecloth, begin your table linen collection by choosing a classic white linen or classic damask tablecloth, along with a matching set of napkins. You can later expand this collection with a solid colored cloth that matches an accent color in your dinnerware pattern, for example.

Don't be afraid to wash real linen tablecloths and napkins. You'll discover that fine linen improves in appearance and feel with every wash. Just as you would with expensive bed linen, iron your table linen while it's still damp, on the wrong side. This will help prevent any shiny patches from forming. Make sure the iron isn't too hot. (For laundering information, see Chapter 10.) When storing fine table linens, always launder and iron (or professionally clean) them properly before putting them into storage. Follow the cleaning and care instructions provided by the table linen manufacturer.

Here's how Procter & Gamble recommends dealing with several common food-related stains.

Coffee and Tea Stains

Before treating any garment, first refer to the care label instructions. Test the effect of the stain-removal technique on a colored item on a hidden area of the item. Pretreat the stain with a liquid detergent, and then soak up to thirty minutes by adding a ½ cup of liquid detergent per gallon of water. (Weigh the item down with a white towel to keep it submerged.) Discard soak solution prior to laundering. Wash the item in warm water using a liquid detergent. Line or air dry, repeating the procedure, if necessary. Avoid using a dryer or iron because the intense heat could cause the stain to become permanent.

Fruit, Juice, and Wine Stains

Before treating any garment, first refer to the care label instructions. Test the effect of the stain-removal technique on a colored item on a hidden area of the item. Rinse the item in cold water to dilute the stain, and then soak the item up to thirty minutes by adding a ½ cup of liquid detergent per gallon of water. (Weigh the item down with a white towel to keep it submerged.) Discard the soak solution prior to laundering. Wash the item in warm water using a liquid detergent. Air dry the item and repeat the procedure, if necessary.

Spaghetti Sauce Stains

Before treating any garment, first refer to the care label instructions. Test the effect of the stain-removal technique on a colored item on a hidden area of the item. Pretreat the stain with a liquid detergent, and then wash the item in warm water using a liquid detergent. Air dry the item and repeat the procedure, if necessary.

Chocolate Stains

Before treating any garment, first refer to the care label instructions. Test the effect of the stain-removal technique on a colored item on a hidden area of the item. Physically remove the stain by scraping with a dull knife, and then shake the item. Pretreat the stain with a liquid detergent, and then wash the item in warm water using a liquid detergent. If any stain remains, soak the item up to thirty minutes by adding a ½ cup of liquid detergent per gallon of water. (Weigh the item down with a white towel to keep it submerged.) Discard soak solution prior to laundering. Repeat the procedure, if necessary.

An Organized Approach to Entertaining in Your Dining Area

When planning a formal gathering, you must preplan every aspect of the event. Depending on the number of people you'll be entertaining and what your role in the event will be, you may choose to hire a professional caterer or accommodator to assist in coordinating and hosting the gathering. Also, make sure that there's always a clear pathway between your kitchen and the dining area. If you'll be traveling back and forth between these two rooms, choose a seat at the table that's the closest to the kitchen, so you avoid disturbing others each time you leave your seat.

Planning Your Event

As you begin to plan your event, consider the following questions:

- What is the purpose of the gathering?
- Will this be a casual or formal dining experience?
- How many people will be attending?
- What will the complete menu include?
- Do you have enough seating, dishes, flatware, glasses, and serving items to accommodate all of the people attending the event?
- What will the schedule for the event be? Create a timeline for serving drinks, hors d'oeuvres, and each course of the meal.
- What music or other entertainment will be incorporated into the event?
- What will the theme of the event be? Do you need special decorations?

What decorating approaches can brighten my dining table?
Use fresh flowers as your dining room table's centerpiece. If you can't always afford fresh flowers, rotate between fresh flowers, realistic silk flowers, and an interesting candle arrangement. Be sure your tabletop is well protected from condensation and accidental spills, however. Water can permanently damage a hardwood table.

Setting the Table

To properly prepare for a gathering in your dining area, set the table properly. The following describes how to take a casual, yet elegant approach to setting the table.

For each place setting, place the dinner plate first. On top of it, place the salad plate/bowl. To the left, position the dinner fork immediately next to the plate. The salad fork goes to the extreme left. On the right side of the dinner plate, place the knife (to be used with the main course), and to the right of that, place the butter knife. The soup spoon should be placed to the right of the knives.

The fork and spoon to be used for dessert should be positioned horizontally, above the inner place. The folded napkin should be placed in the center of the plate. Finally, position the water glass above the dinner plate, to the right (at a one o'clock position). The wine glass should be to the immediate right of the water glass (at a two o'clock position).

Using place cards on your formal dinner table lets guests know where to find their seats. By preplanning where people will sit, you can ensure that people with similar interests (and who get along) will be seated together.

For a more formal (multi-course) dining experience, some etiquette experts recommend that you start with the outside utensils and work your way in. Western Silver, however, offers this advice for setting a formal place setting:

Begin with the dinner plate in the center of each place setting. On top of the dinner plate, place the soup bowl and plate. Working from left to right on the left side of the dinner plate, place the napkin, followed by the fish fork, dinner fork, and salad fork.

To the right side of the dinner plate (going from left to right), position the dinner knife, followed by the fish knife and the soup spoon. Above the dinner plate, to the left (on a diagonal at the eleven o'clock position), place the bread and butter plate, with the butter knife placed horizontally on top of this plate. Directly above the dinner place, position the dessert (cake) fork, and above that, the dessert spoon.

Also above the dinner plate, to the right (on a diagonal at the one o'clock position), place the water glass, red wine glass, and white wine glass (going from left to right).

The following is a brief description of each piece of formal flatware you may find as part of a formal place setting.

- **Butter knife:** Used to spread butter, soft cheeses, chutneys, and relishes.
- **Cocktail fork:** Used for seafood or fruit cocktail, lobster, and for serving pickles or olives.

- **Demitasse spoon:** Used to stir an after-dinner coffee, serve condiments or eat caviar.
- **Dinner fork:** Used to eat all main entrees, except fish.
- **Fish fork:** This utensil is used in place of the dinner fork when fish is served.
- **Fish knife:** Used in place of a dinner or steak knife when fish is served.
- **Iced beverage spoon:** Used to stir any tall beverage or eat some desserts.
- **Salad fork:** Used to eat salads, fish, pies, pastries, and cold meats.
- **Soup spoon:** Used to eat desserts, cereal, and soup, or used as a small serving spoon.
- **Steak knife/dinner knife:** Used for cutting meats.
- **Teaspoon:** Used for coffee, tea, fruits, and some desserts.

Caring for Your Flatware

In general, when washing your fine flatware, use only warm, sudsy water. Carefully rinse away traces of food from the flatware. Especially for expensive flatware avoid using harsh dishwashing detergents that contain chlorides. Also, avoid lemon-scented detergents, which contain acids that may harm the metal. It's also important to hand-dry silver, especially knife blades, to avoid spotting and pitting.

If you'll be washing both silver and stainless steel flatware in the dishwasher, don't put them in the same basket section. You want to avoid allowing one metal to touch the other.

While sterling silver is beautiful, it tarnishes over time. There are many different metal polishes on the market that you can use to keep your fine silver sparkling like new. Tarn-X from Jelmar (800-323-5497, www.jelmar.com), for example, is an excellent metal polish that's available from retailers nationwide. Tarn-X works on silver, silver plate, gold, platinum, copper, and diamonds. To use this product (or polishes like it), Jelmar recommends the following:

1. Use household gloves when polishing silver or other metals.
2. Dip a cotton ball or soft cloth in Tarn-X and wipe on the tarnished areas of the metal. Rinse the metal thoroughly under soapy water and wipe dry. For large items, apply Tarn-X to about $1/3$ of article at a time, and then rinse thoroughly. Don't soak any object in Tarn-X for over two minutes.
3. For heavily tarnished pieces, repeat above process until all the tarnish is dissolved.
4. Tarn-X only removes tarnish. You can apply a companion product, Tarn-X Silver Glaze, after using Tarn-X for optimum shine and luster.

Protecting and Storing Your Fine China

If you choose to display your fine china in a cabinet, it will be pretty well protected behind closed glass doors as you show off the beauty of your pieces. If your fine china will be stored in drawers or closed cabinets, however, you'll want to take steps to properly protect these expensive and fragile items. Using quilted vinyl cases for china, for example, will help keep dust away, and at the same time will help prevent chipping and scratching. The China Protector Set (item #64490) from the Solutions catalog (✆ 800-342-9988, ✎ *www.solutionscatalog.com*), for example, protects a sixty-four-piece set, with separate cases for dinner plates, salad plates, bowls, saucers, and cups. To prevent chips and scratches while storing china in these padded vinyl cases, a separate soft foam protector is placed in between each item. These cases can then be safely stored in a drawer or cabinet. Dinnerware storage pouches, manufactured from quilted cotton with acrylic felt inserts and zippered tops, can be purchased from Old China Patterns Limited by calling ✆ 800-663-4533 or by visiting the company's Web site (✎ *www.chinapatterns.com/pouches.html*). After placing your fine china in these pouches, it will be protected when stored in drawers or cabinets.

If a piece of your fine china, crystal, or formal flatware happens to break, chip, or get badly scratched, and your pattern or design has been discontinued, you can find companies that buy and sell discontinued china patterns and other formal dinnerware. For more information on these companies and a list of dealers, visit the International Association of Dinnerware Matchers' Web site (✍ *www.iadm.com*). The Set Your Table: Discontinued Tableware Dealers Directory (✍ *www.setyourtable.com*) is also a useful resource when you need to replace fine china, flatware, or crystal pieces.

Organizing Your Liquor Cabinet

Whether you have a stand-alone liquor cabinet or a wine rack built into your buffet or credenza, keep all of your related supplies together in one area. In addition to the actual bottles of wine and liquor, some of the supplies you'll want on hand in or near your liquor cabinet include a bottle opener, bottle stoppers, cocktail napkins, cocktail shaker, corkscrew, decanter, foil cutter, ice bucket, pitcher, wine glasses, shot glasses, and *The Everything® Bartender's Book* (Adams Media). Some wine racks have special shelves or cabinets to store these accessories and items.

Many companies specialize in custom-designed and ready-made wine racks and cabinets and also sell a wide selection of wine accessories. In addition to visiting a local wine merchant, check out these online retailers: American Wine Essentials, Inc. (✍ *www.amwe-store.com*), Artisans on Web (✍ *www.aoweb.com*), International Wine Accessories (✍ *www.iwawine.com*), the Wine Enthusiast (✍ *www.wineenthusiast.com*), and Wine Racks USA (✍ *www.wineracksusa.com*).

FACT

If you have a wireless Palm PDA, you can access the Wine Lover's Page and obtain a wide range of wine-related advice. For example, if you're planning a formal dinner gathering, this free service will help you choose the perfect wine based on your menu and budget. Point your Web browser to ✍ *www.wineloverspage.com/pocketwinelist* or from your wireless PDA (such as the Palm with OmniSky service, for example), access ✍ *www.PocketWineList.com*.

CHAPTER 5

Creating a Comfortable Great Room or Family Room

Depending on the size of your home and your living habits, your living area may have many uses. As the name suggests, your living area is a place for living. Thus, you want to ensure that it's as comfortable as possible, clutter-free, and reflects your personal style and tastes.

Assessing Your Needs

Starting with the basics, think about exactly what you use (or want to use) this room for. Next, determine what furniture and other fixtures you need in order to accommodate these activities. For example, if the living area is where you and the people living in your home will relax and watch television, you'll need an entertainment center and plenty of comfortable seating, along with a coffee table and/or end tables, plus adequate lighting. If this is the room where your art collection or collectibles will be stored and displayed, you'll need to accommodate those items with adequate wall space, shelves, or display cabinets, plus appropriate lighting. When spending quality time with a loved one or just curling up on a chilly evening to read a book, perhaps you'll want to utilize your fireplace. If this is the case, the furniture in the room should be situated around the fireplace, but not be too close so it creates a fire hazard. Likewise, you'll need a rack to store the various tools and items associated with the fireplace.

By thinking carefully about how the room will be utilized, you'll be able to figure out exactly how to get the most comfort and functionality out of the room.

As you begin to create the perfect living area environment, consider alternate uses for the room, as well. If, for example, you install a sofa bed in the room, can it double as a guest room when you have guests that plan to stay over? Will this room also be used as a part-time home office? If so, what additional furniture (such as a desk and file cabinets or computer workstation and extra phone jacks) will you need?

> Virtually any living area can be transformed into a comfortable guest bedroom in minutes using a traditional pullout sofa bed, an air mattress (such as the Aerobed—check out *www.aerobed.com/ beds.html)*, a rollaway bed, or a portable cot. You may have to temporarily rearrange tables and other furniture to create space for the guest beds.

Furnishing Your Living Area

The actual living room furniture you select will ultimately be a matter of personal taste, based on the level of comfort and the décor you select. The physical size of the room, however, plays a major role in determining how much furniture actually fits within the room. After all, placing too much furniture within the room, no matter how fancy and comfortable it is, will create a cluttered look and take away from the functionality of the room itself (see **FIGURE 5-1**).

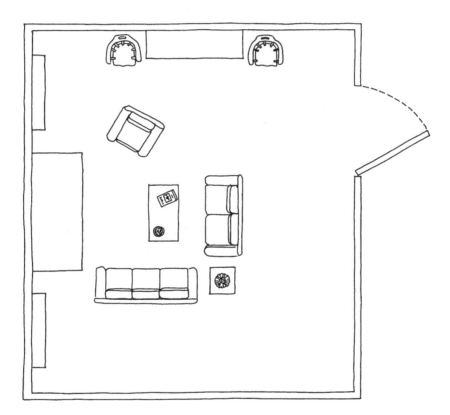

FIGURE 5-1: A cluttered living area layout

Before going out and investing in all new living room furniture, consider rearranging the furniture you have now and accenting or accessorizing that furniture to create a whole new look in the room. Simply by rearranging the furniture into a more functional design, and perhaps adding new curtains and lampshades, you can create an entirely new room for little or no money.

If you use your living area for entertaining, to make it conducive to conversation consider arranging your furniture in clusters (see **FIGURE 5-2**), as opposed to having all of the seating facing the television. Clusters make for a warm and inviting feeling. Also, make good use of any alcoves or recessed walls by lining them with shelves to create additional storage and display space.

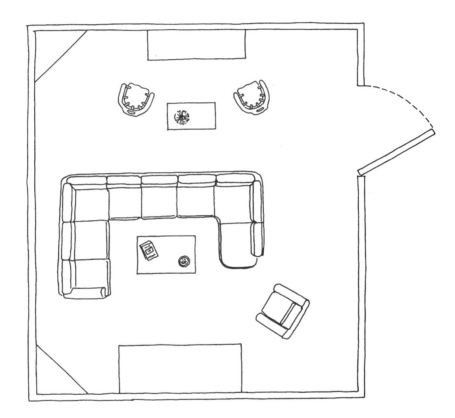

FACT

To plan how your redesigned and well-organized living area will look, consider using the Room Planner, a free service available from HomeStore.com (*www.homestore.com*). With this interactive tool, you can build, decorate, and furnish rooms in your home without all the heavy lifting! It's an easy-to-use online application that will ensure the furniture you select (or currently own) fits comfortably into the available space, and that all of the space within your living area is being fully utilized.

After you understand the overall purpose and main functions of your living area, consider which living room furniture pieces you currently own and which you're interested in adding based on your needs. For furniture, less is more, so choose pieces that will be truly utilized within the room. Common living room furniture pieces include a sofa, love seat, chair and ottoman, recliner, sectional, bookcases and shelf unit, entertainment center or wall unit, coffee or cocktail table, end tables, floor and table lamps, and piano.

Placing a wall unit or entertainment center in the best spot in your living area isn't an easy task. When choosing a wall unit or entertainment center, first inventory all of the electronics that you plan to store on/in it. Does this piece of furniture have ample room for your television, cable box, DVD player, VCR, stereo, video game system(s), surround-sound system and speakers (left, right, and middle)? Are ample electrical outlets located in the area? Will the unit hide all of the wires that go with your audio/visual electronics? Is there a nearby phone jack? If you'll be using WebTV, TiVo, or certain other types of electronics, you'll need access to a phone jack and probably don't want phone wires running across your living area.

If your space is extremely limited, consider mounting your TV, VCR, and stereo on a wall using specially made brackets. This will free up floor space. The Frontgate catalog (✆ 800-626-6488, ✍ *www.frontgate.com*) offers several different wall-mounted media centers and TV pedestals.

How can I maximize my storage space?
As you install bookcases and shelving, utilize as little floor space as possible through the use of tall bookcases or shelving. On the higher shelves, display items or books that you don't access very often, but use clear containers so that you can see what you've stored.

After your entertainment center/wall unit is in place and you begin to add your various pieces of audio and video electronics, be sure to label all of the wires associated with each piece of equipment. Use a Brother P-Touch label maker (available from any office supply store) or a pen to write labels on tape that can be wrapped around each wire. You can also purchase color-coded wires and use different colored ties to wrap related wires together for easy identification.

Shelving is an easy and economical way to add extra storage space to your living area. And don't worry. You don't have to be Bob Villa to build or install shelving! This project doesn't typically require a lot of skill or specialized tools. And unless you decide to use hardwood, (which can be costly), building or installing your own shelves won't cost a bundle either. Before you go shopping for shelves and shelving kits, determine what will go on the shelves and how much the items actually weigh. The weight of the objects will determine the type of shelving, brackets, and fasteners you need and will tell you how far apart to install shelf supports. Attaching the shelves to studs in the wall is the key to secure drywall and plaster installations. To find the studs, use an electronic or magnetic stud finder.

The living area is also where many people choose to keep a computer. Invest in a computer workstation or desk that offers ample space for your entire computer system and related peripherals (printer, scanner, modem, and so on), plus space to spread out your papers and to work. You'll want to position your computer in an area of the living area that's conducive to allowing the person using it to concentrate. Also, consider incoming glares from sunlight through the window and how this will impact your ability to see the computer's monitor during daylight hours. Make sure the computer is positioned near both an electrical outlet and phone jack. See Chapter 9 for more information on setting up a home office.

If you want to keep your computer within your living area, but not make it a highly visible focal point in the room, consider utilizing a closable office center, such as the ones offered by Hold Everything (✆ 800-421-2264, ✎ *www.holdeverything.com*). These cabinets are usually hardwood and offer a pullout keyboard tray and drawers and room for a nineteen-inch monitor, CPU, and other accessories. The doors may contain a wipe board or metal memo holder, plus a built-in magazine/file rack. Ikea, which has retail stores across America, plus a mail-order catalog and Web site *(✎ www.ikea-usa.com)* also offers a wide selection of innovative and highly functional living room furniture selections which are extremely economical.

For additional ideas on how to lay out your living room furniture, check out design and home decorating magazines, visit the showrooms of furniture stores, or contact an interior decorator. Always be thinking in terms of functionality and comfort in addition to appearance.

FACT

You can utilize the corners of rooms by installing shelving in this otherwise unused area. You can also purchase special cabinets, CD storage racks, lamps, and entertainment centers designed for the corner of a room. Another excellent way to save floor space and creating additional room within your living area is to utilize ceiling mounted track lighting, recessed lighting, or wall-mounted lamps.

Living Area Storage Tips

Storage in the living area can be a tricky thing. First, determine what you need to store, and then tap your creativity. For CDs, DVDs, video games, and videocassettes, purchase a display rack/organizer that holds your entire collection. This can be a freestanding unit, one that is mounted on a wall, or one that fits in your entertainment center or wall unit. If it's a freestanding unit, consider placing it in an unused corner of a room so that you can better utilize this space.

You may also want to invest in a multi-functional universal remote control so that you can replace the separate remotes for your TV, cable box, VCR, DVD, surround-sound system, and stereo with one unit. An alternative is to place a remote control caddy on the coffee table or near the TV, to help you keep track of all your different remote control units. The Frontgate catalog (✆ 800-626-6488, ✍ *www.frontgate.com*), for example, offers several different remote control caddies.

For items that don't necessarily need to be displayed, consider a coffee table with drawers beneath it or an ottoman that doubles as a storage box. A wooden chest and an armoire with multiple shelves or closed cabinets is also excellent for storage.

Displaying Artwork and Collectibles

Displaying a collection of artwork, statues, trinkets, memorabilia, or collectibles can be tricky, especially if your space is limited. Begin by going through your collection and throwing away items that are broken or that you no longer wish to keep. Next, pick out any items that you want to store, but don't necessarily want to display. You want to avoid making your display look cluttered, because this won't be visually appealing. Start off by choosing the best method of display for whatever items you have to show off. Consider grouping similar items together. Basic display options for knickknacks, artwork, and collectibles include cabinets with glass doors, pedestals, shelves, wall space (by hanging objects), and floor space (by standing objects on the floor).

Make sure your collections or items are properly lit and that the display you create is visually appealing and lacks clutter. According to some interior designers, the secret to elegant displays—even when working with everyday objects—is lush layering. To create your own elegant displays, begin with one tall object that you place in the center of the collection, and then loosely create a triangle shape as you work down to the display surface (such as the tabletop or shelf). If the items need wall space to be displayed, consider filling a blank wall with multiple items with a similar theme (and matching frames or frames that are similar in style that are artistically positioned on the wall).

In addition to displaying a collection, some people choose to display and store their personal libraries in the living area. This can be done with relative ease by installing a bookcase and/or shelving for this purpose. Your bookcase can be a freestanding unit, or you can choose have a bookcase or shelving built directly into a wall (see the "Furnishing Your Living Area" section of this chapter for more information). Whichever option you choose, be sure to consider the heavy weight of the books and ensure that the shelving/bookcase can hold this excessive weight.

To create a well-organized personal library, begin by sorting through your entire collection. Weed out books you no longer want and consider giving them away to friends or donating them to a local library. Next, sort your books by category (fiction, nonfiction, short stories, poetry, plays, travel, religious, how-to, children's books, textbooks, and so on).

Determine how much bookcase or shelf space you need, and then arrange your book collection by category. If you want to prominently display certain books, such as your family scrapbook, position these books face out on a shelf using a small bookstand.

You can add a personal touch to your library by selecting decorative bookends or by placing various trinkets on the shelves in conjunction with your books. Magazines can be displayed separately on a coffee or cocktail table or by using a freestanding magazine rack. Depending on your décor, you may be able to find end tables with built-in shelves that can also be used for storing books, magazines, remote controls, or your knitting items.

Displaying and Organizing Photographs

You can display, organize, and store your personal photographs and memorabilia in many ways. Because you probably don't have enough wall space to frame and hang all of your pictures, consider a few alternatives, such as creating a scrapbook or using labeled boxes for storage.

Organizing Photos and Negatives

Begin by finding a method for organizing all of your photographs, including labeling the negatives, writing about the pictures, and storing the photographs until you are ready to mount them in your scrapbook. After you establish a method, every time you have a new roll of film developed, implement your organizational strategy immediately.

The Graceful Bee NewBees Web site offers the following photo storage tips:

- Use acid-free labels to document your negatives with a date range and the subject matter of photographs.
- Keep a film log of pictures taken.
- Store photographs in resealable bags.
- Use acid-free strips of paper and an acid-free permanent pen to document your photographs. Include the journaling basics of who, what, where, why, and how. Even if you never get these pictures into albums, by documenting your pictures, you're ahead of the game.

If you're going to be storing photos and memorabilia in an attic, garage, or other non–climate controlled area, at the very least, the photos should be stored in airtight plastic containers. For normal storage in climate-controlled areas, cardboard, wooden, or leather boxes designed specifically for storing photos work perfectly. (If you're on a budget, use shoe boxes.) Make sure you properly label each box.

Making Scrapbooks

After you've reviewed and organized all of your photos, choose your favorites for incorporation into your photo album or scrapbook. Choose an actual album or scrapbook that conveys a specific theme, such as family vacations, holidays, family memories, or a child's album. After you've decided which album to begin with, determine the sequence of the album—chronological, by themes, or by events.

As you put the album/scrapbook together, the number of photographs you can get on a page will depend on the page size, the size of the photographs, and how much you crop the background of the photographs. You can, of course, be creative and overlap your photographs.

Scrapbooking.com (*http://scrapbooking.com*) and Scrapbook Tips.com (*www.scrapbook-tips.com/OurGurus.asp*) offer countless ideas for creating a highly personalized scrapbook with your photographs and other memorabilia.

In addition, the Graceful Bee NewBees Web site (*http://gracefulbee.com/newbees/organization.html*) offers plenty of useful advice for organizing your photos and creating a well-thought-out scrap book. The Iowa Conservation and Preservation Consortium offers the following archival tips for organizing your photographs into an album:

- Use archival plastic page protectors and photograph pages (make sure they're PCV-free), including cellulose triacetate, DuPont Mylar polyester, polyethylene, and polypropylene.
- Attach your photographs, postcards, and other items with archival photo corners, which are usually made of Mylar, or with Tape Runners, Photo Splits, Photo Tape, or similar products. (Avoid using tape because it will eventually cause yellowing and may ooze and cause items and pages to

stick together. Also avoid using rubber cement or any glue with an odor. Some glue sticks are acid-free and safe, but after time, the glue tends to dry up, causing the photos to fall off the pages.)

- Attach newspaper clippings to the pages with a water-soluble or washable non-toxic glue stick, such as those by 3M and Loctite.
- Make sure to identify the origin of your clippings, photographs, and other memorabilia, including the date, source of the item, names, and places.

You'll find a wide selection of photo album and scrapbook accessories at photo supply stores, Hallmark stores, and on the Internet. AlbumSource.com (✆ 866-772-7200, ✍ *www.albumsource.com*) offers literally hundreds of photo albums and photo organizational products that you can order online.

ALERT!

Acid can cause your photos to deteriorate and can cause paper to become brittle. When creating a scrapbook with your photos, use acid-free papers, cardstock, album pages, stickers, inks, and so on. For a list of acid-free products, point your Web browser to ✍ *www.telepath.com/bcarson/scrap_happy/acidfree.html*.

Converting to Digital Photos

An alternative to storing traditional paper-based photographs is to convert to an entirely digital system and store your photos electronically. You can scan your existing photos to create high-resolution electronic files on your computer's hard drive, on Zip disks (from Iomega), or on writable CD-ROMs. The Hewlett-Packard Photo Smart Photo Scanner, for example, is relatively inexpensive and allows you to scan photos, negatives, or slides using any PC-based personal computer. You can also edit and touch up electronic images using special software, such as Microsoft's PhotoDraw program.

Another way to get digital pictures is to purchase a high-resolution digital camera and begin taking all of your photographs digitally. With this method, you no longer have to deal with film, negatives, and storage issues. If you are interested in exploring digital photography, check out *The Everything® Digital Photography Book* (Adams Media).

America Online's "You've Got Pictures" service is another way someone with little or no computer literacy can create electronic images from their photographs, organize these images, and store them. To take advantage of the "You've Got Pictures" service, take your regular 35mm film to a photo developer in your area (as you'd normally do). When ordering your prints, check the AOL box and fill in your AOL screen name on the envelope. Your photos will be developed as prints as they typically are, but within forty-eight hours, AOL will e-mail electronic versions of your photos to your account. You can then share these electronic images with friends and family via e-mail or by posting the images on a Web site. You can also store them for future reference on your computer's hard drive (or other electronic storage media). There is an additional processing charge for this service; however, it'll save you the trouble of scanning your pictures. For details, while on the AOL service, enter the keyword "pictures." In the same way, you can get a Kodak CD with your print film order by checking the Kodak CD box.

Tips for Living in a Small Space

If you live in a studio apartment, college dorm room, or even a small apartment, space is a huge premium. Most likely, you have to use every room or area of your home for multiple purposes. For example, your living area may also double as your home office, guest room, and dining area. Your kitchen may also serve as your laundry area, and your bedroom may need to provide the majority of your storage space (in addition to being a place to sleep).

Every inch of otherwise unused space should be utilized for storage, so be sure to experiment with the various storage and organizational ideas described throughout this book. Utilize under-bed storage, add extra shelving wherever there is room to do so, maximize the use of floor and wall space (and even the ceiling), and think in terms of using multipurpose furniture. For example, by putting cushions on top of a sturdy wooden storage chest, you can create a comfortable seat or bench.

That same chest could also be used as a coffee table. If you have a traditional coffee table, store smaller items in decorative yet functional baskets (with lids) and keep the baskets under the table.

Organize your living space into areas or zones by using room dividers, large plants, or bookcases to separate your dining area from your living area or home office area. You can also build a loft-style bed and utilize the space beneath the bed for drawers, shelves, or a desk. A well-built sofa bed can be used as a couch by day and a bed by night to save additional space (just make sure you have a quality mattress).

In smaller living spaces, instead of a full-sized couch and coffee table you may be able to better utilize your living area by using a love seat or two recliners, plus a set of smaller tables that can be moved around as needed or placed side-by-side to create a full-size coffee table to accommodate guests.

When you're forced to live in a small space, fully utilizing your closets becomes critical. Chapter 2 explores a wide range of closet organizing options and the use of organizational tools. If your closet is tall, install additional upper shelves, where you can store seasonal items, such as blankets, boots, and heavy sweaters. Also, determine whether you can install a double row of clothing rods. Slacks and long coats need full-height vertical space, but you may be able to double up on suits, jackets, shirts and blouses.

If your small living space has a walk-in closet, you can create even more storage space in it by forfeiting its walk-in capacity and installing additional hanging rod storage. For example, you can install one rod behind the other; place your everyday garments (your daily wardrobe items) on the front rack or rod, and your less frequently worn garments, such as formal wear, on the rear rack/rod. Make sure, however, that your clothing isn't being pushed together too tightly as a result of insufficient closet space.

As you design and decorate your living space, focus on your priorities and living habits. Allocate the most space to the activities you do most within your home. While you'll definitely need a bed, could you forgo a living room set and use the space for exercise equipment? If you're a student and spend most of your time studying or reading, a desk with a comfortable chair and ample lighting should be a priority. If you spend a considerable amount of time using your computer, consider investing in a laptop computer as opposed to a full-size desktop computer, and then create a computer workstation area that's comfortable and functional.

In terms of shelving and storage, think vertical. The most underused space in any room is the two or three feet just below the ceiling. Instead of a three- or four-foot-tall bookcase, think about a seven-foot-tall one. If you can, mount shelves high up on the walls, over windows and doors, and above kitchen cabinets.

When purchasing furniture and other items for your small living space, always think fold-up, pull-out, and multi-purpose. For example, a dining table can also function as a desk. An armoire can be used for storage, but also serve as a computer workstation. A couch-futon can be used to sleep at night, but during the day can double as a sofa.

Finally, the best thing you can do to make your limited living space more comfortable is eliminate clutter. Discard or store (in a storage facility) anything you don't use on a regular basis or that you don't need. Getting rid of clutter helps you to best maximize whatever space is actually available. In most cases, clutter is caused by one thing—failure to designate a specific place for each item. After you figure out a home for each thing you own, you'll know where to find it and where to put it away. Adopt this practice on an ongoing basis, and your clutter will disappear.

CHAPTER 6

Uncluttering Your Bathrooms

O ther than the obvious, what do you use your bathroom for? Whether you have plenty of room in your bathroom, or you're confined to a tiny space, this chapter helps you organize this area of your home and create a room that's functional and comfortable.

Utilizing Your Space to the Fullest

Before you can make your bathroom more organized, you must determine the functionality you require from this particular living space. For example, is the bathroom where you shave, apply makeup, store toiletries and linens, keep medications, do your laundry, get dressed, take long baths, style your hair, or spend time reading while doing "other things"?

As you plan how you'll utilize your bathroom space, consider who else (your spouse, kids, teens, guests, and so on) will be using the bathroom and what their needs are. Next, evaluate what space you have available to work with by following these steps:

1. Measure your bathroom.
2. Determine which fixtures are or will be installed, including the sink, commode, shower, bathtub, whirlpool, medicine cabinet, mirror, washer and dryer, towel racks, shelving, lighting, seating, and so on.
3. Determine what style, theme, or décor you plan to incorporate into your bathroom.
4. Determine what you will store in the bathroom (medicines, toiletries, towels, robes, dirty laundry, reading materials, makeup, hairstyling products, and so on). Where will these items go (shelves, cabinets, closet, towel racks, hampers, baskets, hooks, and so on)?

Organizing, Redecorating, and Remodeling Your Bathroom

Reorganizing a bathroom can be a pretty major project, so do one bathroom at a time, starting with the most used bathroom in your home. Divide up the bathroom into sections (countertops, cabinets, shelves, shower, closet, and so on). Thoroughly clean and then reorganize one section at a time.

Bathroom Organization Tips

Take the time to do a thorough reorganization, even if you don't have the time or money to do a major remodeling job. For example, clean out your medicine cabinet, linen closet, and other cabinets. In the medicine cabinet, for example, remove and group the items. Check the expiration dates and discard old medications. When the cabinet is empty, clean the shelves and the interior, and then return everything in an easy-to-find order. Separate each family member's prescription medications and place them on separate shelves. Likewise, put all of the over-the-counter medications on a separate shelf.

When organizing your bathroom's cabinets, begin by taking everything out and dividing the contents into defined categories—hair care products, makeup, toiletries, prescription medications, nonprescription medications, first-aid supplies, and so on. (Keep in mind that cleaning supplies don't belong in the medicine cabinet and should be kept elsewhere.) Take mental notes about what kind of organizational accessory may be useful.

Store together items you use every day, such as makeup and hair care products. If you have a cabinet under the sink, utilize this storage space for items that aren't used daily or that are too large to fit in a medicine cabinet or on the bathroom counter, such as cleaning supplies, extra toiletries, and your hair.

Like every other closet or storage space in your home, keep your towel closet organized. After you arrange towels by size and color, fold them and group by putting like-size towels together. In other words, your bath towels stay together, hand towels stay together, and washcloths stay together. Keep less frequently used towels, such as beach or guest towels, on a less accessible shelf or in a guest bedroom, for example. Store towels that are no longer used for personal care (but are great for bathing the dog or washing the car) out of the bathroom, with your pet or automobile supplies.

In addition to your towels, your bathroom closet will likely be the ideal storage place for bulky items, such as tissues, toilet paper, diapers, and storage containers filled with extra bathroom items. All of these items can be stored at the bottom of your linen closet. By organizing your space efficiently, you may be able to buy larger quantities of certain items that you use frequently, saving yourself time, money, and trips to the store.

To fully organize your bathroom, the following accessories, fixtures, and organizational tools will be useful. You probably won't need all of these items, so pick and choose which will be the most beneficial for you, based on your needs:

- Clock
- Corner caddy (corner shelving for the bathtub/shower)
- Cosmetic tray
- Cotton ball/cotton swab holder
- Hair dryer organizer
- Hamper(s)
- Liquid soap dispenser
- Magazine rack
- Over-the-commode shelves
- Radio and/or television
- Shower caddy
- Telephone
- Toilet tissue stand
- Toothbrush holder
- Towel racks/towel bars (wall-mounted, over the door, or free-standing)
- Tub caddy (shelf that extends across the bathtub)
- Under-sink organizers (for storing cleaning supplies and other bathroom items)

> A nice basket with a lid, that can be placed on a counter or on the floor, is one possible storage solution for your hair dryer, curling iron, and other hair care products.

Each person in the household needs his or her own bath towel, hand towel, and washcloth in a place that's easily accessible. A towel bar that hangs on a door hinge is an excellent space-saving device. To keep every family member's towels better organized, use different colored towels for each family member and give each person an area of the bathroom to store towels.

FACT

Your closet will remain more organized if you fold your clean (and dry) towels before storing them. If you have a 46" × 28" bath towel, for example, start folding it in half horizontally, so that it measures about 23" × 28". Now fold the towel again horizontally (11.5" × 28"). Next, fold the towel into thirds to create a neatly folded package (11.5" × 9.33"). This allows towels to be stacked and easily identified by their size.

If your bathroom lacks the necessary wall space for a towel rack (near the bathtub, shower, or sink), consider purchasing an inexpensive, freestanding floor towel rack. One such unit is available from Stacks and Stacks HomeWares (*http://shop.yahoo.com/stacks/6123.html*). Restoration Hardware (*www.restorationhardware.com*) also offers a collection of highly functional bathroom organization tools and items, such as the Beragamo Drying Fan that mounts in any bathtub or shower and provides hangers for drying hanging multiple garments at once.

Brookstone's Hard-to-Find Tools catalog (800-926-7000, *www.brookstone.com*) features a variety of well-made bathroom organization products. For example, the solid brass Wall Mount Bath Organizer is a vertical organizer that frees up counter space by keeping bathing basics within easy reach for your morning routine. This organizer attaches to a wall and contains a cup holder, soap holder, and two swiveling towel bars. Brookstone also sells a Bath Étagère, which easily transforms wall space into valuable storage space. This unit fits over most commodes and offers two shelves inside polystyrene-paned doors, plus an open lower shelf. The unit is made from high-density fiberboard (which is mildew resistant) and features a lacquered finish. A matching free-standing bath organizer (sold separately) offers additional storage and counter space. For redecorating your bathroom and adding functionality, Brookstone sells a wide selection of decorative bathroom fixtures made from solid brass. Towel bars (in various sizes), towel rings, vanity shelves, showerheads, showerhead caddies, bath tissue holders, and various sized hooks are all available. You'll also find similar accessories at any home improvement or hardware superstore.

ALERT!

Store medications, both prescription and nonprescription, out of reach of children, even those medications with childproof packaging. Pay attention to expiration dates on medicine bottles and packaging. Some medications simply lose their effectiveness after time; others actually become dangerous. Store medications in their original packaging and read and follow all label directions.

After clearing out the clutter, paint or wallpaper the walls, choose artwork, select fixtures, and choose your bathroom accessories (such as a bath mat and towels), and then start putting your bathroom together. Of course, if you're doing a major renovation at this time, you'll want to hire a contractor, electrician, and plumber, among other experts.

Choosing Bathroom Fixtures

As you choose your bathroom fixtures and accessories, pay attention not just to price but also to quality, size, functionality, warrantee, and style. Any hardware or home improvement store can work with you to choose the best bathroom fixtures to meet your needs. When choosing your fixtures, you'll have a wide range of choices, especially when selecting a sink (or sinks), toilet, bathtub, shower, whirlpool, or washer and dryer. (For information on choosing the best washer and dryer to meet your needs, see Chapter 10.)

After your primary bathroom fixtures are in place, think about your bathroom accessories. Refer to your list of what you'll be using the bathroom for and who will be using the bathroom. This will help you determine details like how many towel racks you'll need and the size of the medicine cabinet, for example, plus help you choose the best placement for these fixtures and accessories. As you select the placement, carefully consider your daily routine. Consider questions like the following:

- Do you want to install a magazine rack near the toilet?
- Do you want a hook to hang your robe near the bathtub?
- Do you need a makeup mirror with magnification on the bathroom counter, near where you'll be storing your makeup?
- Is the lighting adequate near where you apply your makeup and style your hair?
- Do you need shelving within your shower/bathtub to store bottles of shampoo and conditioner or different types of soaps for the various people who use the bathroom?

Making Your Bathroom More Energy-Efficient

To help control moisture in a bathroom, use a properly sized ventilation fan. By removing moist air and drying out your bathroom, a ventilation fan helps to prevent mold and mildew. Some new fans can operate continuously and quietly while using less energy.

In addition, seal air and water leaks with caulk or expanding foam and install insulation, especially around the tub. Adding extra insulation around your bathtub will keep the bath water hot for longer periods of time while you soak, which ultimately saves energy and water and keeps you warmer.

To save money when replacing the lighting in your bathroom, the EPA recommends using residential lighting fixtures with the Energy Star label. These lighting fixtures provide quality, color, and brightness with compact fluorescent lighting technology.

When replacing the windows in your bathroom, the EPA also recommends using replacement windows with the Energy Star label. These windows are warmer in the winter and cooler in the summer. New technologies in the glass and frame systems will help make your home more comfortable and lower heating and cooling costs too.

Bathroom Lighting

The American Lighting Association (✆ 800-274-4484) reports that "in the bathroom, you need plenty of even, shadow-free lighting for shaving, grooming, and applying makeup. In small bathrooms, mirror lights will illuminate the entire room, but in larger bathrooms, an additional ceiling fixture is needed for general lighting. A recessed infrared heat lamp will give you added warmth on chilly mornings."

To add lighting around small mirrors, use decorative wall-bracketed lighting on each side in order to illuminate both sides of your face evenly. You can also mount a wall bracket across the top of the mirror. An alternative for lighting the areas around larger mirrors is to use theatrical lighting strips.

"Tub and shower enclosures, for example, can be lighted by placing an enclosed damp-location recessed down light in the ceiling. These down lights are also recommended over whirlpool baths or in saunas," reports the American Lighting Association.

ALERT!

To avoid injuries during nighttime trips to the bathroom, install nightlights near the entrance to the bathroom and near the commode. The Indiglo nightlight (available from hardware stores and Brookstone stores) plugs into any outlet, requires no light bulb, lasts for years, and uses less than five cents worth of electricity per year.

Bathtub Refacing

If you own your home, apartment, or condo and your bathroom is extremely outdated and downright ugly, instead of replacing the shower/bathtub, you can give it a much less costly facelift.

A custom bathroom liner can be installed over your existing tub with no mess and no odor, usually in less than a day. Acrylic walls are then installed over your existing tile walls. If your tile walls have water damage, installers will repair the damage prior to installing the new acrylic walls. The durable acrylic surface will not chip, dent, crack, or peel and is completely colorfast, which means it won't stain, yellow, or fade. It is warm to the touch and has a beautiful mirror-like, high-gloss finish. The high-gloss acrylic used in installation is twice the thickness of acrylics used in the finest spa manufacturing and retains heat three times longer than porcelain. This nonporous, high gloss material is easy to clean and is more acid-resistant than porcelain or ceramic. Because there are no grout lines to clean or maintain, general household cleaners can be used with ease.

In addition to refacing your tub, you can also reglaze the wall tiling in your bathroom. Often in just one day, your tiles and bathtub can be beautifully regrouted, repaired, and recolored with an acrylic coating that will last for years. You can change the color to match your new sink and toilet or renew the one you have.

If you're considering a complete replacement of the tub, keep in mind that the actual price of the bathtub itself is the least expensive part of replacing this fixture. Hiring a contractor, tiler, electrician, and plumber to replace a bathtub/shower is must more costly than the price of the tub. As part of a complete bathtub/shower replacement, ceramic tile must be removed and replaced. Full retiling may become necessary, and the drywall or plaster behind the tile may need to be repaired. If, for example, the tub was originally installed before the floor was installed, the contractor may have trouble removing the tub and may have to remove (and later replace) part of the floor. The disposal of the tub requires a plumber. The result is that the replacement of a bathtub/shower that costs under $200 to purchase can easily wind up costing thousands of dollars, creating a lot of inconvenience, and taking days or weeks to have installed.

Keeping Your Bathroom Clean

The bathroom is probably the toughest room in any home to keep clean and sanitary. The best way to do this is to develop a regular cleaning routine. Every day or two, pick up clutter in the bathroom and clean and disinfect high-touch zones, such as bathroom floors, bathroom faucets, and toilet flush handles. Every week, thoroughly clean the tub, toilet, sink/fixtures/drain, mirrors, floor, and cabinets. If you keep up with this routine, the chore of cleaning the bathroom won't ever get too overwhelming or disgusting. (Most people dread having to scrub bathroom mold and mildew that has built up over several weeks or months.)

To avoid harboring germs, thoroughly clean sponges, mops, and scrubbing brushes after every use. Replace them regularly to reduce germ buildup. Throw out any cleaning tools or equipment that smell bad or look mildewy.

Some of the cleaning items you'll want on hand to make the bathroom cleaning process easier include the following:

- All-purpose cleaner
- Disinfectant
- Glass cleaner
- Mold, mildew, and soap scum remover
- Mop and bucket
- Paper towels
- Plastic organizer to hold cleaners/tools
- Plastic garbage bags
- Rubber gloves
- Scrubbing brush and an old toothbrush (for small areas)
- Soft cloths
- Sponge
- Toilet bowl brush
- Vacuum cleaner

OxiClean (the stuff you may have seen advertised on TV) is an excellent cleaning product that you can use for a wide range of purposes in a bathroom, especially for eliminating mold, mildew, and soap scum. Yes, this stuff really works as advertised!

For smaller cleaning jobs, try Clorox Disinfecting Wipes. These are 7" × 8" disposable wipes that are premoistened with bleach and can be used around the bathroom to quickly clean and disinfect household surfaces.

CHAPTER 7

Organizing Your Master Bedroom and Guestrooms

T he master bedroom in your home has several primary purposes. Most importantly, it provides you with a comfortable place to sleep. This chapter focuses on how to design and organize your master bedroom and your home's guestrooms. It also discusses how to choose, maintain, and store a mattress and bed linens.

Taking an Inventory of Your Bedroom

Before you can begin to design and organize your bedroom, you must determine what you have to work with. Start by measuring the room. Then, take an inventory of the pieces of furniture you own or want in your bedroom. Your bedroom furniture may include an armoire, bed, bureau, desk, dressers, entertainment center or TV stand, exercise equipment, full-length mirror, lamps or lighting figures, nightstands, seating, shelves, and a storage chest. If you're thinking of purchasing new bedroom furniture, consider the approximate size of each piece and determine exactly how it will be used and where in the room it will go. For example, if you're buying a new dresser to store clothing items for you and your spouse, how much space is available in the room for this piece of furniture and how many dresser drawers do you and your spouse actually need? What, specifically, will be stored in each drawer?

Go through everything you currently store in your bedroom, including your wardrobe. Figure out which items actually belong in your bedroom and which can be kept or stored elsewhere. For example, can your winter jackets be stored in a foyer closet or in the basement (attic or garage) during the off-season? What about personal items, such as framed photographs and other belongings? Do you need shelves, wall space, or the top of a dresser, for example, to display these items?

Carefully analyze each piece of furniture in your bedroom and determine whether it's being used to its maximum potential. Could you better utilize your dresser drawer space if you reorganized them? If you were to store your sweaters and/or linens in a container under your bed, could you free up valuable closet space? If you installed a shoe rack in your closet, could you save space by organizing your shoe collection? See **FIGURES 7-1** and **7-2** for examples on how eliminating a few pieces of furniture can make a bedroom seem much more spacious.

FIGURE 7-1:
A bedroom stuffed with furniture

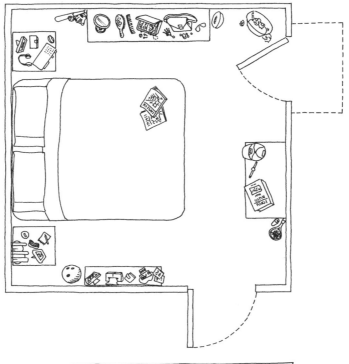

FIGURE 7-2:
A more spacious bedroom

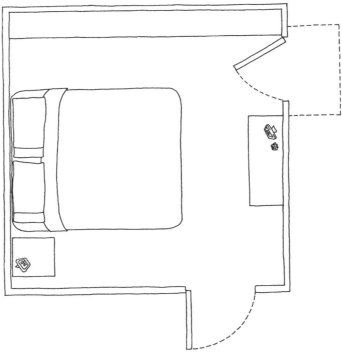

If pieces of furniture in your bedroom aren't being used properly, consider getting rid of them. If, for example, you have some type of seating or exercise equipment in your bedroom that never actually gets used for its intended purpose (and only offers a place to pile laundry), consider removing the furniture or equipment. You may decide to free up the space completely or replace it with something more functional or that provides more adequate storage space.

Knowing what space you have available in your bedroom and what your needs are, choose the pieces of furniture that will provide the most functionality and comfort.

Meshing Attractiveness with Functionality

As you focus on décor and add those personal touches to the room using photographs, artwork, trinkets, silk flowers, and so on, think about functionality as well as visual appeal. When choosing your nightstand, for example, determine what will be stored on this piece of furniture (alarm clock, books, telephone, lamp, reading glasses, TV remote control, food, drinks, and so on). Are there personal items you'd prefer to store in a nightstand drawer? Does the nightstand have ample drawer space? Also, make sure the nightstand is the proper height when placed next to your bed. Ideally, you want to easily be able to reach over to grab the TV remote or turn on a lamp.

What about lighting? When you're comfortably lying in bed, can you reach the light switch? Do you have a lamp on your nightstand that will provide ample lighting between the time you get into bed and actually go to sleep? During the day or evening, when you're using the bedroom for activities other than sleeping, is the room amply lit? For example, when choosing your outfits and getting dressed, is there enough light to differentiate between navy and black garments?

As you choose the placement of your bedroom furniture, pay attention to the location of electrical outlets, light switches, cable TV jacks, and phone jacks. Try to avoid having to run an unsightly (and potentially dangerous) extension cord across the room. Can you plug in your television in a location where it can be easily seen from your bed? Can the telephone be placed on a nightstand?

Purchasing Furniture

If you're on a limited budget when purchasing bedroom furniture, focus first on the most important pieces in the room—your bed frame and mattress. This is where you'll most likely be spending between six and ten hours per day, so it's important that the mattress you choose provides the comfort and support you need. Choosing the best linens, pillows, and blankets is also important for ensuring the best night's sleep possible.

FACT

The Rise & Shine Natural Alarm Clock ($199 from Verilux Corporation, ℆ 800-786-6850) is a specially designed lamp with built-in alarm clock and natural sound generator that replicates the natural process of waking when the sun rises and falling asleep when the sun sets. At night, the lamp slowly fades; in the morning, it gradually increases in brightness. You can also choose soothing sounds of nature to enhance your waking experience.

Choosing and Caring for Your Mattress

When purchasing a new mattress, wear loose and comfortable clothing to simulate how the bed will feel when you're wearing pajamas at home. As you test various mattresses, pay attention to the amount of padding and support. Is the mattress comfortable when you're lying down and sitting up in bed? To see a wide variety of products, visit several different mattress retailers and try out at least a handful of different mattresses before making your decision, paying careful attention to the warrantee that's offered.

Choose the size mattress you need based on your space limitations in the bedroom and the number of people who will be sleeping on the mattress. For two average-size people, a queen- or king-sized mattress is a must. Beds come in six basic sizes: king (76" × 80"), California king (72" × 84"), queen (60" × 80"), full/double (54" × 75"), twin (39" × 75"), and twin extra long (39" × 80"). When determining whether a bed will fit in your bedroom, remember to leave at least fifteen inches on either side of the bed so you have ample room to move around.

Beds can be expensive, so pay attention to prices. To save money, consider purchasing the mattress and box spring together as a set. In addition to the actual price of the mattress, ask about delivery charges. (Ask about delivery time, too.) Also ask if there's an additional fee to have your old mattress removed and disposed of. Don't rely on the sales pitch of any single salesperson. Instead, try beds for yourself in the showroom, and then visit other mattress dealers before making a final decision. And remember that no matter where you shop for your mattress, negotiate the price!

Purchase the highest quality mattress you can afford, even if it means buying slightly less expensive bedroom furniture. The look of the bed frame, for example, is less important than the quality of the mattress you'll be sleeping on night after night.

Understanding Mattress Options

According to HomeStore.com (✑ *www.homestore.com),* when buying a mattress, you have several options. Some of the more popular types of mattresses are covered in the following sections.

Innerspring Mattresses

These mattresses contain springs that are connected in various ways. Whatever the spring design, look for more than 100 coils in a crib mattress, more than 200 in a twin mattress, and more than 300 in a larger model. The wire gauge of a mattress is also important. In this case, the lower the number, the stronger the wire. Thirteen is the heaviest gauge, while twenty-one is the lightest. You also want to pay attention to the layers of cushioning and insulation that are added to the mattress. The more layers, the more comfortable the mattress will be. HomeStore.com suggests that if you'd like a cushy surface coupled with firm support below, look for a soft-top model.

Box Springs and Mattress Bases

Innerspring mattresses can be used on many kinds of bases and frames. Typically, the more solid the base is, the longer the mattress will last. A simple sheet of plywood or even the floor can provide adequate mattress support. According to HomeStore.com, besides promoting air circulation, the only advantages of a box spring or other mattress base are the additional resiliency to the mattress and the additional height.

Foam Mattresses

A high-quality foam mattress can be just as good as a well-constructed innerspring mattress. The benefit to this type of mattress is that it can be manufactured to fit an odd-size bed. As a general rule, the higher the density of the foam, the better. HomeStore.com recommends getting a minimum density of at least 1.15 pounds per cubic foot in a crib mattress or two pounds per cubic foot in an adult-size mattress.

Water Beds

HomeStore.com reports that many newer water mattresses come with a solidly comfortable foam edge. Others, however, use an air baffle or rows of springs along the mattress perimeter, and baffles of various designs inside some mattresses slow down wave motion. A polyurethane liner contains the water in case of a leak.

Protecting Your Investment

A mattress is an investment that should last anywhere from five to twenty-five years, depending on the quality of the product. After the mattress is in place in your bedroom, use a cotton mattress cover as a layer of protection between your sheets and the mattress itself. You'll also want to rotate the mattress 180 degrees at least twice per year. Some people choose to rotate their mattress four times per year or every month. Check with the mattress' manufacturer for the recommended rotation frequency.

If possible, allow the mattress to air out daily or at least weekly. When you wake up in the morning, remove the blanket and top sheets for at least thirty minutes before making the bed. Also, try to avoid sitting at the same place along the very edge of a mattress too often. Some people sit at the same place on their mattress every morning when getting dressed, for example. This causes sagging to occur faster.

Finally, most mattresses come with a manufacturer's warrantee. To ensure this warranty doesn't become void, don't remove the "Do Not Remove" tag that's attached to the mattress when it's purchased.

Choosing and Organizing Bed Linens

Just like your mattress, the linens (sheets, pillowcases, comforter cover, pillow shams, bed skirt, and so on) you choose are an investment. If properly cared for, they'll last for many years and provide much needed comfort as you sleep. To ensure that you experience the most comfort possible, understand what you're buying.

Bob Hamilton is a spokesperson for the Pillowtex Corporation, a company that manufactures a wide range of well-known home-textile products under a variety of brand names, including Fieldcrest, Royal Velvet, Charisma, and Canon. The company has been in existence for over 100 years and continues to offer some of the best-made sheets, pillows, blankets, towels, and other textile products in the world.

No matter what your budget is for buying bed linens, Hamilton suggests looking at three details: the fabric, the color, and the construction. "When purchasing sheets, the quality of the fabric is measured by its thread count. The more threads per square inch, the finer the cloth. The other variable is whether the sheet is manufactured from 100 percent cotton or whether it's made from a blend of polyester and cotton. The problem with all-cotton sheets is that they wrinkle a lot. For easy care, many people turn to a blended fabric. Up until a few years ago, the best quality sheets had a thread count of 180 threads per square inch. In the past few years, manufacturers have begun offering sheets up to a 700 thread count," said Hamilton.

After a thread count goes above 350 threads per square inch, the consumer won't notice a difference in quality. Some foreign manufacturers are using a technique called double-pick insertion to boost thread count, without enhancing the fineness of the cloth. "The best quality sheets sold in America range from 250 to 360 threads per square inch," added Hamilton. The price of bed linen is directly related to the thread count.

Aside from the thread count, however, consumers also needs to select the color of their sheets and the appropriate sizes. "Fitted sheets don't fit every mattress," said Hamilton, "because even standard-sized mattresses vary greatly when you start adding various types of padding and other features that impact mattress height. The trick to finding a fitted sheet that will stay on your mattress is to find sheets with elastic that's sewn all the way around the entire sheet, not just in the corners. When looking at the packaging of a sheet, it should clearly state the mattress size it should fit. Don't just rely on using standard twin, full, queen, and king sizes. Pay attention to the depth [height] of your mattress when purchasing fitted sheets."

Does higher thread count equal greater warmth?
No. Sheets with higher thread counts will be more comfortable, but they won't necessary provide greater warmth.

No matter what type of cotton bed linen you purchase, if you care for it correctly, it'll last for many years. "The only things that destroy most of the fabrics in this world are usage and laundering," said Hamilton. "Many people overlaunder their bedding, using too much detergent or detergent that's simply too strong. A dryer that's set too hot will also cook the fabric. The intense heat decreases the fabric's life because the natural oils and natural resins of the cotton dry out. Read the care instructions on the label carefully and follow them."

Before heading to the store to purchase your bedding, determine what your exact needs are for each bed in your home. For example, the linens you purchase for each bed may include a fitted sheet, a flat sheet, two pillowcases, pillow shams (for decorative purposes), a bedskirt (for decorative purposes), and a comforter or comforter cover.

FACT

To keep bedding sets together, store your sheet sets inside their matching pillow cases. Fold the pillowcase around the sheets and stack them in the linen closet. Using this method, you won't have to search your closet for matching fitted and flat sheets, along with pillowcases. Everything you need for each bed will be stored together within its own storage bag (the pillow case).

To keep your bedding organized, Hamilton recommends that for each bed in your home, you maintain an inventory of three complete linen sets. This way, one set can always be kept on the bed (in use), one can be in the laundry, and one can be in storage. Rotate the three sets regularly. How often you change your bedding is a matter of personal preference; however, most people choose to make this a weekly habit. Rotating your linens will extend their life dramatically; however, acquiring three sets of top-quality sheets can be extremely costly. A single bed linen set could cost over $1,000. Of course, this is for top-of-the-line linens. A complete bedding set made from lower quality linen can cost under $100.

One way to save money on top-quality bed linen is to shop for irregulars. At least once a year, Charisma linen that's deemed irregular is put on sale through the company's online store and through some of the company's retailers. A product labeled irregular is not defective. According to Hamilton, "This simply means that the product has a slight imperfection, usually having to do with the weaving or dying of the cloth. It has absolutely nothing to do with the function or construction of the product. These are imperfections that deem it as not being of first quality; however, purchasing irregular linens is an excellent way to obtain the very best linens possible, yet stay within a reasonable budget." In many cases, irregular linens sell for between 50 and 75 percent off the suggested retail price.

In addition to having three sets of bedding linen and rotating them, another way to make cotton linens last longer is to line-dry them as opposed to putting them in the dryer. "Not subjecting the fabric to intense heat from a dryer," said Hamilton, "especially if it's a high-end sheet, will greatly increase how long the item will last. Also, avoid harsh chemicals. I recommend that people avoid using detergents with a lot of whiteners. Most detergents will negatively change the color of the bed linen or fade the colors. In reality, the color doesn't fade; it's the optical whitener in the detergent that changes the color of the fabric. The obstacle whiteners will dull the real color of the fabric. Based on our extensive research, the one detergent that we have found that works best to preserve high-end bed linens is Cheer from Procter & Gamble."

When bed linens aren't actually in use on a bed, store them properly. Linens should always be laundered before being stored. Sheets and pillowcases, for example, can be kept in plastic bags in a cool and dry closet, out of direct light. Linens should be stored in a way that keeps them away from moisture. This will eliminate mold and mildew. Storing the items in a plastic bag also ensures against damage from moths or other insects. Higher quality sheets are often sold in resealable packages that can be used for storage during the life of the item.

Storing fitted sheets can be a bit tricky, because they're not easy to fold after they've been laundered. According to Fieldcrest, use the following steps for folding a fitted sheet before storing it:

1. Fit one pocket at the top of the fitted sheet into the opposite pocket by inserting your hand behind one pocket and stuffing it inside the other.
2. Smooth the sheet lengthwise and fold length in half again.
3. Fold the sheet from the bottom to top several times to achieve a bundle about 12" × 10".
4. Store in a plastic bag in a closet, in a dresser drawer, or under your bed in an airtight container.

In addition to the mattress and bed linens, choosing and taking care of a good comforter, blankets, and pillows will help ensure that you're comfortable while sleeping. How you launder your comforter or blanket will vary depending on what it's made from. Read the manufacturer's care instructions carefully.

When storing your comforters and blankets, always launder or dry-clean them first. Also, don't overfold or crush a down comforter or pillow. Allow it to remain as fluffy as possible. Loosely wrap the comforter or blanket in plastic, and then store it in a cool, dry place, such as a closet, wooden (cedar) storage chest, dresser drawer (if the drawer is large enough), or in an airtight plastic container. Fold blankets, place them in a cotton pillowcase, and then place them in a closet. Keep blankets and comforters out of direct sunlight when storing them.

Blankets and comforters can also be stored using a freestanding blanket or quilt rack. These are typically made of wood, are placed near the foot of a bed, and provide places to hang various types of blankets out in the open (when they're not actually on a bed). This type of rack can add to the décor of a room and is a standalone piece of furniture that doubles as a storage solution.

FACT

Space Bags (described in Chapter 2 of this book) offer an ideal storage solution for many types of sheets and blankets. However, this storage method shouldn't be used for down comforters or down pillows. You don't want to crush the comforter or pillow by removing all of the air from the bag in which the item is stored.

Organizing Your Dresser Drawers

A dresser is where most people store pieces of their wardrobes that don't readily fit in the closet. This typically includes underwear, shirts, socks, pajamas, shorts, bathing suits, and other garments.

When organizing your dresser, remove everything from the drawers and lay the items on a bed or the floor. Take a careful inventory and determine what actually needs to be kept in the dresser.

Next, group all like items together (either by season or clothing type). Figure out how many physical drawers your dresser has, and then determine where each group of like items will be stored. Store items you use everyday, such as socks, pantyhose, and underwear, in the drawer that's the most convenient to access.

To organize your dresser, insert one or two shoeboxes or small containers in your dresser drawers to keep socks, pantyhose, and other small items from spilling over onto other clothes in the drawer. These are inexpensive drawer dividers/organizers.

To maintain organization, if two people are sharing a dresser, each person should have his or her own drawers. In order to maximize space, keep all items laundered and folded neatly before being placing them in a drawer. Certain types of garments, however, are best stored rolled as opposed to folded. Check the garment's care label for details.

Your jewelry can be stored in a dresser drawer, but to keep it organized, place the pieces into divided containers in a drawer. You may also choose to keep your most frequently used jewelry on a jewelry holder or in a jewelry box. Instead of using an expensive jewelry box that may take up lots of room, consider using plastic ice cube trays or foam egg cartons to store your jewelry in a dresser drawer. You'll find this system works great with earrings, rings, pins, bracelets, and some necklaces, and the cost is under $1. A fishing tackle box with many small compartments also works as an alternative to an expensive jewelry box.

Utilizing Underbed Storage

Underbed storage is an ideal place to keep off-season clothing, bedding, and other bulky items. This storage space can be managed using airtight plastic bins or hide-away drawers. Stacks and Stacks (✆ 877-278-2257, *www.stacksandstack.com*) offers a large selection of storage solutions for use under a bed, including a unit that fits most twin through king-sized beds. The unit's oak finish and brass handle give this hide-away drawer a look that will complement any bedroom. Installation requires the temporary removal of your mattress and box spring, and it works with metal bed frames only.

Stacks and Stacks also markets an underbed cedar storage container. This wooden chest is ideal for shoes, sweaters, and year-round storage, and makes the most of unused space beneath the bed. The unit features a hardboard bottom and sliding top that have an easy-to-clean lacquer finish. Removable casters allow units to be stacked.

Airtight plastic containers (with wheels) designed specifically to be stored under a bed are another alternative. These plastic containers, available at most mass-market retailers, are ideal for storing items like off-season clothing shoes, linens, and holiday decorations. These containers are see-through, so you can easily see what's inside, and because they're on wheels, they can be pulled out from under the bed with ease, no matter how heavy they are.

For a listing of companies that specialize in storage solutions and organizational tools for the bedroom, point your Web browser to the Real Home Guide's Web site at ✍ *http://directory.ceramlinks.com/ furnishings/housewares/organization-and-storage.*

Guestroom Considerations

In most people's homes, space is tight. If you've designated a room to be your guestroom, but you don't have guests too often, you probably want to utilize this space for other activities as well. Perhaps you'll use your guest room as an exercise room, a room to participate in your hobby, a room to display your knickknacks or collections, a reading room, or a home office.

When guests do use this room, make sure it's equipped with all of the amenities they need to make their stay comfortable. This includes a complete bed linen set, two pillows, extra blankets, towels, and toiletries (especially soap and shampoo). You also want to create space for guests to store their luggage and perhaps unpack into a few empty drawers in a dresser. At the very least, provide space for the guest to hang up several garments in a closet. If closet space is tight, purchase a freestanding clothing rack from any hardware store or mass-market retailer. It's also nice if you can offer your guests a television and/or radio in the guestroom.

Think carefully about what you'll be using the guest bedroom for in addition to housing guests. Measure the room carefully, and then determine what type of furniture is required to make the room function the way you need it to. As with all of the rooms in your home, take advantage of organizational products, like specialty hangers, underbed storage bins, dresser drawers, and shelving to organize and properly store your belongings. To save space in your guestroom, you may not want to use a full size, traditional bed. You have many alternatives, discussed in the following sections.

Air Mattress

The AeroBed (✑*www.aerobed.com/beds.html*) is an excellent choice. AeroBed is a self-inflating bed that fully inflates in less than a minute and deflates in fifteen seconds. It has a powerful built-in electric pump for fast, easy inflation. Just plug it in, touch a button, and the AeroBed inflates into a thick and comfortable mattress. AeroBed is made of durable, heavy-duty vinyl with electronically welded seams to withstand years of use. The coil system design provides reliable support and keeps air evenly distributed for comfort all night long. With AeroBed, you always have a comfortable place for guests to sleep without having to store a rollaway bed, a lumpy futon, or a pull-out sofa bed. AeroBed is inexpensive, comes in several popular bed sizes, and uses standard size sheets. When not in use, it deflates to the size of a sleeping bag and can be stored in a closet.

Futon

The biggest benefit to futons is that they're much more affordable than sofa beds. When not used as a bed, a futon can also be used as a couch. Unless you purchase a high-end futon, however, these units tend to be uncomfortable, and they take up the same amount of space as a full-sized couch or sofa bed.

Sofa Bed

When not used as a bed, these pieces of furniture double as full-sized couches that come in a wide range of styles. When a bed is needed, they typically unfold into king- or queen-sized bed. Some sofa beds have custom size mattresses. The cost of sofa beds varies greatly, based on the quality of the couch as well as the type and quality of the mattress built into it. Some sofa beds can be uncomfortable to sit and sleep on.

Portable Cot

These metal frames on wheels fold in half for easy storage in a basement and utilize a thin (often foam) mattress. They come in several different sizes and tend to be extremely inexpensive. Most people, however, don't find them very comfortable.

Wall Bed

If you're building a home office and want it to double as a comfortable guest room, Techline (*www.techlineusa.com*) offers a stylish, well-constructed home office furniture system that includes a pull-down wall bed. This system allows you to utilize the room space available to include a full-sized desk, shelves, cabinets, plus the pull-down bed that sets up in minutes. See Chapter 9 for information on setting up a home office.

CHAPTER 8

Putting Your Kids' Room in Order

O kay, the title of this chapter may be misleading. After all, the word "order" probably shouldn't be in the same sentence as the word "kids." That being the case, this chapter helps you design and organize a relatively clutter-free bedroom/playroom for the young people in your home.

Evaluating Your Needs

Begin the process of organizing a room for your child by asking yourself the following questions:

- How much space is available? (Measure the room carefully.)
- How old is your child and what are his or her primary needs in the bedroom?
- Is this an area where your child will spend a lot of free time playing or studying?
- What are your child's special interests? How can these interests be accommodated within the room?
- Is the room going to be used by one child or two? (If two children will be sharing a room, you'll want to seriously consider privacy issues.) Also, will the bedroom have space so that your child can have a friend sleep over?
- What type of equipment (computer, TV, stereo, telephone) will be used in the room? Does any wiring, electrical outlets, or phone jacks need to be installed or replaced?
- Does the child's bedroom offer privacy from both within and outside the home?
- What type of closet space is available?
- Where will toys, equipment from hobbies, sports equipment, collections, and so on be stored? Do you need to invest in a toy chest, bookcases, a dresser, and/or shelving?
- Is the bedroom furniture you plan to utilize in your child's room suitable for someone of his or her height? Will, for example, your toddler or child be able to reach the drawers in the dresser?
- Based on the age of your child, how long will this room be utilized before a major renovation or redesign is required?
- What are your immediate décor ideas?
- As you begin to choose furniture, what space limitations do you have to consider? If there room for a standalone twin bed? Do you need bunk beds?
- Is the existing lighting suitable for a child's bedroom?

- What type of flooring is currently in the room? Does the hardwood floor need to be refinished? Do you want wall-to-wall carpeting?
- Based on what needs to be done to the room to create a suitable environment for your child, what is your available budget?

Based on these questions, you can develop a general idea of your needs. Using **TABLE 8-1**, write out what needs to get done or be acquired.

TABLE 8-1

ASSESSING YOUR NEEDS IN THE KIDS' ROOM	
AREA OF THE ROOM	WHAT NEEDS TO BE PURCHASED OR COMPLETED
Bed/crib/bassinet	
Changing table (infants)	
Closets	
Dresser/armoire	
Electrical equipment*	
Electrical outlets/wiring	
Floor	
Lighting	
Mirror	
Rocking chair (infants)	
Seating	
Shelves and bookcases	
Toy chest	
Under-bed storage	
Walls**	
Windows	
Other furniture	
Other fixtures	

  * Computer, telephone, stereo, television, radio, alarm clock, and so on
** Wallpaper, paint, and so on

After you have a list of what tasks need to be done and the items that need to be purchased, create a timetable and budget for yourself. If you need to hire someone (electrician, contractor, plumber, and so on), start making appointments.

Getting Free Design Assistance

One of your first steps as you begin planning your child's bedroom may be to visit a furniture store that offers free interior design services (or at least free design consultations). For high-end furniture, Ethan Allen (✎ *www.ethanallen.com*) is one example of a furniture store chain that offers the services of their highly trained interior designers.

What can you expect when you utilize the services of an interior designer to help you properly plan out a room's décor and functionality before making renovations or purchasing any furniture? According to Ethan Allen, their interior designers can help you plan a budget for your furniture purchase, provide an objective opinion on the room plan you've developed, assist you in pinpointing the pieces of furniture you need and selecting the best furniture to meet your needs, create a room design for you and help you determine your needs, and incorporate new pieces of furniture into your existing décor.

Finding More Space

When designing and creating a comfortable and functional bedroom for a child, one of the biggest issues you'll most likely face is available space. After all, children tend to have ever-growing toy collections, not to mention an ever-changing wardrobe and an abundance of other toys and equipment that they need to store. If you're living in a tight space, as you plan your child's bedroom, consider the following space-saving options in order to maximize the space available:

- Add hooks on the closet door(s) and inside the closet (on the side walls) for jackets, shoe bags, and other items.
- Free up valuable floor space by utilizing a loft bed for your child. The sleeping area is on the top, while a desk, dresser, shelves, or other forms of storage space can be built beneath the bed.
- If you need to accommodate more than one child, consider bunk beds to free up space.

- Install shelving on the walls as opposed to using a freestanding shelf unit that would take up floor space. On these shelves, store books, toys, collectibles, trophies, and other items.
- Install underbed drawers and use underbed storage bins for off-season clothing, toys, sports equipment, and so on. It may make sense to raise the bed slightly to create additional under-bed storage space.
- Keep the number of actual furniture pieces to a minimum. Whenever possible, choose pieces of furniture designed with multiple uses in mind. For example, some children's beds already have shelving or drawers built in.
- Make full use of closet organization tools (described in Chapter 2) to utilize every inch of available closet space.
- Take advantage of the storage space that a good-sized toy chest provides. This can be a central location where toys are kept. Within the toy chest, use plastic bins or shoe boxes to separate toys with lots of small pieces, such as building blocks, toy cars, board games, action figures, dolls (and accessories), and trading cards.
- Display shelving can sometimes be installed about a foot down from the ceiling line. You can use this shelf space to show off collections, trophies, artwork, and other items that don't need to be readily accessed.

In small spaces, your child's room must be as clutter-free as possible. The first step to achieving this is to get rid of anything that's not needed. If you buy a month's supply of diapers in order to save money, for example, don't store them all in the middle of the nursery where they'll take up valuable space. Get rid of toys that are broken or that your child has outgrown. Also, keep drawers and closet space from getting filled with clothing that no longer fits or that your child will no longer wear.

FACT

Limit the number of toys that can be out at one time. Make a rule that any toy that isn't being actively used be put away before a new toy can be taken out and used. For an infant or toddler, keep only a few toys out in the open and rotate them every few days. If a toy breaks or no longer gets played with, give it away or throw it out.

Choosing Furniture for Children

Finding the right furniture that's well built, functional, visually appealing, durable, and within your budget will likely require some searching on your part. Be prepared to visit a number of furniture stores to see the available options. If this is furniture that will be used by young children, pay careful attention to the quality of construction and think in terms of product safety. Don't try to save money by purchasing poor-quality furniture or second-hand furniture (especially for an infant or toddler) that may not meet the latest safety guidelines issued by the U.S. Consumer Product Safety Commission (☎ 800-638-2772).

If you're extremely budget-conscious, shop around by visiting your local furniture retailers (including children's furniture specialty stores and department stores), and then use the Internet to compare prices from online retailers. It's not a good idea, however, to purchase children's furniture you haven't seen, touched, and examined firsthand.

No matter where you buy furniture, keep the following tips in mind:

- Decide on a basic look, style, or theme. To get some ideas, read a few home-decorating magazines and visit several furniture store showrooms. Also surf the Web for online furniture retailers.
- Figure out what your overall budget and time frame are.
- If you're not sure where to start, contact an interior decorator. Either pay an independent decorator to come to your home and work with you to create the room or utilize the interior-design services offered at many high-end furniture stores.
- As you see what's available, compare value, workmanship, durability, and safety features.
- Think in terms of storage. You can utilize several different types of storage in a bedroom, including open storage (shelves and baskets), closed storage (armoires, bins, chests, underbed storage, and dressers), convenient storage (closets), and remote storage (closets and storage options in other areas of your home, such as the basement, attic, or garage).

ALERT!

As you examine children's furniture, pay attention to its quality. Determine what materials the furniture is made from. Beware of sharp edges and splinters. Check that all moving parts, such as drawers, work smoothly and are well constructed. Stick with well-known and name-brand furniture that comes with a good warrantee.

Make sure the individual pieces of furniture you choose will fit properly into the layout of the room (based on size and décor) as well as into your budget. For example, if you're purchasing a large dresser, is there ample room to open the dresser drawers? After you know the exact measurements of the bedroom as well as the individual pieces of furniture you're interested in, sketch out on paper the room's proposed layout.

Budget Issues

After you find furniture you like, check the price. Based on where you're shopping, the prices may be negotiable. Also, determine whether and when the items will go on sale. Make sure you determine, in advance, what extra costs may be involved. For example, does the furniture store charge extra for certain colors or finishes? What are the setup and delivery charges? Does the price you're being quoted include all of the accessories you see in the showroom? Watch out for hidden costs and make sure you understand exactly what you're paying for and what you'll receive. Also ask about delivery time. Make sure there's not a three or four month wait to have the furniture manufactured and delivered.

Based on the costs and your budget, consider purchasing only a few pieces of furniture at a time, putting off buying furniture that you don't need right away. For example, if you're creating a nursery for your newborn baby, you won't be needing a crib for several months. You can put off the purchase of this expensive piece of furniture until it's actually needed and use a bassinet in the meantime for the newborn.

Also, look into financing and layaway options. Pay attention to interest rates and the fine print when using a store credit card versus a bank-issued credit card. Preplanning your finances and understanding your options will make paying for the new furniture much easier.

Preparing the Room

Prior to having the furniture delivered, consider how you need to prepare the room itself. For example, does the room need to be painted or wallpapered? What about flooring, window treatments, or electrical work (outlets and lighting)? Before the furniture is delivered and set up, make sure the room is totally prepared and well cleaned. You'll also want to remove all of the clothing, toys, and other items from the room. After the new furniture is in place, sort these items and place them in their new storage locations.

FACT

Wall-to-wall carpeting, area rugs, hardwood floors, linoleum, and tile are some of the flooring options available for bedrooms. As you choose the flooring for the child's bedroom, think in terms of safety, functionality, and your ability to keep the floor clean. Some experts suggest utilizing a vinyl floor with area rugs for an infant's room, but this is a matter of personal preference.

Organizing a Baby's Nursery

If you're about to be a first-time parent, your life will be turned upside down when your new baby is born. As part of taking a well-organized approach to the pregnancy, you probably want to prepare the nursery before the baby is actually born. This means determining what your needs will be.

As you begin to design your nursery, think in terms of functionality. For example, you'll want to choose a room in your home that's close to a bathroom. Likewise, if the nursery is located close to your bedroom, you'll be able to react that much faster in the middle of the night when your infant wakes up and requires attention.

As you consider purchasing furniture and fixtures for your nursery, make sure they meet the safety guidelines issued by the U.S. Consumer Product Safety Commission (✆ 800-638-2772).

Knowing What Furniture You Need for a Nursery

For a newborn baby's nursery, some of the essential pieces of furniture and equipment you'll ultimately need are discussed in the following sections.

Furniture for Sleeping

At first, this will be a bassinet, but within a few months, the baby will need a crib.

Dresser

Your baby will quickly build up his or her own wardrobe. You'll need drawers to store the clothing. As you do when organizing your own bedroom (see Chapter 7), organize the dresser drawers by storing similar items together.

Changing Table

Until your child is toilet trained, you're going to be changing a lot of diapers. The area where you'll be changing diapers should provide a safe area for your child, plus have storage (shelves or drawers) for all of the items you'll need. While the baby is being changed, everything you'll need (wipes, creams, diapers, and so on) should be within arm's reach for you, but not for your baby. You don't ever want to turn your back on the child. The changing table should have a concave shape in which you can nestle your child to discourage his or her rolling over. A changing table with drawers and/or shelves beneath it will prove to be highly functional.

Diaper Bin

Most parents rave about the Diaper Genie from Playtex (✆ 800-843-6430, ✑ *www.playtexbaby.com/diapergenie.htm*). The Playtex Diaper Genie is the only diaper pail system that individually seals each diaper, locking in odor and germs. The patented design wraps each diaper in a fragrant film to produce a chain of sealed diapers easily emptied from the base. The Diaper Genie unit can store up to twenty-five medium-sized diapers before it needs to be emptied. The wide opening makes it easy to dispose of even larger diapers. It can be conveniently operated with one hand, so you can use it while changing your baby.

Clothing Hamper

Many companies offer hampers designed to fit the décor of a child's nursery or bedroom. Baskets, for example, come in different shapes. The Everything 4 Baby Web site (✍ *http://everything4baby.freeyellow.com*) offers an elephant-shaped hamper that can double as a storage box for toys as your child gets older. It's hand-woven from durable wicker.

Toy Bin

After your child is born, he or she will probably start to amass a large toy collection. You'll want to keep these toys organized and keep them from cluttering the space available. A closet is an excellent place to store larger toys and accessories (such as rockers, walkers, bouncers, swings, and so on) when they're not in use. A toy bin is ideal for small to mid-sized toys, while shelves or a basket (placed in the floor or on a dresser) can be used to display teddy bears and other stuffed toys in a decorative manner. If you choose to utilize a toy chest, make an effort to keep it organized; that is, don't just toss toys in willy-nilly. Also, pay attention to the construction of the unit and make sure it's totally safe. The lid should not be able to slam shut, nor should it be able to entrap your child.

Nursing Chair

A comfortable rocking chair is ideal for nursing an infant.

Electronic Monitor

Keeping tabs on your infant when he or she is alone in the crib is critical. A wide range of video and audio child monitors available. The Dorel Juvenile Group (✆ 800-723-3065, ✍ *www.safety1st.com*), which manufactures childcare products under the Safety 1st name, offers a range of monitors, plus an entire catalog of infant and childcare products available from children's specialty stores nationwide. The Sound & Sight Television Monitor is a wireless monitor system that connects to any television within a 300-foot radius of the camera location. This system turns any television into a video and audio monitor. The Held-Held Monitor & Television offers similar technology, except the receiver includes a two-inch, color, handheld TV monitor that can be carried anywhere within a 300-foot radius of the camera.

Smoke Detector

Make sure you install a quality smoke detector in the nursery. Check the battery monthly.

Arranging the Furniture

After the room is selected, consider what your daily routine with the infant will be, and then position the furniture accordingly. Near the rocking chair, for example, you may want a bookcase and a table (where you can place whatever you'll need to nurse the baby). You'll probably also want a telephone with a speakerphone in this area, plus you may want to have a view out a nearby window. Keep a dresser with your child's clothes close to the changing table, so that you can easily reach various garments while dressing your baby. If the clothes will be kept in a closet, consider placing the changing table as close to the closet as possible.

Choose the location of the crib first, because this will probably be one of the most used and largest pieces of furniture in the room. Make sure the crib and the changing table are positioned as far from any hazards (such as windows, heaters, air conditioners, drapes, and so on) as possible.

As your child goes from being an infant to a toddler, floor space will become increasingly more important, because this is where your child will play. As you arrange furniture, try to maximize floor space as much as possible. To generate more floor space, utilize lighting that attaches to the ceiling or walls (as opposed to floor lamps) and take advantage of vertical storage spaces (tall bookcases or dressers with more drawers stacked vertically as opposed to being wide).

Always think in terms of safety when planning and organizing your nursery. Be conscious of electrical cords, curtain cords, and toys with small parts or pieces. Never hang any artwork, mirrors, or items directly over the crib, where they could fall on your child.

To make certain your nursery and your entire home are properly childproofed, you can hire a professional baby safety expert who will visit your home and help you organize it. The International Association of Child Safety (☎ 888-677-IACS) can offer referrals. Keep in mind, however, that no matter how well you organize your nursery and no matter how many safety precautions you take, nothing replaces the need for constant supervision of your child, especially during the first two years of his or her life.

FACT

If the décor you choose involves a large wall mural consider whether this wall space would be better utilized by installing shelves or bookcases. Could you free up floor space by moving furniture against the wall? Before committing to a wall mural as part of your décor, make sure you have ample space for everything else. A wallpaper border around the ceiling, for example, may be a more efficient way of introducing more color or style into the room.

Designing a Bedroom for an Older Child or Teen

As your child gets older, his or her needs will change dramatically. Instead of a crib, you'll need a bed. Instead of a changing table, you'll need a dresser and/or a desk. Storage space becomes more of a premium, and issues such as privacy become increasingly more important.

Organize your child's room in much the same way you organize your own master bedroom (see Chapter 7). First, determine what you have to work with. Start by measuring the room, and then take an inventory of the pieces of furniture you own or want in the bedroom.

If you're purchasing new bedroom furniture, consider the size of each piece and determine exactly how it will be used and where in the room it will go. For example, if you're buying a new dresser to store clothing items, what, specifically, will be stored in each drawer?

Clearing Out Clutter

Together with your teen, sort through everything currently stored in your teen's bedroom, including his or her wardrobe. Figure out what items actually belong in the bedroom and what can be stored elsewhere. For example, can winter jackets be stored in a foyer closet or in the basement, attic, or garage during the off-season? What about personal items, such as trophies, toys, or collectibles? Can you use shelves, wall space, or the top of a dresser to display these items?

Carefully analyze each piece of furniture in the bedroom and determine whether it's being used to its maximum potential. If your dresser drawers were to be reorganized, could you better utilize the space? If you were to store your child's sweaters or linens in a container under the bed, could you free up valuable closet space? If you installed a shoe rack in the closet, could you save space by organizing his or her shoe collection?

Just as with a closet, when organizing your child's dresser, remove everything from the drawers and lay the items out on a bed or on the floor. Take a careful inventory and determine what actually needs to be kept in the dresser. Next, group all similar items together (either by season or clothing type). See how many physical drawers your dresser has, and then determine where each group of similar items will be stored. Items your teen uses every day, such as socks and underwear, should be placed in a drawer that's the most convenient to access.

Finding Furniture for Teens

Most furniture stores display collections of furniture designed specifically for children or teenagers. This furniture should be well-made and maximize storage space. For example, a loft bed (with a desk or dresser below it) will save space and make the most out of a small area because the wall space (in addition to floor space) is being utilized.

Bunks 'n' Stuff (☎ 800-355-1997, *www.bunksnstuff.com*) is just one online source of furniture for a child or teen's bedroom. This company specializes in space-saving bunk beds and loft beds. The company's bunk/loft system offers a complete bedroom set in one unit. The set includes two twin beds, as well as a built-in three-drawer desk, two-shelf bookcase and a twenty-two-inch deep five-drawer chest with European-style metal drawer guides. The price includes delivery to the room and carton removal (some simple assembly is required). The desk and bookshelves can be placed on either side and are reversible, giving versatility to any room.

For a single twin-size bed with plenty of drawer storage below it, Bunks 'n' Stuff offers what it calls the Captain's Bed. This standard twin bed has plenty of drawers beneath it, including an oversized center drawer that can be used for anything from a toy chest to a file cabinet. A matching dresser, desk, and nightstand are available.

Bunk Beds Plus (✆ 219-672-3491, ✍ *www.bunkbedsplus.com*), Bhome.com (✆ 612-861-0102, ✍ *www.bhome.com*), and the Great American Bunk Bed Company (✆ 866-4US-BUNK, ✍ *www.greatamericanbunkbed.com*) are other online retailers of bunk beds and storage solutions for a child's bedroom.

While functionality and construction are key considerations when purchasing a bunk bed, consider the following safety guidelines as well:

- The bed should be made of strong, durable materials with edges that are smooth and rounded. After this unit is installed, shake the bed vigorously to be sure it's firm and stable.
- The guardrails should run the length of the bed on both sides of the upper bunk.
- The ladder should be wide, securely attached, and at a comfortable climbing angle.
- The mattress used with the bed should be the proper size and have a snug fit (some bunk beds utilize custom-sized mattresses). The mattress should be supported by strong slats that are tightly screwed into the side of the bed.

In the child/teenager's room, take full advantage of underbed storage and consider using closet organizers to fully utilize closet space. Think carefully about what the room is being used for and plan accordingly. If your child will be doing homework, practicing an instrument, or using a computer, create a quiet environment that's well-lit. Because most teens have an abundance of electronic equipment (computer, TV, VCR, DVD player, video game system, alarm clock, stereo, telephone, and so on), make sure the room has ample electrical outlets and that these outlets are in locations where extension cords won't have to be overused. Instead of storing diapers and other baby items, your child might need a place for a

CD collection, baseball card collection, video game and software library, trophies, books, Barbie dolls, and/or model airplanes.

After your children reach their preteen years, allow them to have input into the design and layout of their bedrooms, because this is their personal space, and they know what their living habits and needs are. Allow them to express their personal tastes and styles by selecting the décor (within reason, of course).

To help your preteen or teen keep his or her room organized, create an environment where everything has its proper place. Then, it'll just be a matter of convincing your teen to put his or her belongings back in their proper places. If a teen is given the opportunity to pile up dirty laundry in the middle of the bedroom, for example, that's what will happen unless you provide a convenient hamper or laundry basket. Likewise, less trash will wind up on the floor if a good-sized wastebasket is placed in the room and is easily accessible.

> For additional storage solutions and information about products that you can use to store various items and belongings, point your Web browser to the Web site of Container World, Inc. (✍ www.storagesources.com).

In order to keep your child or teen's room clutter-free, take some time every season for the two of you to go through their drawers and closet and discard any clothing that's worn out, doesn't fit, or is out of style. Take an inventory of your child's wardrobe and determine what new items are needed. The shorts that fit your child last summer probably won't fit this summer. Likewise, at the end of each school year, go through your child's bookshelves and piles of paper to determine whether you can get rid of or store old textbooks and papers to make room for new books.

Teenagers have responsibilities. One of them is to study and do their homework. While you probably don't have time to look over your teenager's shoulder every minute of the day, you can ensure that he or she has a special area designated for studying, reading, and doing homework. Ensure that your teen has a desk or some sort of flat surface to do work.

ALERT!

While the Internet can be a valuable tool for your child or teen, cyberspace also contains content that's not suitable for your child. Don't allow your child to surf the Web alone. In addition, invest in software that limits Web access and provides a summary of the sites visited.

CHAPTER 9

Organizing Your Home Office

Whether you have the opportunity to work from home full-time or part-time, or you simply want to establish a space in your home to handle your personal business, creating a well-designed and properly organized home office environment will greatly impact your productivity and comfort.

Determining Your Needs

Your needs in a home office depend on the type of work you do and your personal work habits. Before you can begin to design and organize your home office environment, create a detailed list of the types of work you'll be doing from this area of your home. Consider the tasks you may perform from a home office, including brainstorming, conducting business-related phone calls and teleconferences, holding in-person meetings, making and receiving phone calls, monitoring the stock market, paying bills, performing research, reading, sending and receiving e-mail and faxes, storing a library of work-related and professional books (for example, a personal law library), storing personal or work-related files, surfing the Internet, writing reports, and writing and sending business letters.

After you determine what tasks you hope to accomplish on an ongoing basis in the home office you're creating or organizing, develop a detailed list of furniture, equipment, and supplies required to achieve your objective. As you determine what's needed, think about ways you can reduce clutter in your workspace. For example, select furniture with plenty of drawers and file cabinets with extra storage space. You should also position equipment close to electrical outlets and phone jacks, so you won't have lots of unsightly and disorganized cords running throughout the room.

Because your desk is the central and most integral part of your home office, decide on its location first. Then determine what other furniture and equipment needs to be nearby and what can be placed elsewhere in the room. This will help you create the most functional design and layout for your work environment.

FACT

To save space yet add functionality to any home office, consider purchasing an all-in-one or multifunctional peripheral that serves as a laser printer, copier, scanner, and fax machine, all in one unit. These units cost considerably less than purchasing each piece of equipment separately, plus you'll save a lot of space.

Visit any office supply superstore or computer center to find out more about these all-in-one peripherals.

TABLE 9-1 is a basic checklist to help you determine the pieces of furniture you want in your home office environment, based on your personal needs and work habits.

TABLE 9-1

HOME OFFICE FURNITURE CHECKLIST				
FURNITURE	NEEDED	OPTIONAL	NOT NEEDED	SIZE REQUIREMENTS
Desk	❑	❑	❑	
Desk chair	❑	❑	❑	
Computer workstation	❑	❑	❑	
Work table/extra desk	❑	❑	❑	
File cabinets	❑	❑	❑	
Storage containers/cabinets	❑	❑	❑	
Shelving	❑	❑	❑	
Bookcases	❑	❑	❑	
Extra seating	❑	❑	❑	
Artwork	❑	❑	❑	
TV and VCR	❑	❑	❑	
Desk lamp	❑	❑	❑	
Other lighting	❑	❑	❑	
Safe	❑	❑	❑	
Bulletin board	❑	❑	❑	
Wastepaper basket/garbage	❑	❑	❑	

Creating the Right Work Environment

Now that you have a basic idea of what you hope to accomplish in your home work space and what equipment you'll need in order to achieve your objectives, design and lay out your home office so that it will maximize your productivity and be a comfortable place to work. Issues such as lighting, color schemes, ergonomics, and functionality all need to be addressed. As with any organizational task, preplanning is crucial, so put some thought into your needs and wants, and then address each issue individually.

One of the most important details to consider when designing a home office is choosing an area of your living space that is closed off or separated from the rest of the home. You want to be able to work within an area that's quiet and away from the hustle and bustle of children running around, babies crying, and dogs barking, for example. If you're building or refinishing a room in your home to be a home office, consider adding extra insulation and/or soundproofing materials to the walls, floors, and ceiling to ensure you'll have a quiet place to work.

Unless you have an extra room in your home that can be transformed into an office, you may consider utilizing your finished basement, sunroom, guest bedroom, finished attic, or media room as your home office. Obviously, some of these options have drawbacks. For example, if your guest bedroom doubles as your office, you'll have to give up your work space every time you have company. Likewise, if your media room doubles as your office, it's impossible for you to work while other members of your family relax and watch television. An extra bedroom, attic, unused garage (finished), or basement are probably your best options for creating a home office.

Before making a major financial investment in remodeling an area of your home to transform it into a home office, try working in the area for a while to ensure that the environment and surroundings will help you maximize your productivity. Remember, you need to pinpoint an area of your home that will provide ample space and the best possible environment (in terms of lighting, temperature, privacy, and sound) for you to be productive. After you know what furniture you'll need, take measurements to make sure it will all fit properly in your current or proposed home office.

In a small area or room, for example, you may not have space for a full-size L-shaped desk, bookcases, and file cabinets, so you may be forced to modify your layout or work habits. Ideally, however, you want to create an environment that will allow you to reach your peak level of efficiency using established work habits, because those work habits have been successful for you.

When choosing your space, therefore, think about the room's temperature and overall climate. Some attics, for example, get very warm, while basements can be cool, damp, and drafty. Consider what extra equipment you'll need to maintain a comfortable temperature. Portable heater, fan, window air conditioner, or a (de)humidifier may be necessary to create an environment that's conducive to working. Damp environments are not suitable if you'll be storing paper-based files or using electronics, such as computers.

In addition to having a place that's quiet, you want it to be properly lighted. Ideally, a home office should have at least one large window and/or skylights to allow natural daylight into the room. The lamps, lighting fixtures, and light bulbs you choose will also impact the overall environment. For example, fluorescent light bulbs may be cheaper and last longer, but they're much tougher on your eyes than traditional light bulbs.

Studies have shown that people exposed to natural sunlight tend to be happier and more productive in a work environment. Natural sunlight can be supplemented by special full-spectrum light bulbs that simulate natural sunlight. Full Spectrum Solutions is an online-based company that sells full spectrum light bulbs and lighting fixtures. According to the company's Web site (✐ www.fullspectrumsolutions.com), some of the benefits of utilizing this type of bulb to supply lighting in your home office include reduced glare, less wear and tear on the retina, and no damage to the skin from natural sunlight.

Choosing Your Desk and Storing Supplies

One of the most important pieces of furniture in any home office is the desk. This will be your central work area. When many people think about desks, what comes to mind is a rectangular shaped top with a small central drawer and file-sized drawers on the sides (see **FIGURE 9-1**). To handle basic paperwork, this type of desk design may be appropriate. A generic desk typically measures between sixty-five and seventy-two inches long, with a depth of thirty-six inches. (The height of a desk is generally between twenty-eight and thirty inches.) After you add a computer, printer, telephone, and a basic desk set to the surface of your rectangular desk, however, you'll probably find that most of the valuable work space is used up and inefficient.

FIGURE 9-1:
A standard
home office
layout

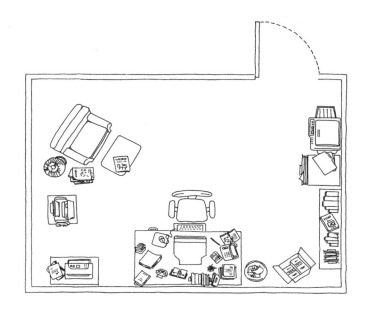

As you choose a desk, consider U-shaped or L-shaped designs that provide ample space for a computer, lamp, papers, telephone, etc., but also give you space to do your work (see **FIGURE 9-2**). If you incorporate a computer desk into your home office, make sure it's ergonomically designed. The ideal height of the keyboard should be about twenty-eight inches, yet the monitor should be at eye level, so that you're not looking up or down at it.

FIGURE 9-2:
A home office
layout with
an L-shaped
desk

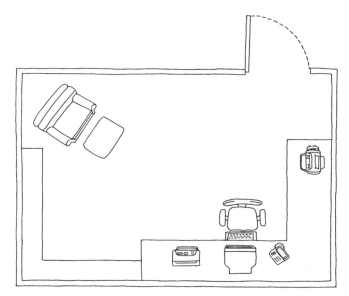

The desk design you ultimately choose should be based upon what you'll be using the desk for. For example, if you'll be holding business meetings around your desk, you'll need ample room for chairs on both sides of the desk, plus a clear line of sight to the people sitting opposite you.

For most people, desk space is a premium. Thus, you want to have at your disposal as much open desk space as possible, based on the amount of room in your home office. Take measurements and create your own blueprint on paper. This allows you to experiment with different room designs so you can have the largest desk possible, yet not feel like this piece of furniture dominates the room or makes for a claustrophobic work space.

Keep in mind that you'll probably want important files, your computer (and printer), telephone, calculator, and/or other items within arm's reach in order to maximize your productivity. To ensure that what you need is readily available, make a point of getting rid of nonessential furniture and other items. For example, if you use a calculator only once per day or every other day, keep your calculator in a desk drawer, as opposed to on the desktop itself. You may, instead, want to utilize the calculator built into Microsoft Windows and create a desktop shortcut on your computer so your calculator is only a click of the mouse away when you need it.

Likewise, while you'll want your computer printer within arm's reach so that you don't have to leave your chair to obtain a printout, your fax machine, for example, can probably be placed farther away and not on your main desk.

Be sure to utilize the available space to its greatest potential. For example, instead of having file bins on your desk, can you utilize hanging files and take advantage of nearby wall space? A computer monitor stand is also an excellent tool for saving valuable desk space. This type of stand also ensures that your computer monitor will be at eye level, thus creating a more comfortable work environment that will inflict less stress on your neck, shoulders, and arms. Office supplies, shipping supplies, and other items should be readily available, yet kept in a clutter-free manner. This can best be done by storing these items in a closet and utilizing plastic storage bins or customized shelving. Chapter 2 of this book focuses on custom-designing and organizing closet space.

To become a well-organized person requires that your desk (your personal work space) become and remain as organized as possible. This means eliminating clutter and distractions. Sure, having a few personal mementos, such as a picture of your kids, is important. But, having many pictures cluttering up your desk is a distraction.

In order to help keep the papers on your desk organized, utilize an in-box/out-box or a to-do box. All of the papers, except for the ones you're currently working with, should be placed within one of these boxes, properly filed in a filing cabinet, or thrown away. Don't allow yourself to create piles of papers, reports, bills, mail, and other documents on the floor or on nearby chairs. After these piles get created, they'll always grow higher and become unorganized. Be sure to utilize a filing system to maximize organization and eliminate clutter.

Office supplies and tools you use regularly—stapler, tape, paper clips, rubber bands, pens, pencils, memo pads and notepads, staple remover, markers, scissors, rulers, and so on—should be kept in a desk drawer that's readily available and within arm's reach. These items should not clutter your desktop when they're not in use. Instead, purchase small containers to divide up your supply drawer so that it remains well organized and each item stored in that drawer is readily available. On a regular basis, sort through the drawer and throw away dead pens, bent paper clips, stretched out rubber bands, and other useless junk that gets accumulated.

To help avoid clutter, don't keep items in your home office that don't belong there. For example, aspirin, food, children's toys, personal photo albums, and so on should be kept in their appropriate places outside of your home office.

Next to each of your telephones, always keep a notepad or phone message pad along with at least two pens. This will allow you to jot down notes or messages and not have to fumble around for a writing instrument.

So, what actually should be kept on your desktop? The answer to this question depends greatly on what you use your desk for. Consider the following common desk items when deciding how you utilize your premium desk space: calculator, computer, desk clock, desk lamp, desk set, in-box/out-box, notepad and pen, office supplies (stapler, pens, blotter, tape, and so on), PDA, personal scheduler or calendar, and telephone/answering machine.

FACT

Invest in a phone shelf. This allows your telephone to be raised slightly (for ergonomic purposes) and also provides ample storage and space for an answering machine, telephone headset, phonebook, notepad, and pen. To save space, consider purchasing a telephone and answering machine that are one unit. Many phones also have built-in digital phone directories for storing frequently dialed numbers, which can save you lots of time.

Home Office Seating

At the end of a workday, does your lower back hurt or do you feel tension in your neck and shoulders? These pains may be caused by your office chair and could be reduced or eliminated simply by purchasing an ergonomically designed chair that better fits your body.

Chairs are one of the most important home office tools, yet they tend to be overlooked. An ergonomically designed office chair may cost a bit more than a traditional chair, but it's designed to support the contours and movements of your body. Ergonomic chairs are also fully adjustable to meet your unique needs based on your height, weight, posture, and work habits.

As you sit at your desk throughout the day and reach for the phone, work at a computer, participate in meetings, or do paperwork, the position of your body is constantly changing. The desk chair you use should automatically adjust to the shifts in your body's position and continue offering much needed support to your back, legs, neck, and shoulders.

While working or sitting for long periods of time, your body needs to be relaxed in order to ensure proper blood circulation. If you aren't relaxed, you start to experience pain and fatigue and run the risk of sustaining long-term injuries. "Above all else, an office chair should offer comfort and full support," advises Bruce Lightly, the president of Lux Company, Inc. (✆ 800-334-7426, ✐ *www.luxcompany.com*), a company that designs and manufactures ergonomic seating products.

Optimally, the chair should also offer some sort of lumbar adjustment, because everyone has a different spinal alignment that needs to be taken into account. In addition, it should have rounded edges with arms that are adjustable. If you're typing at a keyboard and using a mouse, your arms will be in a different position than if you're simply doing paperwork at your desk. A chair also needs to be moveable, so it should be on wheels and have a swivel capability.

Studies show that people who use ergonomically designed chairs are more productive, because they're more comfortable throughout the day. These people take fewer breaks, their bodies undergo less stress, and their lower bodies experience improved circulation.

"There's more to ergonomics than a chair that moves up and down, so don't get caught up in buzz words when shopping around. A truly ergonomically designed product should be able to meet the needs of the user by adjusting to the unique size and shape of their bodies, and at the same time, accommodate their work habits," said Lightly of the Lux Company.

Ergonomically designed chairs come in a wide range of styles. Some are considered executive seating, while others are classified as task-seating products, which are similar to the seating products currently in use by the majority of the people who work in a traditional office environment. The price of a quality, well-designed ergonomic chair will typically range from $500 to $700 (or more), depending on its features.

The following manufacturers, retail stores, and mail-order companies can provide you with information about the latest developments in ergonomically designed office chairs and help you choose the design that's best for you:

- Amotek (☎ 800-242-4777, ✐ *www.amotek.com/product.html*): Manufacturer of ergonomic office chairs.
- BackSaver Products Company (☎ 800-251-2225): Offers an assortment of chairs, desks, and products designed to protect your back from pain and stress in an office environment.
- Ergomax Seating System (☎ 800-332-5635, ✐ *www.americanergonomics.com*): Manufacturer of ergonomic office chairs.
- Home Office Furniture System (✐ *www.hofs.com*): An online home office furniture showroom.
- OfficeMax (☎ 800-283-7674, ✐ *www.officemax.com*): An office supply superstore.
- Relax the Back (☎ 800-596-2225): This chain of retail shops specializes in back-care products, including office chairs.
- Reliable Home Office (☎ 800-869-6000): This catalog is filled with home office furniture, small business equipment, and other products useful to people who work from home.
- Staples (☎ 800-333-3330, ✐ *www.staples.com*): An office supply superstore.

Organizing Your Files

Keep all of your files, papers, and documents, whether they involve your professional work or personal business, in file cabinets or bins where they are readily accessible, yet kept out of the way when they're not needed. One of the most unorganized approaches you can take is allowing papers, receipts, and other documents to pile up on your desk, on the floor, or on chairs.

File cabinets come in a wide range of sizes. Some are approximately 15" × 21" × 36" (for a single, letter size file), and some have two, three, or four drawers stacked horizontally. It's an excellent strategy to utilize as much vertical space as possible by investing in a four-drawer file cabinet. This takes up the least amount of actual floor space, yet can store the most papers. Your most time-sensitive and important papers can be kept directly on your desk using stackable files. It's common for people to utilize an in-box or to-do file directly on their desks. The trick, however, is to be disciplined enough to process those important papers properly, so they're appropriately dealt with as opposed to simply being allowed to stack up on your desk and stored there indefinitely.

From an organizational standpoint, use separate file cabinets for your personal and business files. Next, divide up your files and label them carefully. For example, in your personal filing cabinet, you may have folders or separate files for the following types of paperwork: auto-related, banking, bills, career, education, financial, health/medical, insurance, investments, legal, mortgage, taxes (keeping current and past information separate), travel, and warranties/receipts/instructions.

All of your files should be divided up, labeled, and kept organized. Files can be sorted and stored alphabetically, numerically, with some sort of color-coding, by date, geographically, by subject, or by using your own criteria. What's important is that you (and anyone using your files) understand the filing system you implement. Whenever possible, keep your filing system straight-forward, up-to-date, and intuitive for others. For example, if you're storing company files, store them alphabetically by company name (or the client's last name).

FACT

Part of being organized is being neat. Invest in an inexpensive labeling system, such as the Brother P-Touch system (✐*www.brother.com/usa/label/label_cntr.html),* available from any office supply store. Use this labeling system to affix labels on each of your file cabinets and individual file folders. Actual files can be kept in manila-colored file folders or you can purchase color-coded files for easy visual identification and sorting.

Keep current files readily available, while dormant/inactive files can be kept in airtight storage containers in an out of the way area, such as a basement or attic. Old files can also be scanned into a computer and stored on a computer's hard drive or in an electronic format (such as a Zip Disk) or on a writable CD-ROM.

As you go through all of your papers, answer the questions in **TABLE 9-2**.

TABLE 9-2

PAPER-SORTING STRATEGY		
QUESTION	IF YES . . .	IF NO . . .
Is this important?	Determine an appropriate filing location.	Discard document immediately.
Is this paper/file timely?	Place in to-do file or on desk.	Discard document or determine an appropriate filing location.
Is it personal?	Store with personal files.	Store with professional documents.
Will you need the file/paper again?	Determine an appropriate filing location.	Discard document immediately.
Can the information be obtained somewhere else (online, for example, or scanned into your computer)?	Discard document immediately	Determine an appropriate filing location.

How can I deal with the papers that come across my desk?
On a daily basis, new papers will come across your desk and have the potential to instantly transform themselves into clutter. To make sure this doesn't happen, set aside at least fifteen minutes a day to review incoming papers and take the appropriate action with them.

As someone who is dedicated to becoming more organized, you probably already have a massive filing cabinet or set of files that needs to be sorted through. Initially, it'll take an investment of time to go through these files and throw out what's not important or necessary to keep. After this initial work is done, make a point to clean out your files periodically to avoid clutter buildup. Spending fifteen minutes per day or an hour a week organizing your paperwork will save you countless time later and keep you more organized. You'll need to go through every piece of paper in your home office (including those in your files), and eliminate the stuff you don't need. You'll also have to put each important piece of paper in its proper place. Finally, after your current files are in order and current clutter has been eliminated, you'll need to make an ongoing effort to stop creating new clutter in your workspace.

The papers that don't get filed within your filing cabinets and that don't get thrown away will probably need to be stored. Depending on what storage facilities you have available, you can invest in cheap cardboard storage boxes (shaped like filing cabinets), or you can spend a bit more and purchase airtight plastic containers. Plastic containers/filing bins are available from a variety of manufacturers, such as Rubbermaid (✎*www.rubbermaid.com*), and are available from office supply stores and other retailers.

ALERT!

Store important papers, such as birth certificates, wills, marriage licenses, contracts, real estate deeds, mortgage papers, insurance documents, and business papers in a safe-deposit box at a local bank or invest in a fireproof safe (make sure the safe is rated to be fireproof for at least one hour).

When controlling clutter in your home office, follow these basic steps:

1. Identify the various clutter-related problems you face, for example, piles of papers everywhere or overflowing closets and file cabinets.
2. Determine exactly how these clutter-related problems are negatively impacting your ability to work within your home office.
3. Figure out how and why all of the clutter in your home office was created in the first place.
4. Ask yourself, "What have I done so far to try eliminating clutter?" and "Why didn't those efforts work?"
5. Ask yourself, "What is required for me to eliminate the clutter?" (The solution may be simple behavioral changes, a refocus on how files and other items in your office are organized, or the use of organizational tools—see Chapter 13.)

Instead of storing back issues of magazines, tear out articles that are worth saving and toss out or recycle the rest of the magazines. In many cases, you'll find that the same information is available online, so you may not need to store the actual printed articles at all.

As you go through your day-to-day life, dozens, perhaps hundreds of papers will go across your desk each day. For those papers that deserve your utmost attention, that can't be forgotten, or that you classify as having top priority, consider placing a special file on your desk or hanging a bulletin board near your desk upon which you can stick only the most important of papers. Depending on the size of the bulletin board, you can divide it up into areas that are labeled, "To Do Today," or "To Do Next Week," for example.

Organizing Your Computer

We're living in the information age, and using the Internet now includes such activities as shopping, communicating (via online chats, message postings, and e-mail), research, financial management (investment management), and entertainment. When connected to the Internet, a computer becomes a powerful communication tool, with a vast amount of information available twenty-four hours per day.

The Internet is probably beginning to have an impact on your life, changing the way you handle everyday tasks. A growing number of people are turning to the Web to handle electronic bill paying, for example. By using one of these bill-paying or electronic-banking services, you can save time and money, keep you financial records more organized, and keep paperwork to a minimum.

The Internet, however, is just one use of a computer in a home office environment. Using off-the-shelf computer software in conjunction with a powerful operating system (such as Microsoft Windows), you can perform a wide range of tasks and better organize the immense amount of information you receive. Because the cost of computers and related equipment continues to drop while the power and capabilities of computers increase, more and more people are relying on technology to handle a greater range of everyday tasks.

Knowing that a computer can handle a wide range of applications, it's important that you, as the user, determine exactly the tasks you'll ultimately be using your computer for. No matter what applications you choose to utilize, think of the computer's hard drive (the place where your files, programs, and data are stored) as an electronic filing system that also needs to be kept organized. After all, you need to be able to just as quickly and easily find your computer files and your paper files.

However, simply by using your everyday programs, your computer generates random files that fill up your hard drive, but that you don't need. For example, the Web browser Microsoft Explorer keeps track of every Web site you visit and stores detailed information about those sites in various cache and temporary folders and files. To delete some of the older Microsoft Explorer files that may no longer be needed, from the Tools pull-down menu in the program, select the Internet Options feature. You can then adjust the Temporary Internet Files settings or delete the unnecessary files.

Sorting through and deleting unnecessary files from your computer can be tricky if you're not computer literate, yet if nothing is done to manage all of your files, they eventually take up tremendous amounts of hard drive space. Using a program like Norton SystemWorks (✍ *www.symantec.com)*, managing your computer files and keeping your system operating properly is much easier. According to Symantec, the company that developed Norton SystemWorks, "this program gives you everything you need in one easy-to-use suite. The new One-Button Checkup makes system maintenance as easy as the click of a mouse. In addition, Norton AntiVirus is the world's leading antivirus software. Norton Utilities optimizes your PC's performance and solves problems easily. Norton CleanSweep removes unneeded programs and files."

Data Back-up Options

Just as with a normal, paper-based filing cabinet, periodically clean up your computer's hard drive and get rid of unnecessary files, data, and programs. Before ever deleting anything from your computer, however, make a backup of the files and data. Backup files can be stored on 3.5-inch disks, writable CD-ROMs, ZIP disks, or using some other form of data backup device. ZIP drives from Iomega (✍ *www.iomega.com*) are an easy-to-use and inexpensive way of backing up data and programs. Any writable CD-ROM drive can also be used for backing up vast amounts of data relatively quickly and inexpensively.

By using a data-storage device, such as a ZIP drive and your computer, you can not only back up and store electronic files, you can also scan paper-based files into your computer and store them electronically. Save your work on a regular basis and then make daily or weekly backups of your most critical data.

When scanning and electronically storing paper-based files, you can use a program called Adobe Acrobat (✍ *www.adobe.com*) to make this process easier. According to Adobe, someone can use Acrobat to "convert any document to Adobe Portable Document Format (PDF). Adobe PDF files can be opened reliably across a broad range of hardware and software and look just like your original files." Thus, when you view a scanned document on the computer screen or print it out later using a printer, it'll look exactly like the original paper-based document that was scanned.

Cables, Cables Everywhere

Have you looked behind your computer lately? If you're like most people who have a CPU, monitor, printer, scanner, mouse, external speakers, and other devices connected to your computer, chances are you'll see a maze of wires all tangled up behind your computer. The thought of adding a new peripheral to your computer or having to physically move the location of your computer is often dreaded, simply because you'll need to sort through all of those wires.

While you can't create a wire-free environment, you can sort through all of those wires one time, bind them together, label each of them, and ultimately create a more organized workspace. Most office supply stores sell Velcro strips for wrapping wires and making them neater. (Twist ties also work perfectly.) Many computer desks also offer special compartments and holes in the desktop for routing wires and keeping them out of open view.

In addition to labeling and wrapping your wires, careful preplanning can also ensure that you locate your computer next to power outlets and phone outlets, for example, so that you don't have extension cords, phone cords, and power strips running across the room. Part of creating a truly productive work environment is creating an atmosphere that's aesthetically pleasing. Organizing your wires and cables will help to create a more organized-looking environment.

Saving Space with Your Monitor

There are many different types of computer monitors. If you're looking to save valuable desk space, consider adding a flat-screen monitor to your computer. These monitors are often only several inches thick, yet offer excellent resolution. They're also easier on your eyes if you use your computer for extended periods of time. Companies like Apple, CTX, Hitachi, Hewlett Packard, NEC, Mitsubishi, Nokia, Philips, Princeton Graphics, Samsung, Sony, and ViewSonic all offer flat-screen monitors in various sizes from fourteen inches to over twenty-two inches.

Organizing Your Contacts and Information

One challenge virtually everyone faces is keeping track of all the people they know. These days, people often have a home address and work address, not to mention multiple telephone numbers (home phone, work phone, cellular phone, fax, and pager number). In addition, people also have Web sites and e-mail addresses, plus other information that is important to keep track of. Even if you have only a small handful of friends, business associates, and acquaintances, keeping track of the information pertinent to these people can be an ongoing challenge.

You could try maintaining a handwritten address book, but each time information needs to be added or changed, keeping those handwritten pages neat and legible may become more and more of a challenge. Keeping a business card file is also an option, but finding the right business card when you need it after your collection starts to grow can be a time-consuming task. In today's information-oriented world, using contact management software offers the ideal solution for keeping track of the people you know as well as other important data.

Computer programs, such as Microsoft Outlook (✐ *www.microsoft.com*) and Act! (✐ *www.act.com),* are easy to use and allow you to store, sort, and retrieve unlimited information about the people in your contact database. These and other programs like them are also designed to help plan your busy schedule and offer a variety of other features that make staying in touch with people by mail, phone, fax, or e-mail easier.

With more than 3.2 million individual users and 11,000 corporate accounts worldwide, ACT! has become the tool of choice for managing and growing business relationships. This program allows you to get instant access to detailed contact and account information, plus a complete history of your contact-related communications. It also offers tools to help you manage your schedule efficiently, sales tips from Dale Carnegie Training, and more. Put ACT! to work for you to give you the power to utilize your personal and professional contact information.

After you've begun developing and maintaining your own contact database, people's phone numbers, addresses, and other information will be available to you almost instantly, as long as you're in front of your computer. By also utilizing a handheld personal digital assistant (PDA), you can take this important information with you wherever you go.

PDAs are battery-powered, handheld computers designed to give you full access to vast amounts of data, anytime and anywhere. These units have recently dropped in price and are now affordable, yet more powerful than ever. While many companies now manufacture PDAs, all operate using either the Palm OS or Microsoft Windows CE (Pocket PC) operating system. Palm Computing (✐ *www.palm.com*) and Handspring (✐ *www.handspring.com*) offer a wide range of PDAs that utilize the Palm OS system, so this operating system currently dominates the PDA market. The price of a good PDA starts under $150; however, the more powerful models, with add-on accessories and peripherals, can cost upward of $500 to $1,000. Some utilize wireless modem technology, allowing you to surf the Web or send/receive e-mail from virtually anywhere using a handheld device. In addition, by using synchronization software, your data (such as your addresses, appointments, and notes) on your PDA can be kept up-to-date and identical to the data stored in your computer. In addition to storing vast amounts of information, PDAs also have built-in scheduling programs and alarms, designed to help people keep track of their hectic day.

Choosing an Office Telephone

Your telephone is your primary connection with the outside world. Depending on the type of work you do, you may find it necessary to have multiple phone lines in your home office: a personal phone line, a work phone line, a modem line and/or a fax line. Think about how many phone lines you'll need and what they'll be used for before purchasing your actual equipment.

When ordering voice phone service from the phone company, you'll be offered many options and service add-ons. In addition to choosing which phone company will provide your local and long-distance phone service, you may be offered call waiting, call forwarding, three-way calling, caller ID, and an incoming toll-free number. Based on what you'll be using your phone for, you can choose the services that will help you be the most productive.

In addition to the phone service you choose, you'll also need to purchase a telephone. As you'll quickly discover, you have many options available. Phones come in all shapes and sizes and have a wide range of features built into them. Many phones also offer features like a built-in answering machine, caller ID, speed dialing, a hold button, speakerphone, a mute button, a headset, and conference calling. Determine, in advance, which of these functions you want to utilize. If, for example, you want the freedom to walk around your home while on the phone, a cordless phone will be a lot more practical than a traditional corded phone. Telephone headsets are also ideal if you want to talk on the phone but keep your hands free to use a computer keyboard, for example. If you'll regularly be making business calls, for example, find a phone that doesn't allow background noise (such as children playing or dogs barking) to be heard in the background. Hello Direct (✑ *www.hello-direct.com*) is one of many mail-order companies offering a complete line of telephone headsets, telephone systems, and accessories that are suitable for a home office.

FACT

The HOAA (✆ 800-809-4622, ✑ *www.hoaa.com*) is an organization dedicated to serving home-based and small business professionals. The organization offers a package of member benefits, including a newsletter available to home business professionals, group savings on health insurance, and many other benefits normally available only to large corporations. Annual membership is $49.

Planning to Be Productive

From this chapter, you've gained insight into how to design a home office that best fits your personal and professional needs. With each piece of home office furniture now in its proper place and all of the necessary equipment installed, it's time to utilize the home office you've created to actually get work done. By preplanning and analyzing your work habits and determining your needs in advance, you can develop the ideal work environment for yourself. Getting into the habit of keeping this workspace organized will probably take some dedication on your part, however. As you begin working from your home office, always be thinking about ways you can improve your filing system, reduce clutter, and ensure that the environment is as neat, clean, and conducive to working as possible.

After you begin using your home office, take an organized approach to your work habits. Try to establish work patterns for yourself. For example, after you create your to-do list each morning, allocate time to open your mail, deal with incoming e-mail, and do whatever other tasks are an important part of your routine. As you plan your day, expect to have some distractions, so don't overbook yourself. After all, emergencies happen, unexpected phone calls come in, and uninvited people tend to drop by when they're least expected. Learning how to deal with unexpected situations as part of your well-organized daily routine helps ensure that you remain focused on what you need to accomplish.

If you still need help designing your home office, consider hiring an interior design or organizational consultant to carefully analyze your needs and help you create the best work environment possible within your budget. If you're employed and plan to work from home (as a telecommuter, for example) some companies will pay to have your home office equipped with the necessary equipment for you to get your work done. You may also be entitled to a tax deduction for maintaining a home office. Be sure to discuss the financial and tax ramifications with an accountant or financial advisor.

Getting Advice from the Professionals

The National Association of Professional Organizers (✍ *www.napo.net*) is a not-for-profit professional association whose members include organizational consultants, speakers, trainers, authors, and manufacturers of organizing products. NAPO's mission is to encourage the development of professional organizers and promote the recognition and advancement of the professional-organizing industry.

According to NAPO, "Organized people save time and money, make more money, and have lower stress and frustration levels. There is no one right or wrong way to get organized, and you need to change what you're doing only if you're not happy with how you manage your time, paper, information, and space. The amount of information available to us continues to grow at a rapid pace, as do the number of demands on our time."

Implementing an organizational system can help you deal with everything from your papers to your professional responsibilities and give you parameters on what to keep, what to toss, and what to take action on. When getting your work done, NAPO offers these suggestions:

- Break large projects down into small, sequential steps, and then schedule these steps into your day using your personal planner, scheduler, or PDA.
- On your desktop, keep only the supplies you need on a daily basis.

- Be clear about the response you need when sending a message (voicemail, e-mail, or a letter) to a colleague. They can then provide a full response, even if they don't reach you directly.
- Keep a file index (a master list of file names). Check the index before creating a new file so you avoid making duplicates and use it when deciding where to file a piece of paper.

CHAPTER 10

Arranging Your Laundry Area

Within this chapter, you'll discover how to select the best washer and dryer to meet your needs, find tips for organizing your laundry area, and learn how to properly care for your laundry. By taking an organized approach to your laundry, you can make doing laundry more enjoyable and reduce the chances of laundry mishaps.

Designing Your Laundry Area

One of the keys to having a well-organized laundry area is placement within your home. Some people place the washer and dryer in the basement, which means they have to constantly lug piles of clothing up and down stairs. (If you're in this situation, consider installing a laundry shoot.) Others choose to place the washer and dryer near the master bathroom for added convenience.

Unfortunately, washer and dryer are big and bulky, so finding a convenient place to install these appliances can be tricky. After all, you probably don't want to give up valuable closet space near your bedroom or in your master bathroom. Changing the location of your washer and dryer can also be a costly endeavor, because plumbing, gas lines, and electrical wiring may have to be rerouted.

Wherever you locate your washer and dryer, you can probably better organize the area of your home that's dedicated to laundry. In a perfect world, a laundry area would offer the following:

- Ample space for a full-sized washer and dryer (remember to leave at least a few inches between each of these appliances and the nearby walls)
- Shelving or cabinets to store detergents and fabric softeners (the room will look less cluttered if you utilize cabinets with doors, so items can be stored out of sight)
- Space for keeping laundry baskets or hampers of dirty clothing
- An area for ironing, steaming, and folding clean clothes
- An area to hang wet clothing that needs to be line-dried
- Storage for hangers and/or a place to hang garments
- A sink for hand-washing garments
- A wastebasket
- A television, radio, and/or telephone to entertain yourself while you fold and iron
- Ample lighting, so you can clearly separate different-colored clothing, identify garments that are badly stained for special treatment, and read the handling instructions printed on the small labels of some garments

- Temperature control, because if the laundry area gets too cold (especially in a basement), the water pipes could freeze; if the room is too hot, it will be unbearable to actually work in the room

Unless you live in a large house or have allocated a section of your basement to accommodate all of the above listed needs for space, chances are you'll have to improvise. For example, you may be forced to set up a clothing line outdoors or in your basement to hang wet garments. In addition, you may be forced to do your ironing and folding in a bedroom and store hampers and laundry baskets of dirty clothing in your bedroom or bathroom until the dirty clothes are ready to be washed.

As you design or redesign your laundry facilities, pay attention to functionality. Having to carry countless loads of laundry up and down stairs will greatly increase the amount of physical exertion required for doing laundry. Likewise, the location of your laundry facilities will determine whether you can easily multitask (do your laundry while also handling other personal or household responsibilities).

No matter where you decide to position your laundry facilities, make sure everything you need is readily available and stored in the immediate area. Keep detergents and fabric softeners within arm's reach of the washer and dryer. The flooring where you place your washer, in particular, should be waterproof linoleum or tiling. You'll also want to place an overflow container under the washer to prevent water from escaping the immediate area, should the washer overflow or leak.

Make sure you create ample space to separate your clothing. Most people choose to separate their whites and colors when laundering their clothes. You may also need to separate clothing based on which family member each garment belongs to or by fabric type. If a garment is badly stained, it may require special attention. When folding your clean clothes, you want ample space to create piles, iron, and hang certain types of garments on hangers.

Nobody enjoys doing laundry. This is a task that we're all forced to do in order to maintain a wardrobe of clean clothing (unless, of course, you send everything to a dry-cleaning or professional laundry service). How you decorate your laundry area can go a long way toward making this task more pleasant. Painting the walls a bright color, adding cheerful artwork to the walls, and installing some form of entertainment (a small TV, radio, and/or telephone) can also help take the tediousness out of doing your laundry.

Everyone develops a personalized system for doing laundry. The layout and design of your laundry facilities should complement your work habits in order to make this task as stress-free and easy as possible.

> The visual look of washers and dryers varies. If these appliances will be readily visible within your home, pay attention to how the units fit within the décor of the room they'll be kept in. The overall look and color scheme may be important considerations.

Choosing the Best Washer and Dryer

Whether you live alone, have roommates, are married, and/or have children, no matter how often you do laundry, dirty clothing always seems to pile up. If you're in a position to purchase a new washer and dryer, you have a lot of options. Ideally, you want to choose appliances that are designed for the amount of laundry you'll actually be doing, based on your unique living situation. In recent years, a lot of technology has also been built into washers and dryers, making them more functional and easier to use. The price range of these appliances has also expanded. For example, a brand-name washer can be purchased for anywhere from $250 to over $3,000.

As you begin looking for the perfect washer and/or dryer, first analyze your needs, and then answer the following questions:

- How many loads of laundry will be you doing per day or per week?
- What features would you like built into your washer and dryer?
- How much space do you have available for these appliances?
- What's your budget?
- What will your future needs be (given that a washer and dryer can last from five to over ten years)?

Determine how much space you have available in your home to install your new washer and dryer and look only at models that fit easily within that space. Pay attention to the capacity size of each unit. Make sure you match the washer and dryer load capacity or else for each load of wash you do, you may have to do two or three dryer loads. This will prove to be extremely inefficient.

By knowing what type of clothes you typically wash, you'll be able to choose a washer and dryer designed to handle those types of garments. When choosing a specific model to purchase, evaluate the construction materials. Some less expensive units, for example, are made of painted steel, while others have rust-resistant porcelain tops. The top-priced units typically feature stainless steel cabinets. In addition to examining the construction materials, pay attention to the controls on the unit. Most units feature either knob or button controls. On higher-end models, touch pads have become a common feature. Ideally, you want to choose a model with controls that are easy to understand and operate.

Energy use is also an important factor to consider, especially if you're responsible for paying your utility bills (gas, water, and electricity). By law, every washer and dryer manufacturer is required to place a yellow sticker on each unit outlining how energy-efficient it is. On this label, you'll see the average cost per year to operate the unit. Obviously, this cost will vary based on the prices you pay for your utilities, but it's a good way to compare the energy efficiency of various models.

FACT

If your space is limited, consider purchasing a washer/dryer combo. These units can typically fit in a small closet. They do, however, have small load capacities. Washer-dryer combos come in two types: one that looks very much like a regular washer and dryer but stacks the dryer on top of the washer and a single washer-dryer unit that both washes and dries clothes without your having to move the clothes from one unit to the other. Both can save a great deal of space.

Washer Features

According to What's the best washer.com (✐*www.whatsthebest-washer.com*), you want to look for nine key features when shopping for a new washer. The features to look for include those listed in the following sections.

Bleach Dispenser

Beach will automatically get added to the wash water at the appropriate time during the wash cycle. The bleach gets diluted before it touches the fabrics directly, which goes a long way toward eliminating bleach spots on your garments.

Hand-Wash Cycle

This feature washes certain types of clothes on a very gentle cycle, protecting delicate garments and eliminating the need to physically hand-wash them in a sink.

Extra-Long Wash Cycle

These features can be used to more effectively clean heavily soiled items, such as grimy work overalls, muddy or grass-stained jeans, and diapers.

End-of-Cycle Alarm

When the wash cycle is done, an alarm will sound. This gives you the opportunity to promptly remove items, thereby reducing wrinkles.

Timer

A timer informs you of how much time remains in a wash cycle, allowing you to better organize your time.

Inline Heater

This feature increases the temperate of the hot water (to 170 degrees), making it more suitable for cleaning clothes (especially white fabrics).

Tub

The tubs in washers come in three common sizes, and they determine the size of the load the washer can handle. The most common size is 2.4

cubic feet; however, you'll see washers with capacities between 1.7 and 3.3 cubic feet. Based on your personal requirements, choose a size that's based on the amount of laundry you do in a given period, the unit's size, and your budget.

Speeds and Cycles

Most washers have three basic washing cycles: regular, gentle, and permanent press. More expensive units offer additional cycles that cater to the cleaning needs of a wider range of fabric types. Be sure to match the speeds and cycles to the types of fabrics you'll be washing.

Water Level and Temperature Settings

Depending on the size of the laundry load, you may choose to select a low water level (for conservation purposes). Some garments are better suited to be washed in either cold, warm, or hot water. These settings offer you greater flexibility to meet your personal laundering needs.

ALERT!

Depending on where your washer and dryer will be used within your home, pay attention to how loud these appliances are while operational. Noise doesn't matter much if you keep washer and dryer in your basement, but if they're located near your bedroom, kitchen, or master bathroom, noise should be a consideration.

Dryer Features

Now that you know what to look for in a washer, you'll probably want to choose a companion dryer. Most dryers cost between $220 and $1,500; the average cost is between $300 and $500. Some of the details to look for when evaluating and choosing a dryer include the following:

- Power source (dyers can be electric, gas powered, or both)
- Capacity (the capacity should match your washer)
- Auto-dry-control feature (this means the dryer stops working when the clothing is dry)

- A number of cycle selections (typical cycles include delicate, permanent press, and regular)
- Number of temperature selections (the more expensive the unit, the more selections you'll have)
- Express dry (used to quickly dry a small number of garments)
- Controls (either mechanical or electrical)
- The space available in your laundry area

Visiting Stores and Showrooms

Visit several reputable stores and showrooms. Try to visit appliance dealers that sell a variety of brand-name washers and dryers and that stock several models within each manufacturer's product line. Sears or Best Buy are always good places to start. Make sure the dealer you purchase your washer and dryer from is equipped to handle future repair work as well as installation.

ALERT!

Before visiting a retailer, visit the Web sites for each major washer and dryer manufacturer you're interested in. Find out as much as possible about the features and prices of each model. This helps you develop a list of intelligent questions to ask the salesperson when you actually visit the store or showroom.

Virtually all name-brand washers and dryers come with a good warranty. Make sure you ask about the warranty and compare what's offered from different manufacturers. For an additional fee, some retailers will allow you to purchase an extended warranty on major appliances. This may be an investment worth considering based on your financial situation.

Organizing Your Laundering Efforts

When was the last time you did several loads of laundry, wound up missing socks, had the dye from a new pair of jeans run all over your other clothes, and then wound up with a wrinkled mess after everything came out of the dryer? Everyone has had these laundry nightmares happen, but virtually all laundry disasters and mishaps can be avoided by taking an organized approach to cleaning your clothes. This section describes the basics of how to properly do laundry, choose the right detergent, and reduce wrinkles, while at the same time extending the life of the garments in your wardrobe.

Most clothing these days use colorfast dyes. This means that when they're washed, the colors don't run. Over time, however, if not properly taken care of, the color of fabrics will fade. Likewise, most clothing made from cotton comes preshrunk. This means that they can be placed in the dryer and not shrink. There are, however, many exceptions to these rules, so be sure to read the labels on each garment carefully before washing it for the first time.

FACT

White fabrics (and colorfast fabrics) are best laundered in hot water. When mixed with pastels or colored laundry, whites, along with permanent press fabrics and 100-percent synthetic fiber fabrics, should be washed in warm water. To prevent fading, colored clothes should be washed in cold water. However, this will vary based on the fabric type and type of detergent you use, so read the garment labels and detergent directions carefully.

The following are the basic steps involved in successfully washing a load of laundry using a traditional washer and dryer with off-the-shelf detergent:

- Separate your clothing by color and fabric types, washing like items together.
- Empty all pockets!
- Turn down the cuffs of pants and shirts (turn jeans inside out to reduce fading).
- Close all zippers, snaps, and hooks.
- Read the care labels on each garment and follow the directions.
- On the washing machine, set the load size.

- Select the cycle type on the washer.
- Choose the appropriate water temperature on the washer (hot, warm, or cold).
- Determine the best laundry detergent, fabric softener, and bleach for the job, and then mix the appropriate amount into the washer when the directions on the detergent say to do so.
- Deal with badly stained clothing separately. This may involve using a special detergent and/or allowing the stained garment to soak before putting it through a normal wash.
- When the washer cycle is complete, remove the garments promptly. Place each garment in the dryer (if applicable), keeping in mind that some types of garments need to be line-dried and shouldn't be exposed to the high temperature of a dryer.
- To minimize wrinkling, as soon as the dryer finishes, remove the garments immediately. You may then choose to iron certain garments to completely eliminate wrinkles.

ALERT!

Avoid overloading a washer (putting too many garments in at once). Overloading can damage the washer along with the clothing. At the very least, an overcrowded washer will prevent the garments from getting as clean as they would otherwise.

Choosing the Best Detergent

When you walk up and down the laundry detergent isle of a supermarket, you're faced with literally dozens, if not hundreds of options. In addition to the many different brand names, detergents come in several forms, including the following:

- **Liquid:** These detergents are easy to measure and dissolve quickly. Liquids can often be used to pretreat stains, but usually don't contain bleach.
- **Powders:** Usually more economic than liquids, powder-based detergent can be used in the dispenser drawer of your automatic washing machine.

- **Tablets:** While tablets offer the same cleaning power as liquid or powder-based detergents, no measuring is involved. Just drop in a single tablet into the washer (as described in the detergent's directions).
- **Capsules:** This is an alternative to tablets and also doesn't require measuring.

As you'll see when you shop for detergents, virtually all of the different brand names offer a complete line of detergent products. In addition to using detergent, you may also choose to add fabric softener into the washer (or dryer, depending on the product). As the name suggests, fabric softeners make clothing feel softer. They also help reduce wrinkles and static cling. For best results, liquid fabric softeners (such as Downy Care) should be added to the washer during the final rinse cycle. Fabric softener sheets, such as Bounce, should be added to the dryer as described in detail on the product's packaging.

ALERT!

If you have a question about how to properly use a specific type of laundry detergent, don't guess! Call the manufacturer of the detergent and ask. Both Tide (✆ 800-879-8433, *www.tide.com*) and Wisk (✆ 800-ASK-WISK, *www.wisk.com*), for example, offer toll-free phone numbers and Web sites designed to answer questions.

Stain-Removal Strategies

Stains are almost impossible to avoid if you live a normal lifestyle, especially if you have kids. Food, drinks, dirt, blood, grass, ink, motor oils, grease, makeup, wine, rust, chewing gum, nail polish, perspiration, and deodorants and antiperspirants are all common causes of stains you'll have to contend with sooner or later. The good news is that if you approach each stain in an organized and calm manner, you should be able to make it disappear with relative ease.

Based on the type of stain and its severity, you may choose to have a garment professionally cleaned. You can also try pretreating, presoaking, bleaching, or prewashing the garment, depending on the type of fabric and what caused the stain. Washing the stained garment in the appropriate water temperature and using the strongest possible detergent or stain remover will also help your battle against even the toughest of stains.

As soon as a stain is created, the manufacturers of Wisk recommend following these five steps:

1. Sponge stains promptly with cool water to prevent the stain from setting.
2. Always test your stain-removal agent on a hidden part of the garment first, to check for colorfastness and bleachability.
3. Before laundering, pretreat stained articles with a liquid detergent. Remember, washing and drying without any pretreatment can set some stains.
4. Air-dry treated and washed items. Some residual stains are not visible when wet, and heat from the dryer could set them, making them tougher or impossible to get rid of.
5. Follow all safety precautions on stain-removal product labels.

To deal with a wide range of stains, pretreat to remove a few small spots. Apply undiluted liquid laundry detergent (such as Liquid Tide with Bleach Alternative), undiluted liquid dishwashing detergent (such as Dawn), or suds from an Ivory soap bar directly on the stained area. Launder immediately.

For deep-set soils, old stains, extensive staining, or protein stains, like blood, grass, or body soils, presoak the garment. For a maximum of thirty minutes, soak stained items in a plastic bucket or laundry tub with the warmest water safe for the fabric and a good heavy-duty laundry detergent. Bleach-sensitive stains, like fruit juice or drink mixes, should be rinsed in cold water, and then washed with a non-chlorine bleach product. If stains remain, colorfast items may be laundered with a colorfast bleach, and bleachable items may be laundered with chlorine bleach.

Prewash for heavily soiled garments, like work or play clothes. Run through the prewash cycle with the recommended amount of detergent. When the wash cycle is complete, drain the prewash solution and launder in the hottest water recommended by the manufacturer.

FACT

OxiClean (☎ 800-781-7529, ✎ www.greatcleaners.com) from Orange Glo International, Inc., is a powerful oxygen-based alkaline cleaner that attacks the toughest organic dirt including mildew, blood, pet messes, mold, wine, juice, baby formula, and more.

Ironing Strategies

The Appliances.com Web site (✎ *www.appliances.com*) offers the following tips on how to properly iron your clothing in order to greatly reduce or remove wrinkles.

Ironing Board Setup

Set up the ironing board at the right height, appropriate to whether you're sitting or standing. You should be able to place your hand on the board without bending your arm or your back. Adjusting the ironing board to the correct height will reduce muscle fatigue.

Temperature Controls

Be sure to correctly adjust the temperature of your iron prior to getting started. Begin by consulting labels for manufacturer's suggestions, especially when dry-ironing. For example, when ironing blended fabrics, use the setting for the lowest-temperature fabric in the blend. Most fabrics can be ironed using the steam setting.

Proper Motion and Handling

Start ironing each garment in the middle and work your way outward. There's no need to press too hard, especially when using steam.

Special Fabrics

Be sure to use extra care with certain types of fabrics. For example, all silks should be ironed on the reverse side. Cultivated silks should be ironed when evenly damp, but should not be sprayed because they may spot; raw silks should be ironed when dry. Velvet, acrylics, corduroy, embroidered pieces, and synthetic leathers should also be pressed from the reverse side with a clean towel or blanket on the ironing board. This will prevent these materials from ending up with an unwanted sheen.

Cooler Fabrics First

Whenever you're ironing clothes with unique fabrics, save yourself time as well as a potential tragedy by sorting the garments and then starting with synthetics that call for the coolest settings. By working your way up to high-temperature cottons, you'll avoid scorching and having to wait for your iron to cool down, which takes a lot longer than heating up.

Avoid Overheating

When using the heat of an iron, more is not always better. Be sure to use the right temperature for each of your garments. An overheated iron is the quickest way to make your clothes go from clean to crispy. Synthetics and silks react best to low or medium temperatures. Cottons and linens react best to the iron's highest temperatures. Wools respond best to medium or high temperatures (and the use of a press cloth to avoid shine).

CHAPTER 11

Clearing Out Your Basement, Attic, Garage, or Workshop

This chapter explores some of the ways you can utilize your basement, attic, and garage space and keep them efficient and well organized, because, after all, any unorganized space will hold far less stuff than a space that's been properly organized. This chapter also provides information on taking advantage of public storage facilities in your community.

Finding a Place for Everything

In addition to eliminating or greatly reducing clutter, one of the steps to becoming truly organized is to determine specific places for your belongings, and then making sure that each item is kept within its proper place. As a storage facility, your basement, attic, and/or garage can easily be organized with the proper use of shelving, cabinets, hooks, and airtight storage bins. After all, if you're going to create a storage space within your home, you want to make full use of the available space—not simply throw items into it in an unorganized manner.

Before you store an item within your basement, attic, or garage, adhere to the following guidelines:

- Clean, package, and/or launder the items. Items that go into storage in good condition are more apt to stay that way longer. For example, polish your jewelry or silver flatware.
- Sort and place similar items together.
- Categorize.
- Place items in appropriate (airtight) storage containers, which come in a variety of sizes.
- Label. Mark each carton, container, or item with a descriptive label that's easily visible. For example, "Summer Clothing," "Baby Clothing," "1998 Personal Financial Records," "Christmas Decorations," or "Winter Jackets."
- Store in such a way that your belongings can be easily found and retrieved without having to dig through endless piles of stuff.

Taking Security Precautions

If you live in an apartment or condo, you may have access to storage space in a basement or attic; however, this space may have to be shared with other tenants or residents. In this situation, you can still store your belongings, but you'll need to contend with security issues and avoid storing anything extremely valuable or sentimental.

When storing items in a communal storage facility, make sure you use containers that can be locked, especially if the area or storage cubicle you have access to is not totally secure. You'll still want to use airtight containers to store your belongings, such as clothing, books, papers, memorabilia, and so on, but you'll also want to take additional security precautions. For example, use containers that are a solid color (not clear or see-through) and don't visibly label your containers. Instead, number them and keep the list of the contents of each numbered container to yourself. If someone happens to break into your public storage space, you don't want to make it easier for them to find valuable items to steal or damage.

If you'll be storing larger items, such as sports equipment (bikes, skis, and so on), make sure you lock these items up separately. Somehow attach or bolt the locks to a wall, floor, or ceiling. Take steps to ensure that these larger and more expensive items are not readily visible to someone casually peaking into the storage facility.

Finally, basements, attics, garages and public storage facilities aren't typically climate controlled and are sometimes prone to leaks. Exposure to extreme temperatures, mold, rodents, insects, and other natural disasters could potentially damage or destroy your belongings. Never store anything extremely valuable in these areas unless you take the maximum possible precautions. Items that can't be replaced, such as family photo albums, valuable antiques, or heirlooms, should not be stored in potentially unstable or insecure areas. Airtight plastic containers are extremely useful for protecting items stored in non-climate controlled areas. In addition, you can utilize storage systems like Space Bags (described in Chapter 2).

When actually placing boxes, plastic storage containers, or other items in your basement or attic, never store them directly on the floor. Insert plastic or wooden pallets on the floor below your items. This will raise your items up slightly as a precaution against flooding.

For the ultimate protection of valuable or important papers, documents, jewelry, and other small belongings, consider investing in a safe, which can be bolted to a wall or floor, making it extremely difficult to steal. Safes also tend to be fireproof and waterproof. If you have just a small number of important documents, you can always rent a safe-deposit box at a local bank or financial institution.

Organizing Your Basement

Your basement can be an excellent storage location for a wide range of large and small items, such as unused furniture, sporting equipment, off-season clothing, and deck furniture. Many people also utilize their basement as a laundry facility (see Chapter 10) or exercise room. Others choose to transform it into a fully functional room.

Knowing that below your house there's a basement, you first need to determine how you plan to utilize this space and what needs to be done to the space to make it usable for your intended purpose. After you know what you'd like to use your basement for, measure the space carefully and make sure it's suitable for your needs.

Next, prepare your basement for its intended purpose. If you plan to finish your basement to make it a fully usable living space, you'll probably want to hire professional contractors, an architect, an electrician, and a plumber to handle the design and construction work for you.

If you'll be using your existing basement as a storage facility, however, examine the space carefully and determine potential hazards you'll want to take precautions against, like flooding, mold, mildew, rodents, insects, extreme temperatures, and so on.

Make sure that you install enough lighting so you can see all areas of your basement clearly. Also, ensure that the fixtures you choose will be able to withstand the harsher temperatures.

Next, decide what you want to store in your basement. Then, on a pad of paper, draw a rough layout of the area and determine how and where you'll be storing your various belongings. Consider allocating space for larger items, such as furniture, bicycles, boxes, plastic storage containers, and luggage first. Figure out whether you'll need to install additional shelving, lighting, flooring, or anything else to make your basement space more usable. If the room is constantly damp, you may want to install a dehumidifier. This will help cut down or eliminate mold and mildew buildup. If flooding may become a problem, consider installing a sump pump. No matter what, make sure you install a smoke detector in your basement and check it at least every six months.

By visiting any hardware store, you'll find a wide range of plastic and metal shelving units, some of which are standalone units and some that need to be bolted and installed directly onto your walls. After you decide what smaller items you'll be keeping and what you will store in your basement, choose the best method for storing these smaller items, using boxes, shelving, cabinets, or perhaps a pegboard with hooks that gets mounted on a wall.

In addition to visiting a hardware store to purchase shelving, you can also visit online-based companies, including the following:

- **APM Shelf Store** (✍ *www.shelvesonline.com*) offers a selection of Closetmaid wire shelves, along with complete shelf kits for your closet, linens, pantry, basement, and garage.
- **Basis Design** (✍ *www.basisdesign.com*) sells shelving and organization units that require no tools for assembly and are ideal for closets, cabinets, and other storage spaces.
- **1-800-BUY-RACK** (✍ *www.buyrack.com*) offers industrial-strength shelving, racks, stacking bins, or other types of heavy-duty cabinets.
- **Dura** (✍ *www.thefittedgarage.com/index.html*) sells modular metal storage units that combine cabinets, shelving, and pegboards. This storage system is perfect for your garage, basement, or workshop.
- **Shelving Direct** (✍ *www.shelving-direct.com*) offers a line of boltless shelves, racks, bins, and workbenches that are appropriate for use at work and at home.

Go through everything (yes, everything!) currently stored in your basement. Throw away, donate, or sell anything that you no longer want or need. In other words, eliminate all unwanted clutter. Throw away anything that's damaged or broken (and is beyond repair) and remove items that are blocking areas where you want to work or play.

FIGURE 11-1:
A cluttered
basement

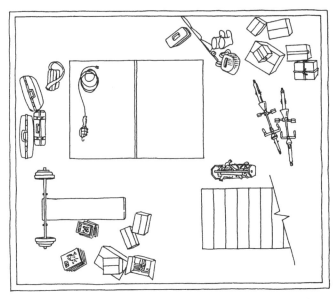

Before carrying down everything you plan to store in your basement, prepare the area. This means emptying the area and cleaning it thoroughly. Next, install the shelving, lighting, or other organizational tools you believe are necessary.

To protect the items to be stored, think about what's required: cardboard boxes, airtight plastic containers, shelves, drawers, coverings (tarps), and so on. You can also store items by hanging them from the basement ceiling.

FIGURE 11-2:
An organized
basement

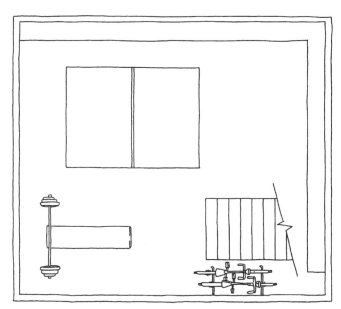

After the room is prepared, fill your basement with the items you plan to store there, starting with the largest items first. Refer to your hand-drawn diagram to figure out where things will go. As you evaluate your storage plan, answer the following questions:

- Are the items you're storing easy to find and readily accessible?
- Are the items you're storing far enough away from your laundry area or workshop area? Is there a clear path to your working appliances, as well as ample space to work and play?
- If you have children, does your storage area provide any potential hazards? Should certain items be locked up separately?
- Have you protected your belongings against natural disasters (flooding, mildew, mold, insects, and rodents)?
- Are your stored items in the way of your home's hot water heater, furnace, fuse box, washer, dryer, or any other appliances in use within the basement? Are all drains and pipes clear from any obstruction?

If you're storing plastic crates or boxes, stack them up against a wall, making sure they are stable and won't fall. Also, make sure the labels (describing what's in each box) are facing outward and are easily readable. Place the larger and heavier boxes on the bottom, and the lighter boxes above them. Items stored in boxes at the bottom of the piles should be the ones you'll be needing the least often. After all, to reach them, you'll need to first remove the boxes or crates above them, which will require additional manual labor.

Remember to divide up and categorize what you'll be storing. Sports equipment should be kept together, as should books, furniture, holiday decorations (and gift wrapping supplies), and other similar items. Make sure you keep flammable items away from your furnace, hot water heater, washer, dryer, and any other potential dangers.

As you decide where your various items will be stored, think in terms of when they'll be used. For example, you may want to store your winter clothing in containers near your Christmas decorations. Likewise, you may want to store your grill near your Fourth of July decorations and lawn furniture. If you tend to go on a family vacation every summer (and use your luggage), you may want to store your luggage near your summer items for easy access.

Your most frequently used items should receive prime storage space so they're most readily accessible any time of the year. If you also use your basement as a workshop, exercise room, or hobby area, make sure your storage area is kept separate. You can use room dividers or other methods to section off each area of your basement, as needed.

Even if you have ample lighting in your basement, keep a high-intensity, battery-powered flashlight near the entrance to this area. If you lose power, you may need to access your fuse box, hot water heater, or furnace. Check the batteries in the flashlight at least once per month.

Organizing Your Attic

The environment of an attic is very much like a basement: cold, dark, and damp. In most homes, however, the attic is more difficult to access. Hence, only consider the attic for storing lighter or smaller items, such as off-season clothing, empty luggage, holiday decorations, empty boxes from electronic equipment (like a computer, DVD player, or fax machine), toys, or sports equipment.

If you'll be using the attic as a storage area and will need to gain access to this space often, consider replacing the basic access panel entrance (which you may need a ladder to get to) with a pull-down staircase. Also, install a light switch or light pull-string near the entrance to the attic. You don't want to be climbing around in the dark. For information on pull-down staircases, visit any hardware or home improvement store. You can also point your Web browser to the Ladder Pros Web site (*www.ladderpros.com/attic.htm*).

Treat organizing your attic in almost exactly the same way you would handle the basement. In other words, know that you'll be storing your items in a non-climate-controlled environment (with potential hazards, such as water, mildew, mold, insects, and/or rodents), and take the appropriate precautions. Airtight plastic storage containers, like the ones available from Rubbermaid (✎ www.rubbermaid.com) will come in handy. Purchase clear containers so you can see what's stored inside, but also label each container.

Unless you're using airtight containers, don't store paper-based items, such as photos, books or other important documents, in the attic. Videotapes and audiocassettes as well as any type of electronic equipment won't do well in a potentially damp environment with extreme hot or cold temperatures.

Throughout the attic-organization process, focus on being a clutter buster. Go through everything you plan to store and throw away, and then donate or sell anything you know you no longer have a use for. Anything that's broken or damaged beyond repair should be thrown out. There's an age-old saying that goes, "Out of sight, out of mind." Just because you're able to hide your stuff in the attic and forget about it doesn't mean you should use this space to simply move clutter from the main part of your home (your living space), to another location. Obviously, if an item has sentimental value or needs to be saved, that's fine. Get rid of items you know have no value to you and won't ever be needed again.

Begin organizing your attic space by determining how you plan to utilize this space. Consider what you plan to store in your attic, and then measure the attic space carefully and make sure it's suitable for your needs. Prepare your attic for its intended purpose, eliminating potential hazards you want to protect against.

Using a pad of paper and your measurements, draw a rough layout of the area and determine how and where you'll be storing your various belongings. Figure out whether you'll need to install additional shelving, lighting, flooring, or anything else first to make your attic space more usable.

Get rid of cobwebs by cleaning the attic thoroughly. After the area is cleaned out, begin placing the items in the attic to be stored. Place items that you won't need often in the back, where they're less readily available.

As you place boxes or items to be stored in the attic, make sure air vents are unobstructed. Also, if there is a ventilation fan in the attic, make sure your items are kept away from it.

Don't place anything heavy on the floor of your attic unless you're confident the floor can hold the weight. You may want to reinforce the flooring by placing a thin wooden board across two or more support beams, and then storing some of your belongings on top of the board.

If you're considering expanding your living space by finishing off your attic and transforming it into a fully functional room of your home, first consider the following:

- Does the attic offer ample headroom?
- After it's complete, what will the room be used for?
- Is there an easy-to-access stairway leading to attic space?
- Are the floor joists large enough to support the added load?
- What will it cost to transform the attic into a finished room? Is the investment worth the added functionality you'll receive from the room after it's in use?

If your primary concern is to create additional storage space in your attic, perhaps you can take advantage of Isobord Enterprises, Inc.'s StorageBord product line (*www.isobordenterprises.com/p_storagebord.htm*). This is a quick and relatively inexpensive system for transforming a totally unfinished attic into an area with a sturdy floor space that can be used for storage. StorageBords are made from premium engineered strawboard. The panel installs easily to attic floor joists to create a convenient storage area in the home. The boards are made with non-formaldehyde resins. Thus, StorageBords contain no harmful toxic resins and are made to withstand the dramatic temperature fluctuations of a normal attic.

Create additional storage space by utilizing the area behind attic knee walls. Within this wedge-shaped space, you can install shelves, individual drawers, or rolling bins that pull into the room.

Organizing Your Garage and Workshop

Like your basement and attic, your garage offers a non-climate-controlled storage space. The potential problem is that you probably need to share this space with one or more vehicles. With this in mind, many people find the garage to be the perfect spot to store lawn equipment, bicycles (and other sports equipment), car parts, tools, and empty suitcases. It's also the perfect spot to set up a workshop, assuming you have room for a worktable and your tools.

After you decide your garage will be transformed into an organized storage space, follow the same basic tips as you did for your basement and attic. These steps include determining how you plan to utilize the space and asking yourself what needs to be done to the space to make it usable for your intended purpose. This may include adding shelves, hooks, cabinets, additional lighting, an electric garage door opener, and so on. Measure the garage space carefully to make sure it's suitable for your needs, leaving room to park your car. (The best way to do this is to empty out your garage and park your car inside it. Take a piece of chalk and on the floor of the garage, draw an outline of your car. Make sure you open the doors to the car to ensure you leave ample clearance to get in and out of your vehicle.) You must also determine potential hazards you'll want to take precautions against, like mold, mildew, rodents, insects, freezing, flooding, oil spills (from your vehicle), and so on.

Clean your garage thoroughly. Then, place the items that need to be stored in the garage. Make sure all cartons, boxes, and crates are clearly labeled.

Remember to lock up all tools, chemicals, and dangerous items. Keep them away from children. And be sure you install both a smoke detector and a carbon monoxide detector in your garage and check them every six months to ensure they remain operational.

The following sections share some organization tools and products designed specifically for a garage. Many of these items are available from hardware or home improvement stores, or they can be ordered directly from the Internet.

Garage Storage Cabinets

Garage Storage Cabinets (✐ *www.gsc-cabinets.com*) offers a modular wall unit system that incorporates shelves, cabinets, and even a workbench. Garage Storage Cabinets are perfect for the garage environment. Modules are designed to fit your needs, from sports to gardening to working on cars. Mix and match cabinets that are available in 12-inch, 16-inch, and 24-inch depths. Garage Storage Cabinets are designed to hang on a steel railing system. This unique system gets belongings off the floor to prevent water damage and to aid in cleaning beneath the cabinets. Because garage floors are poured at a sloping angle, the hanging system ensures that doors close smoothly, drawers slide easily, and cabinets hang straight for long-lasting performance.

Wood Logic Storage Products

Wood Logic Storage Products (✆ 800-303-4393, ✐ *www.woodlogic.com/products.htm*) is an online retailer of innovative products designed to organize a wide range of items typically stored in a garage, such as tools, gardening equipment, bicycles, fishing gear, and so on.

Stack-On Products Company

To keep track of and organize your tools, car parts, or other items, Stack-On (✐ *www.stack-on.com/tool_and_hardware/garage*) offers a complete line of cabinets and garage-organization products. Stack-On Products Company is a leading manufacturer of top quality tool storage systems, accessories, and security cabinets. Stack-On supplies a wide and diverse line of tool storage products to meet the needs of mechanics, maintenance personnel, trades persons, homeowners, and hobbyists. Its product line includes steel and plastic hand boxes, specialty storage products, chests, cabinets, and steel security cabinets.

StoreWall

Instead of cabinets, StoreWall (✆ 414-224-0878, ✐ *www.storewall.com/residential/garage.htm*) offers a contemporary and well-designed variation of a pegboard with hooks for storing and displaying tools and other items. To solve the tough garage organization assignments, you can find a wide range of accessories available, including shelves, hooks, bins, baskets, and many specialty storage products. You can use StoreWall inside or outdoors (it's waterproof and can be easily cleaned), and the system is available in a variety of solid colors and wood grains. Each tongue-and-groove panel is $3/4$" thick, 15" high, and available in either 4' or 8' lengths.

Organize Everything

A metal, stand-alone shelf unit requires no installation and stands freely on your garage's floor. A wide range of shelving alternatives can be found at any hardware or home-improvement store. One such shelving unit is available from Organize Everything (✐ *www.organize-everything.com/ garstorun1.html*). The InterMetro shelves are priced under $160 (for a four-shelf unit) and are made of heavy-duty steel construction. Each individual shelf will hold 300 to 500 pounds. Shelves can be adjusted up or down and offer easy snap-together assembly. This particular shelf unit measures 18" deep × 48" wide × 74" high.

Organize-It

Organize-It (✐ *www.organizes-it.com/garage.htm*) offers a variety of different tools, hooks, and organizers designed for use in a garage. One product, for example, allows you to neatly store extension cords, while the Heavy Duty Lawn & Garden Rack will keep all of your gardening tools (large and small) in their proper place.

InterMetro

InterMetro (✐ *www.metro.com/consumer/index.cfm*) is the world leader of home shelving and storage. The company's wire shelving can brighten any room in the house including general storage areas like the garage. With its extensive line of home shelving, Metro's products provide quality storage and durable workmanship at a reasonable cost. These units come in a variety of colors and are very easy to assemble. Pieces of this system can be mixed and matched, so you can create a customized shelving system that meets your size specifications and needs. These products are available from hardware stores and authorized dealers nationwide.

How can I find room for recyclables?
Using several large bins or garbage pails, separate aluminum cans, glass bottles/jars, and newspapers from your regular garbage and store these items separately in your garage. Make sure the recycling bins you use for bottles and cans have tight lids so that you can keep wild animals out. Ideally, you also want bins with wheels.

Utilizing Public Storage Facilities

When the storage space available in your closets, basement, attic, and garage just isn't enough, you have other options. Public storage facilities are available across the United States that provide extra storage space for a flat monthly or annual fee. Public Storage (☎800-44STORE, ✐www.publicstorage.com) is just one nationwide chain of public storage facilities. Public Storage manages over 1,400 self-service storage locations in eighty U.S. and Canadian cities. In addition to offering just storage facilities, the company offers pick-up service, which is particularly useful for transporting large and heavy items from your home to the storage unit you rent.

Public Storage's self-storage service makes storing your belongings easy. Your items are kept in a safe, convenient facility. Storage units range in size from 5' × 5' (25 square feet) up to 10' × 30' (300 square feet). The facilities are well-lit, modern, and accessible seven days a week. For security, Public Storage locations utilize computerized gate-controlled access, plus all of the storage units have their own locks.

To find other self-storage facilities in your area, check the Yellow Pages or point your Web browser to Self Storage Net (✐www.selfstorage.net), which offers a directory of facilities plus tips on how to maximize this type of storage space.

The storage facility provides a written agreement when you rent the space. Make sure you read this agreement carefully. Check the paperwork for your payment date and determine whether the agreement covers prorated rental periods. Also ask how and when your security deposit will be refunded.

Knowing How Much Space You Need

How much outside-of-the-home storage space will you need? See **TABLE 11-1** (compiled by Self Storage Net) for help to make this determination.

TABLE 11-1

DETERMINING HOW MUCH STORAGE SPACE YOU NEED	
STORAGE SPACE SIZE	EXAMPLES OF WHAT FITS IN THIS SPACE
5' × 10'	A couch and chair, chest of drawers or dresser, mattress set, plus small items and boxes. Outdoor furniture, lawn mowers, garden tools, and so on. Bicycles and/or motorcycles.
10' × 10'	Furniture from a one-bedroom apartment or small house, also small items and boxes. Also may be used to store a car or truck and other small items.
10' × 15'	This unit is about the same size as a typical one-car garage. What will fit includes furniture from a one-bedroom apartment and small boxes.
10' × 20'	Furniture from a two-bedroom house with appliances, miscellaneous items, and cartons. This size also may be used to store a car or truck and other small items.
10' × 30'	Furniture from a three-bedroom house with miscellaneous items and cartons. Will hold the contents of a 40-foot moving van. Also may be used to store a car or truck. Boats or RVs may fit, along with some furniture and cartons, depending on the height of the garage doors.

The following are questions to consider when evaluating self-storage:

- What size units are available?
- What is the monthly/annual fee for renting the space?
- Can you rent month to month or is a long-term agreement required?
- What type of security is offered? Is there always a guard on duty?
- Are the facility and the individual storage units climate-controlled?
- How much of a deposit is required?
- What are the guidelines in terms of what can and can't be stored at the facility?
- Can you obtain access to your storage unit twenty-four hours per day, 365 days per year?
- What paperwork are you required to sign to rent a storage unit?

Deciding Whether You Need Climate Control

According to Storage USA (☎ 800-STOR-USA, ✍ www.sus.com), another nationwide self-storage facility with over 500 locations, "Climate-controlled space guarantees that nothing will be damaged by extreme hot or cold temperatures. We, for example, keep our storage units between sixty degrees in the winter and eighty degrees in the summer. Thus, your belongings will be protected against any rapid change of external temperatures. Our climate-controlled space also provides a cleaner environment by filtering dust particles out of the air. This will keep items cleaner and fresher."

Utilize climate-controlled storage space for items such as books, business files/records, cleaning supplies, computers, crystal/glassware, electronic equipment/devices, fine linens and clothing, leather furniture, mattresses, musical equipment, oil paintings, paint supplies, pharmaceutical products, pianos, and retail inventory items.

Organizing Your Storage Space

After your storage unit has been rented, Migson Public Storage (☎ 877-564-4766, ✍ www.migsonstorage.com) offers these suggestions for organizing the space to ensure you can get the most organization possible:

- Lay down cardboard, pallets, or skids on the floor of your storage space.
- Create a walkway inside your storage space to allow for easier access.
- Keep items that you need to access frequently at the front of your storage space.
- Draw and label a map of where everything is located in your storage space.
- For better ventilation, leave a few inches of space between your items and the storage space's walls.
- Stack similar boxes together.
- Stack heaviest items on the bottom and lighter items on the top.
- Stack pictures and mirrors on their sides.
- Disassemble table legs to save space.
- Place mattresses on end so they stand straight up.
- To protect items against dust, cover exposed items with old blankets.
- Store sofas on end to conserve space.
- Always lock the door to your storage unit when leaving.

CHAPTER 12

Organizing the Outdoors

This chapter focuses on how you can best utilize the outdoor area where you live, by taking advantage of your deck, garden, greenhouse, patio, and storage shed. It also focuses on ways to better organize your outdoor living space, making it more functional and visually appealing. As with any area of your living space, one trick to establishing organization outdoors is to eliminate clutter.

Designing and Building a Deck or Patio

Your deck or patio may not be surrounded by four walls, along with a floor and ceiling, but it can still be utilized as an additional room of your home where you can relax, barbecue, dine, sunbathe, read, socialize and entertain, or do a wide range of other activities. Depending on where you live, your deck or patio may be utilized year-round or at least during several seasons of the year.

If you have a choice about where your deck or patio will be built, consider the best possible site on your property, paying attention to the following.

The View

Choose the location that offers the best possible view of the outdoors. You can always minimize less desirable views by planting trees or shrubs.

Weather Patterns

Choose a site that offers maximum exposure to the sun, but pay attention to wind, rain, and snow patterns to determine how these weather conditions will impact your outdoor living space.

FACT

If your deck or patio faces north, it will most likely receive the least amount of direct sunlight. A south-facing deck or patio will be warmer, because it will be exposed to sunlight throughout the day. An eastward facing deck or patio will receive sunlight primarily in the morning, so the afternoons and evenings will be cooler. If your deck or patio faces west, chances are it will receive direct sunlight for the majority of the afternoon and evening.

Topography

Study the deed map for your home (available from your city hall, county office, title company, or bank or mortgage company), and look at the boundary lines of your property and the location of your home on the property. Also, take a careful look at the existing landscaping, the design of the terrain, and the views available.

Functionality

Depending on how you'll be using your deck or patio, make sure you'll have ample room. For example, if you plan to use the space for barbecues and outdoor dining, is there ample space for a table and chairs along with the actual grill? Can you easily enter and exit your home? Choose a location that offers the maximum amount of privacy but that won't make you feel confined. Consider what you will be using the outdoor space for.

Local Building Codes

Depending on where you live, chances are that local laws and ordinances affect what you can build on your property. Before you start construction or remodeling of your deck or patio, contact the local building department in your area to determine whether you'll need a building permit. If you live in a condo, gated community, or other type of community, make sure you won't be violating any of the bylaws created by the homeowners' association.

Your Budget

As with any type of home improvement, construction, or remodeling, building or remodeling a deck or patio can be a costly endeavor. As you begin to develop your plans, obtain multiple price quotes, set your budget, and then stick to it.

Design

To help you plan your deck or patio building or remodeling, a wide range of computer software CAD (computer aided design) packages are available to help you create your own plans, set a budget, and explore various design ideas. One such software package, called Deck Designs, is available for PC CD-ROM from Decks USA (☎ 330-788-7882, *www.decksusa.com*). This software offers hundreds of deck design plans for single-level, multi-level, L-shaped, and basic decks that can be fully customized. The software will help you create blueprints, floor plans, and even 3-D models. There's also a materials calculator and other useful tools built into the software to help you create a budget and choose the best possible tools and construction materials for the job.

As you decide what type of deck or patio area you want to create, pay attention to the design of your home, and then choose a style that fits your needs and personal taste. You'll find that decks and patios can be created around a wide range of themes or styles, all of which are highly functional and have the potential to be extremely beautiful. Some of the popular styles include: Asian, eclectic, Mediterranean, naturalistic, period (such as Victorian, for example), rustic, and tropical.

In addition to the layout and design of your deck or patio, as you consider its functionality and what you'll be using it for, think about your outdoor heating, bug control, and lighting requirements. For example, for heat, you may consider building an outdoor fireplace or utilizing a freestanding or permanently installed gas, electric, or propane heater. The location of the heating fixtures is important for creating a comfortable environment on chilly days or evenings. For example, you'll probably want to ensure that a heating unit covers the radius of your seating or eating area.

As for lighting, you have many options. Consider safety, functionality, security, and decoration when choosing how your deck or patio will be lit. You can hardwire lighting fixtures to the electricity in your home, install solar-powered lighting, use torches, or use other sources of portable light (such as battery-powered lanterns).

Professional Assistance

Unless you plan to build or remodel your deck or patio yourself, chances are you'll need to work with professionals to actually design and then build your outdoor living environment. Consider seeking out the advice of architects and/or landscape architects, landscapers, and general contractors.

While you probably want to hire someone based on a recommendation from a reliable source, such as a relative, coworker, neighbor, or friend, you can find people to work with in the Yellow Pages or using an online search. THE Directory (*www.gardenbuildings.com*), for example, offers a comprehensive online listing of suppliers of garden and leisure buildings, as well as other professionals associated with designing and building decks, patios, storage sheds, and other outdoor structures.

Organizing Your Deck or Patio

With space usually at a premium, one of the biggest concerns you'll need to deal with when trying to organize your deck or patio is clutter. Don't choose equipment and furniture that's too big for the space available. Keep in mind that you may not always be alone on your deck. You may invite guests for a barbecue and have four, six, ten or more people on your deck or patio, in addition to your grill, plants, decorations, tables, and chairs.

To help keep your patio or deck organized, keep all unused items in storage (in a shed, deck box, or garage). Don't keep lawn equipment and other items on the deck or patio, out in the open. As for patio furniture, choose items that can withstand all weather conditions. It may be necessary, however, to bring in chairs and tables, for example, during severe weather. If you'll be storing your outdoor furniture during the off-season, select models that can be folded and easily put into your basement or garage. Whatever type of patio furniture you end up with, always store the cushions inside when they're not in use to avoid exposing them to the elements.

In an effort to conserve space but still decorate your patio or deck, utilize the railings or surrounding areas. Instead of placing flower pots on the ground (which takes up space that can better be utilized by patio furniture), use flower boxes or over-the-rail planters, irdfeeders, or other decorative items that can be attached to the railings. Lighting can also be hung from walls or placed on railings to conserve space.

Grilling Equipment

Keep your grilling area several feet (or more) away from your dining or sitting area. This is for safety as well as for better organization. Before buying a grill, define what your needs will be. For example, if you'll be using it only once every few weeks (and only during the spring and summer months), choose a grill that's on wheels and that can be stored in a shed or garage. This will free up valuable patio or deck space. You'll also need to decide what type of grill you want. Some operate using propane gas, while others are gas-powered or use charcoal.

You never want to store filled propane tanks in your house, basement, or garage for safety reasons. If storage of flammable materials is a problem, consider a gas grill that can be permanently installed on your deck and hardwired (connected directly) to the gas lines coming into your home. With a direct gas connection, you never have to worry about refilling your propane tank or running out of propane when you start cooking your July 4th picnic.

When planning a cookout, gather up all of your items near the grill. After you're done with the lighter fluid and matches (if you're using a charcoal grill), remove these flammable items from the area. Place the grill away from where children will be playing and far away from anything that could catch on fire, such as plants, trees, shrubs, table cloths, napkins, or even the apron worn by the chef. If the weather is bad, never consider wheeling your grill unit inside to do your cooking.

A small storage chest kept on your deck or patio is the perfect place to keep grilling utensils, citronella candles, and other items. These items, however, should not be stored with unrelated items, such as outdoor sporting equipment, which your children will likely have access to.

Outdoor Furniture

Like traditional furniture for the inside of your home, patio furniture is available in a wide range of styles, colors, and designs. Before purchasing a complete patio furniture set and spending a fortune on pieces you don't need and will never use, answer the following questions:

- How much deck or patio space do you have available? (Take careful measurements of your available deck or patio space and carefully measure the furniture, before purchasing it, to ensure all of the pieces will fit in the available space.)
- Will you be dining outdoors? (If so, consider a traditional table and chairs.) How many people will need to be accommodated around the table (two, three, four, six, or more)?
- Do you want reclining chairs/lounge chairs?
- Will the furniture be kept on the deck year-round or stored during the off-season? If storage is necessary, do you have ample space in your garage, shed, or basement?
- Do you want cushions on the chairs? Where will the cushions be stored when not in use?
- Do you want ottomans or small tables to accompany the patio chairs?
- What style of furniture are you looking for?
- What material would you like the furniture to be constructed from?
- Will you have a large umbrella or awning on the deck or patio?
- In addition to the patio furniture you choose, what else will be stored on the patio (grill, plants, decorations, heating units, fountains, and so on)?
- What's your budget?

If space is a serious issue, and you want to be able to utilize your deck or patio space for a variety of different purposes, consider purchasing folding patio furniture. This will allow you to place a table and chairs on your deck or patio when dining or entertaining, yet replace these items with folding reclining chairs when you choose to relax and lie out in the sun. The Gardener's Supply Company (☎ 800-427-3363, ✎ www.gardeners.com) offers a line of extremely comfortable folding recliners that adjust to an infinite number of positions, yet fold up for easy storage in a shed, closet, garage, or basement.

When looking to purchase the perfect patio furniture to meet your needs, think about how often the furniture will be utilized, what the function of the furniture will be, how you'll be spending time on your deck or patio, and what your personal tastes are in terms of colors and styles.

In addition, look for durability. Make sure the pieces are sturdy and well manufactured, and that all of the seams and joints are firm. Think about how much time you want to spend maintaining the furniture. Consider whether the furniture will require a lot of upkeep and maintenance, such as regular staining for wood, or frequent cleaning. How much effort are you willing to put into the furniture? Finally, be sure the patio furniture you choose can withstand all types of weather based on the climate you live in. Be sure that screws and nuts are rustproof. Also, make sure the furniture won't fade in the sun. The cushions should be water-resistant or waterproof, even if you plan to store them indoors (the garage, basement, shed, or attic) when they're not in use.

Patio furniture can be manufactured from aluminum, iron, wicker, wood, resin, fiberglass, plastic, and a wide range of other materials. Each of these materials has advantages and disadvantages in terms of cost, maintenance, and how long the furniture will last.

Aluminum

Patio furniture created from aluminum is strong, won't rust, and retains its good looks through summer suns, thunderstorms, and heavy usage. Quality aluminum furniture is durable and can last for a decade or more. It's also lightweight, which makes it easy to move, and requires minimal maintenance. Patio furniture made from cast aluminum is distinctive and elegant and often features classic designs with roots in the cast-iron styling made popular in the eighteenth century. Like tubular aluminum, it is durable and easy to maintain.

Iron

Patio furniture manufactured from iron has been popular for more than a century. It is versatile, stylish, strong, and often less expensive than furniture made from other materials. This type of furniture, however, tends to weigh a lot, making it difficult to move.

Resin and Polyvinyl Resin

There are two categories of resin furniture: molded resin and tubular resin. Your local mass-merchant retailer may have a resin chair for under $5, while better-quality stores offer what appears to be an identical chair for over $50. With resin, the general rule is that you get what you pay for. Quality chairs are usually heavier and roomier, and the resin combinations last longer than lower-quality versions. Tubular resin offers a wide choice of styles and strengths.

Wicker

For a handcrafted, natural, and always distinctive look, wicker adds charm and style to any patio or deck. In terms of styles, wicker furniture can look contemporary, elegantly Victorian, or tropical. One drawback to wicker furniture is that it can easily be damaged by direct exposure to the elements. It's best utilized in sheltered areas, such as on covered porches, within screened rooms, in sunrooms, or indoors. Quality wicker can be exceedingly durable. With proper care, it will last for decades. Well-made older pieces can command top dollar among antique collectors.

Wood

Outdoor furniture manufactured or handcrafted from wood is always in style. In days gone by, wood patio furniture was comprised of those oversized redwood sets and rustic-looking picnic tables. Wood patio furniture has come a long way, however. It's now very fashionable and durable. You'll find a wide range of front-porch rockers, classic garden benches, dining sets, Adirondack chairs, curved chaises, and tables of every size and shape. Wood patio furniture is extremely versatile. It may be used with or without cushions. You'll find elegant patio furniture made from pine, oak, cypress, teak, jarrah, mahogany, cedar, maple, birch, and beech, as well as a collection of exotic hardwoods. Wood may be stained, oiled, or painted. Some woods, like teak, can be almost carefree if you allow them to weather to a handsome silver/gray color. You must, however, be willing to re-oil, restain, or repaint your wood patio furniture from time to time.

In addition to visiting a local nursery or greenhouse, outdoor furniture/patio store, or hardware superstore, you can find a wide range of home and garden products online. Outdoor Décor (✍ www.outdoordecor.com), for example, offers everything from patio furniture to birdhouses and gardening supplies.

Outdoor Storage Sheds

People enjoy their lawns and outdoor property in many different ways. Whether you've created lush gardens, pride yourself on maintaining immaculate landscaping, or allow your children to use the backyard as a play area, chances are you own landscaping equipment (such as a lawnmower, rakes, garden hoses, sprinklers, shovels, and so on) and other items that you use to maintain your lawn and garden.

These items, along with patio furniture, need to be properly maintained and stored when not in use. To avoid cluttering your basement, garage, or other in-house storage areas, many people choose to utilize an outdoor storage shed. These are relatively small, standalone structures that are built to withstand the elements and provide non-climate-controlled storage space outside the home.

Defining Your Outdoor Storage Needs

When defining your outdoor storage needs, answer the following questions:

- What elements and weather conditions will your storage shed be exposed to?
- What will you be storing in the shed?
- Do the contents of your shed need to be kept in a waterproof environment?
- Does the shed have to be temperature-controlled?
- Will you need electricity in the shed?
- Based on what will be stored, what size shed do you need? (For example, if you have three bicycles, a lawnmower, and a leaf blower, these items will take up considerable space.)
- Where on your property will the shed be built or situated?

For basic storage needs, whether it's for a lawnmower and gardening tools or to store patio furniture during the off-season, Rubbermaid (✐ www.rubbermaid.com) offers several relatively inexpensive outdoor storage sheds. These units are designed to be freestanding, weather resistant, lockable, and assembled in less than thirty minutes.

Priced under $300, the Large Vertical Storage Shed from Rubbermaid is comprised of eight interlocking panels. The inside space can be designed to contain three separate shelves, while the main structure can be anchored into the ground or attached to a house. Approximately fifty-two cubic feet of storage space is offered in a unit that measures 56" wide × 32" deep × 77" high. Rubbermaid also offers a Large Horizontal Storage Shed (priced under $200) that offers thirty-two cubic feet of storage space in a unit measuring 60" wide × 32" deep × 47" high.

If you're looking for a unit to store lawn equipment, bicycles, and other larger items, the Sliding-Lid Storage Shed from Rubbermaid provides an excellent solution. Priced under $400, this unit offers ninety-two cubic feet of storage space and measures 60" wide × 79" deep × 54" high. Like many of Rubbermaid's outdoor storage sheds, it's available in taupe, evergreen, and black. Combining additional functionality with a basic storage shed, Rubbermaid's Patio Storage Bench works as a fully functional bench that can be placed to overlook a garden, used on a patio or porch, or placed by a pool or tennis court. The unit contains four cubic feet of storage space and measures 48" × 25" × 36". As a bench, the Patio Storage Bench comfortably holds two adults. As a storage unit, it's perfect for storing gardening tools, hoses, cushions, and other small items.

Whether from Rubbermaid or another manufacturer, storage sheds are available in a variety of shapes, sizes, and orientations: horizontal or vertical, top- or front-loading, with lifting or sliding roofs. They require simple assembly (usually less than an hour), not long hours of building, and need little or no maintenance.

In addition to being easy to construct and designed to fit visually into any landscaped environment, most storage sheds are durable. Sheds with tough resin construction provide protection to the items inside.

When someone thinks of a shed, however, he or she may not think of a heavy-duty plastic storage unit, such as those available from Rubbermaid. Many people think of small standalone structures made from other materials, like wood or metal. These units sometimes resemble small barns or even tiny houses. They come in a wide range of styles and colors. Sheds can also be custom-built to meet specific size requirements.

Contact Backyard America, a company that sells a wide range of outdoor storage solutions via the Internet (☎ 703-392-5152, ✎ *www.backyardamerica.com/sheds.htm*), for a variety of storage sheds, some of which even include vinyl siding, windows, shutters, and doors.

FACT

Sheds can be placed on several types of foundations depending on your site and application. If the shed is to be in your yard, it can usually be placed on a 3–4" bed of stone. If the site is soft or you want protection from frost, use a pier foundation with pressure-treated columns on concrete footings. Sheds can also be placed on concrete or stone patios that are in sound condition.

Styles of outdoor storage sheds from Backyard America include the Mini Barn (a traditional barn style, offered in a compact, economical package measuring 4' × 8' × 8'). The company also offers the types of sheds in **TABLE 12-1**.

TABLE 12-1

TYPES AND DIMENSIONS OF SHEDS (Height × Width × Depth)	
UTILITY SHEDS	**LEAN-TO SHEDS**
2' × 4' × 4'	4' × 6' × 7'
4' × 4' × 5'	4' × 8' × 7'
4' × 6' × 5'	4' × 10' × 7'
4' × 8' × 5'	6' × 8' × 7'
	10' × 8' × 8'
	6' × 10' × 7'
	8' × 8' × 8'

Backyard America also offers an exclusive, under-deck shed system. These outdoor storage solutions are available with a variety of exterior finishes, door and window styles, and flooring choices. These units are custom-built for each customer. In addition to storage, these structures can be used for potting, as playhouses, and as pool/spa cabanas. According to the company, "Our unique roof/ceiling system allows for construction under existing decks without having to disturb the deck flooring or structure. These economical structures are built on-site so there's also no need to move fences or landscaping."

Backyard America is just one company that offers a wide range of outdoor storage solutions. To see some of these solutions first-hand, consider making a visit to your local hardware store or hardware superstore. Some gardening-supply stores and nurseries also sell various types of sheds and outdoor storage solutions.

Organizing Your Shed Space

In addition to your lawnmower, leaf blower, gardening equipment, bicycles, and other large items, you'll probably discover that your shed is an ideal place for storing smaller items. Place these smaller items on shelves or in a special area of your shed where they're easily reachable without having to remove the lawnmower, for example. Also, place the items you'll be using the most often closest to the front door of the shed for easy access. Keep the items you'll use only once a month or even once a year in the back corner of the shed, where they're not as readily accessible.

Consider installing hooks in addition to shelves. From hooks, you can hang certain types of tools and other items so they're out of the way, yet easily visible so you can retrieve them when they're needed. Utilizing the wall space of a shed with shelves and hooks is an excellent use of space.

Just because you have extra storage space, don't allow your shed to become transformed into an alternate clutter storage location. Just as you've learned to do within your home, discard unwanted or unneeded clutter, such as broken tools or unwanted flowerpots.

Organizing Your Garden/Landscaping Tools

Organizing your collection of garden and landscape tools is what this section is all about. Your lawnmower, leaf blower, mulcher, rake, watering can, shovel, hoe, garden hoses, sprinklers, hedge trimmers, edger, spade, trowel, and pruner are just some of the tools you probably use on a regular basis when caring for your garden or landscape. You also probably have flowerpots, potting soil, seeds, bags of mulch, and countless other items to keep track of.

FACT

Never risk a back injury by trying to carry heavy items. Instead, invest in a garden cart or wheelbarrow to transport these items. A garden cart or wheelbarrow is also ideal for transporting heavy bags (or piles) of leaves and lawn refuse. The Gardener's Supply Company (✆ 800-427-3363, ✑ *www.gardeners.com*) offers high-quality, Vermont-built garden carts in two sizes.

For hanging tools with long handles, like rakes and shovels, the Long Handle Tool Organizer is perfect for your garage or utility closet wall. This is a 19"-long wall bar that attaches with the supplied screws. The three grippers will support round handles from $^3/_4$" to $1^1/_4$" in diameter, even very heavy weights like sledgehammers. Simply lift off to release and remove the tools being stored. The Long Handle Tool Organizer is available from the Garrett Wade Tool Catalog (✆ 800-221-2942, ✑ *www.garrettwade.com*), but similar products are available at most hardware stores.

Another tool-organization product is the SureLock from Tidy Garage (✆ 888-4-GARAGE, ✑ *www.tidygarage.com/surelock.html*). This wall unit allows you to organize shovels, brooms, rakes, and other hard-to-store items in one compact place. The Surelock Tool Organizer mounts easily to any wall and holds a multitude of garden and household tools, from a light broom to a heavy sledgehammer. Its two self-adjusting, spring-locking arms hold any handle size and shape securely with the heavy, sharp parts nearest to the ground. Six large, permanently attached hooks offer a multitude of valuable storage options.

For organizing, storing, and carrying around smaller hand tools, Cody Mercantile (📞 800-443-4934, ✍ *www.codymercantile.com*) offers the Rolling Tool Organizer. Using this tool carrier on wheels, you can organize your tools in fifty-two pockets in and outside the foldable rolling crate. The unit's telescoping handle collapses for storage. Side handles let you carry this tool organizer over obstacles as well as load it easily into your vehicle. The organizer is sewn from tough nylon fabric reinforced at all stress points. It measures 15" wide × 14" deep × 15" high, with a 33" fully extended handle.

The Garden Rover, available from Plow & Hearth (📞 800-627-1712, ✍ *www.plowhearth.com*) is the ideal storage unit on wheels for storing large and small garden tools. The Garden Rover is both compact and mobile. It's designed to keep you and your tools organized. Load it with up to eighteen tools and push it to your work site. The four-compartment front pouch holds hand tools, seed packets, and other garden supplies, and is made of vinyl-backed 600-denier fabric. The unit itself is lightweight and well constructed, and has a 100-pound capacity to hold bags of mulch or seed. The 8" molded tires are designed so that the unit can be pulled or pushed along rough terrain.

The Plant Factory (📞 334-653-7043, ✍ *http://theplantfactory.com/accessories-index.html*) takes a traditional five-gallon bucket and transforms it into a handy storage unit that's portable and highly functional. In the same way, the Fiskars Bucket Tool Caddy Plus (*✍ www.fiskars.com)* turns any five-gallon bucket into the ultimate tool organizer for your garden. It features thirty pockets, including nineteen exterior and eleven interior pockets, to organize all of your gardening tools and accessories.

The Harriet Carter Garden Tool Organizer (📞 800-377-7878, ✍ *www.hcgifts.com/gartoolor.html*) is a metal, floor-standing storage caddy that allows you to have your rakes, brooms, shovels, and other tools standing upright in storage. The caddy has twenty slots to keep tools neatly in place, plus a side rack that holds a garden hose. There's even room for pots, fertilizer, trowels, seeds, and more. The unit can be kept in a garage, greenhouse, basement, or utility closet.

The Step2 Company (📞 800-347-8372) offers the Yard Butler, an organizational and functional tool designed to make cleaning up the yard much easier. It contains a thirty-gallon paper or plastic trash bag holder and four storage slots for long-handled tools, such as rakes and shovels. It also provides three slots for hand tools, a storage bin, and an easy-grip handle. It can be easily pushed anywhere on its four 7-inch poly wheels.

When utilizing the tools you own, become familiar with what each was designed for and be sure to use the right tool for each specific task.

FACT

Regular watering is one of the keys to growing a successful lawn and garden. If you're like so many people, your schedule is probably hectic, so making time several times a week to water your lawn and garden isn't always possible. Any garden supply store, however, offers electric or battery-powered water timers. These small devices connect between your gardening hose and faucet and can be preprogrammed to turn on and off a sprinkler automatically.

To take a completely organized approach to every aspect of your gardening and landscaping, you may consider utilizing a PC-based software package called Garden Organizer Deluxe (from PrimaSoft). This computer program can be used on a desktop or laptop computer. The software offers a handful of different functions and modules. For example, the Plant Organizer allows you to catalog your favorite plants (enter plant name, description, attributes, maintenance notes, pictures, and more). Other functions built into the software include an idea organizer to store information about different garden solutions, a work organizer to organize new garden projects and maintenance tasks, an address organizer to organize your garden-related contacts, and a Web resource organizer to keep information about Web resources related to gardening and landscaping. You can download a free, fully functional trial version by pointing your Web browser to PrimaSoft's Web site at *www.primasoft.com/ deluxeprg/goodx.htm*. You can also purchase a full version of the software online.

CHAPTER 13

Taking Charge of Your Day

At the same time you begin to harness the power of organization within your home to create a comfortable living environment, you also need to understand how to take control of your time in order to maximize your productivity, reduce stress, and make the absolute most out of your free time (or the quality time you have to spend with your friends and family).

Organizing Your Morning

Every morning you wake up to the same basic routine—you're tired, you're running late, you have half a dozen things to get done, you need to decide what you're going to wear, you can't find your car keys, and you realize that you forgot to put the cell phone in its charger last night. While you probably can't change the tasks that comprise your daily routine, you can take a more organized approach to make the early morning hours less stressful. After all, if your morning goes smoothly, you've set the stage for the rest of the day.

To better organize your morning routine, first determine exactly what your routine is comprised of and how much time you have to accomplish it. Begin by asking yourself at what time you need to leave for work in the morning and how much time you need to complete your morning routine. Based on the answers to those two questions, do the math! What time do you need to wake up in the morning? (Make sure you leave yourself a few minutes extra.) Now, set your alarm clock!

The next step is to determine the activities that comprise your morning routine. After you fully understand what you need to get accomplished each morning, you can devise ways of taking a more organized approach to these activities, cutting down the amount of time they take and reducing your early-morning stress.

Starting from the moment you wake up in the morning, what does your morning routine consist of? Make a complete list, preferably in order. **TABLE 13-1** gives you a few common activities, but you'll need to customize this list (and place it in chronological order) for yourself.

Use modern technology to make your mornings easier. For example, purchase a coffee machine with a timer that can be set the previous night, so that the machine will automatically switch on and have your morning coffee ready when you reach the kitchen in the morning.

TABLE 13-1

MORNING TASKS	
TASK	**TIME NEEDED**
Apply makeup	
Brew coffee	
Brush teeth	
Choose what to wear	
Defrost dinner for the evening	
Exercise	
Find your car keys	
Grab your cellular phone and pager	
Iron clothing for the day	
Make breakfast	
Pack your briefcase	
Prepare lunches for the kids and/or yourself	
Read the newspaper	
Shave	
Start and warm up your car	
Style hair	
Take a shower	
Watch the morning news	
Write out your day's to-do list/schedule	

Next to each item on your list, write down approximately how long each task takes. For example, shaving may take ten minutes, while brewing your morning coffee may take eight minutes. As you evaluate your list, consider how you can multitask. When you first wake up in the morning, can you get the coffee machine started, so that the coffee starts brewing while you're in the shower? Can you warm up the iron while you're choosing the day's outfit to wear? Can you have the TV or radio on while you're in the shower and getting dressed?

Out of all the items on your morning list, what can be done the previous night? Perhaps you can spend twenty to thirty minutes before bedtime creating the next day's to-do list and schedule, deciding what you'll wear, and ironing those clothes, making the kids' lunches, locating your car keys, and packing your briefcase. If you prepare breakfast for several people, you can also save time by setting the breakfast table and deciding the night before what you'll make for breakfast.

Purchasing a hardwood valet, for example, will allow you to lay out, hang, and organize your outfit the night before, so everything is ready (and wrinkle-free) in the morning. The Frontgate catalog (✆ 800-537-8484, ✍ *www.frontgate.com*), for example, sells the Hardwood Gentleman's Valet, which offers ample hanging space for a complete business suit, small drawers (for change or cufflinks), a shelf for your personal accessories, and hooks for a belt and necktie. The unit also has a built-in shoe rack.

A smaller dresser top valet can be used for organizing those smaller accessories (glasses, jewelry, watch, wallet, keys, pen, PDA, pager, and so on) that you normally keep in your pockets. A well-designed dresser top valet will be stylish, have multiple compartments, and may have one or two small drawers.

In the kitchen, instead of fumbling around through the various drawers, figure out everything you need to prepare breakfast and coffee in the morning, and keep those items in a specific area of the kitchen—all in one convenient place. Group and store opened breakfast condiments, such as honey, jelly, and syrup in a small container or basket in the refrigerator, so you can put them all out at once. Also, consider sorting out your vitamins and medications the night before so that everything is ready for you in the morning. If you're half-asleep, this will help keep you from accidentally taking the wrong pill or wrong dosage.

If you find it incredibly difficult to get yourself together and out the door each morning, set multiple alarms for yourself. In addition to your wake-up alarm, set a separate alarm that gives you a thirty- and/or fifteen-minute warning for when you have to actually leave.

Prepare and organize your bathroom to accommodate for your daily routine. Begin by creating a sublist of everything you do in the bathroom and what items you'll need for shaving, applying makeup, styling your hair, taking a shower, and so on. If room allows, create separate areas for each of these activities and group together the items you'll need for each activity. An alternative is to use small, portable storage bins or trays. Keep all of your shaving gear together, for example, apart from your hair-care products.

If you constantly lose your keys, create a place near your front door where you can organize various items. You can use a small shelf or board (with hooks) to hold keys, outgoing mail that needs to be dropped in a mailbox, shopping lists, your cell phone or pager, and other items you tend to forget in the morning. Get into the habit of putting your keys on the hook or shelf near the front door every time you come home. Also, get into the habit of plugging your cell phone into its charger at night and keeping it near your keys. After all, you can't leave home without your keys, so if your phone is with the keys, you're less apt to forget it.

To keep yourself on schedule in the morning, position easily visible clocks in the bedroom, bathroom, and kitchen. Also, try to predict what distractions or morning emergencies you'll encounter and determine in advance how you'll deal with these situations in a timely and stress-free manner. For example, if your car is unreliable and won't start, what will you do? If you forgot to pick up your clothing from the dry cleaner and you have nothing to wear to work, how will you handle it? What happens if the kids miss their school bus?

How can I take less time to apply makeup?
Consider working with a professional makeup artist to find out how to become more adept at quickly applying your makeup. In many cases, less is more. Most high-end cosmetics and skin care stores as well as many department stores have highly trained makeup artists on staff who will work with you.

Make the Most of Your Commuting Time

No matter where you live, if you commute to work by car, one of the things you'll probably have to deal with on a regular basis is heavy traffic. Instead of cursing at the other drivers on the road, this section shows you several ways you can make your commuting time more productive and relaxing. To avoid getting into an accident, however, never attempt to read or write while driving and always pay attention to the road while using a cellular phone. Even eating in the car can be a distraction that can result in an auto accident if you're not careful.

Listening to Books on Tape

The radio is a wonderful tool for listening to news and keeping track of current events when you're in the car, and listening to music is an excellent way to help you relax and unwind. But if your car is equipped with a cassette or CD player, you can also use your commuting time to learn new skills or enjoy listening to a best-selling novel that you don't have time to read. Learning cassettes, such as those from Nightingale-Conant (✆ 800-647-9198, ✐ *www.nightingale.com*), are easy to use. In addition, Audio-Tech Business Book Summaries (✆ 800-776-1910, ✐ *www.audiotech.com*) offers a monthly audiocassette program that summarizes two business books in thirty and forty minutes each. The Audio-Tech Business Book Summaries service is offered on an annual subscription basis and is designed to help you stay up-to-date on the latest business trends, no matter what type of business you're in. If you're more interested in listening to an unabridged how-to or self-help book or a popular novel, Simon & Schuster Audio (✐ *www.simonsays.com/audio*) offers an extensive catalog of audio books that are sold at bookstores.

Talking or Taking Notes

Instead of just listening to someone else speak, using wireless communications, you can also do the talking. With the cost of wireless communications becoming increasingly more affordable, using a cellular or digital PCS phone to check your voice mail, return important phone calls, hold business meetings via conference calls, or even chat with a friend or loved one is now a viable option. If you're going to use a cell phone in your car, however, use a phone with a headset or speakerphone so that your driving is not distracted. Sprint PCS (✆ 800-480-4PCS, ✐ *www.sprintpcs.com*) is one of the most affordable wireless communication options, but shop around for the best deals. Based on your needs, many cellular and digital PCS services offer specials or customizable rate plans. Check newspaper ads and visit several wireless communication stores in your community.

In addition, by using a microcassette recorder while sitting in traffic, many people boost their overall productivity by dictating letters and memos, keeping track of ideas when they can't write them down, and reciting a daily to-do list on their way to work.

> If you tend to get bright ideas while driving, have a microcassette or digital recorder handy in your car so you can record your ideas instantly. Don't endanger yourself by trying to write things down using a pad and paper or entering them into your PDA while driving.

Using Non-driving Commutes Effectively

What you're able to accomplish when commuting depends on whether you drive yourself to work or carpool, take the train, or use some other form of public transportation. If you have downtime when commuting to and from work, you can take this opportunity to do the following:

- Make phone calls and review voicemail messages (via cellular phone)
- Surf the Web (using a wireless modem and a laptop or a wireless PDA)
- Read the newspaper or magazines to stay up-to-date on current events
- Read trade journals to keep up on industry-oriented news relating to your career
- Do your schedule planning for the day

Taking Control of the Rest of Your Day

Most people spend five days per week (and at least eight hours per day) on the job, pursuing a career. This primarily leaves nights and weekends to spend with your friends and family and to deal with your personal responsibilities. You've probably discovered, however, that by the time you're finished with all your professional and personal responsibilities, there's little or no time remaining for you. By better taking control of your time, you can create more time for yourself, pursuing the activities you thoroughly enjoy in life.

Becoming a more organized person and taking control over your time are skills that you can easily learn and master (with practice).

The first step is to determine exactly how you're spending every minute of your day right now. Using a calendar or a blank sheet of paper, spend at least two or three typical weekdays (and at least one full weekend) creating a detailed diary of how you spend your time. This detailed summary should include all activities, from sleeping to eating to spending time in your car to watching television. Complete the activity log worksheet in the following section to help you better determine how you're spending your time.

Tracking Your Activity

Create one activity log (see **TABLE 13-1**) for each day of the week you choose to track in your personal and professional life.

TABLE 13-1

ACTIVITY LOG	
DATE _____	DAY OF WEEK _____
TIME OF DAY	ACTIVITY
6:00 A.M. – 6:30 A.M.	
6:31 A.M. – 7:00 A.M.	
7:01 A.M. – 7:30 A.M.	
7:31 A.M. – 8:00 A.M.	
8:01 A.M. – 8:30 A.M.	
8:31 A.M. – 9:00 A.M.	
9:01 A.M. – 9:30 A.M.	
9:31 A.M. – 10:00 A.M.	
10:01 A.M. – 10:30 A.M.	
10:31 A.M. – 11:00 A.M.	
11:01 A.M. – 11:30 A.M.	
11:31 A.M. – 12:00 P.M.	
12:01 P.M. – 12:30 P.M.	
12:31 P.M. – 1:00 P.M.	
1:01 P.M. – 1:30 P.M.	
1:31 P.M. – 2:00 P.M.	

ACTIVITY LOG (CONTINUED)

DATE _____   DAY OF WEEK _____

TIME OF DAY	ACTIVITY
2:01 P.M. – 2:30 P.M.	
2:31 P.M. – 3:00 P.M.	
3:01 P.M. – 3:30 P.M.	
3:31 P.M. – 4:00 P.M.	
4:01 P.M. – 4:30 P.M.	
4:31 P.M. – 5:00 P.M.	
5:01 P.M. – 5:30 P.M.	
5:31 P.M. – 6:00 P.M.	
6:01 P.M. – 6:30 P.M.	
6:31 P.M. – 7:00 P.M.	
7:01 P.M. – 7:30 P.M.	
7:31 P.M. – 8:00 P.M.	
8:01 P.M. – 8:30 P.M.	
8:31 P.M. – 9:00 P.M.	
9:01 P.M. – 9:30 P.M.	
9:31 P.M. – 10:00 P.M.	
10:01 P.M. – 10:30 P.M.	
10:31 P.M. – 11:00 P.M.	
11:01 P.M. – 11:30 P.M.	
11:31 P.M. – 12:00 A.M.	
12:01 A.M. – 12:30 A.M.	
12:31 A.M. – 1:00 A.M.	
1:01 A.M. – 1:30 A.M.	
1:31 A.M. – 2:00 A.M.	
2:01 A.M. – 2:30 A.M.	
2:31 A.M. – 3:00 A.M.	
3:01 A.M. – 3:30 A.M.	
3:31 A.M. – 4:00 A.M.	
4:01 A.M. – 4:30 A.M.	
4:31 A.M. – 5:00 A.M.	
5:01 A.M. – 5:30 A.M.	
5:31 A.M. – 6:00 A.M.	

After you've completed several activity log worksheets (one for each day), evaluate them carefully to determine exactly how you're spending your time. Calculate how much time you spend each week doing important tasks and how often you engage in time-wasting activities. Use the formulas in the following sections to calculate specifically how much time you're spending on various work-related and personal tasks and activities. Be sure to add any additional activities or tasks that are appropriate to your personal/professional life.

Work-Related Activities
Commuting to and from work

____ Hours per day × ____ Days per week = Total hours spent:_____

Reading mail and e-mail

____ Hours per day × ____ Days per week = Total hours spent:_____

Talking on the phone

____ Hours per day × ____ Days per week = Total hours spent:_____

Sitting in meetings

____ Hours per day × ____ Days per week = Total hours spent:_____

Performing important work-related tasks

____ Hours per day × ____ Days per week = Total hours spent:_____

Performing unimportant work-related tasks

____ Hours per day × ____ Days per week = Total hours spent:_____

Dealing with unexpected interruptions

____ Hours per day × ____ Days per week = Total hours spent:_____

Dealing with unexpected emergencies

____ Hours per day × ____ Days per week = Total hours spent:_____

Doing paperwork and completing reports

____ Hours per day × ____ Days per week = Total hours spent:_____

Time spent working specifically toward work-related goals

____ Hours per day × ____ Days per week = Total hours spent:_____

Other Task: _____

____ Hours per day × ____ Days per week = Total hours spent:_____

Personal Activities

Cooking and eating

____ Hours per day × ____ Days per week = Total hours spent:_____

Sleeping

____ Hours per day × ____ Days per week = Total hours spent:_____

Personal grooming

____ Hours per day × ____ Days per week = Total hours spent:_____

Cleaning and laundry

____ Hours per day × ____ Days per week = Total hours spent:_____

Driving

____ Hours per day × ____ Days per week = Total hours spent:_____

Spending quality time alone

____ Hours per day × ____ Days per week = Total hours spent:_____

Spending quality time with loved ones

____ Hours per day × ____ Days per week = Total hours spent:_____

Reading (books, magazines, newspapers, and so on)

____ Hours per day × ____ Days per week = Total hours spent:_____

Watching TV

___ Hours per day × ___ Days per week = Total hours spent:_____

Paying bills and doing paperwork

___ Hours per day × ___ Days per week = Total hours spent:_____

Running errands

___ Hours per day × ___ Days per week = Total hours spent:_____

Participating in a hobby

___ Hours per day × ___ Days per week = Total hours spent:_____

Time spent pursuing personal goals

___ Hours per day × ___ Days per week = Total hours spent:_____

Other activities: _____
Hours per day × ___ Days per week = Total hours spent:_____

As you see your schedule laid out before you in writing, you should be able to pinpoint some of the activities you engage in on an ongoing basis that take up time unnecessarily. By looking at your schedule, perhaps you can come up with ways of better combining tasks in order to save time.

Because you know yourself better than anyone, not only should you determine exactly how you spend your time, but also determine at what times of the day you're the most productive. Are you a morning person? Do you find you're able to concentrate best after lunch? Also take a few minutes to consider what aspects of your life cause you the most stress. What is it about these activities that actually causes the stress? What could be done, starting immediately, to eliminate some of this stress? Are you overworked and don't get enough sleep? Are you faced with serious personal or professional issues that are constantly on your mind? Are you always working under tight deadlines? Do you find yourself always missing deadlines and running late for appointments?

Setting Goals for Yourself

One reason why so many people never achieve their goals and never seem to have time in their day is because of a lack of organization and planning. One way to begin taking control of your life (and your time) is to set detailed short- and long-term goals for yourself. As you go through each day, work toward achieving those goals and focus your primary energy on the tasks necessary to accomplish your daily objectives. This is something that fewer than 33 percent of all Americans ever take the time to do.

The people who have achieved success in their lives (whether it's personal or professional success as they define it for themselves) have almost always mastered the ability to set goals and plan, plus they have mastered time-management and organizational techniques. Take time to consider what is (or what you want to be) truly important in your life, and then outline the steps you need to take to get there. If you're unsure how to set goals and plan tasks, you may want to take a time-management course that includes a section on goals and values.

Day-Timers, one of the world's leading developers and manufacturers of personal planners and time-management tools, found that 62 percent of American workers feel they are always or frequently rushed to do the things they have to do, yet only 8 percent of American workers describe themselves as extremely happy with their lives.

It's within your power, using basic time-management and organizational skills, to be among the relatively few Americans who aren't constantly rushed and who are truly happy in their personal and professional lives.

Managing Your Time

In your twenty-four hours per day, you must meet your personal and professional responsibilities, as well as eat and sleep. If you're like most people, you probably find that you simply run out of time each day and never get to accomplish everything you hoped to achieve. This happens to people who are full-time students, homemakers, or full-time employees. No matter who you are, juggling personal and professional responsibilities isn't easy!

Avoid falling into the pitfall of trying to take on too much at once. Studies show that most highly productive managers in the workplace have learned to take on only about three major tasks or priorities each day. By spending time focusing on only a few important tasks at once (plus a few less important obligations), you can focus your attention and dedicate the time necessary to accomplish what needs to get done.

Part of becoming a better organized person means finding ways to deal with and eliminate all forms of clutter, including mail, paperwork, e-mail messages, phone messages, old magazines, old newspapers, piles of laundry, bills, knickknacks, dirty dishes, memorabilia, and trash. Without clutter, whether it's physical clutter in the form of piles of paper or more abstract clutter, you'll be able to more easily focus your time and energies on what's important in your life.

Based on the activity logs you've created, what needs to change? How can you modify your habits and be able to spend your time being more productive and less stressed out?

As you examine how you spend your day, pinpoint the biggest time wasters that are keeping your from getting your most important work done. According to the Day Timer's 4-Dimensional Time Management program, a course that teaches time-management skills, to successfully manage your time, you must begin to do the following:

- **Focus:** Determine what's really important and what duties you're responsible to perform in a timely manner; learn to differentiate between what's important and what's not in terms of how you spend your time.
- **Plan:** Discover how to properly prioritize the items on your to-do list. Establish tasks based on your goals and decide in advance how much time each task will take.
- **Act:** Based on your planning, take an organized approach to completing each of the high-priority tasks and items on your to-do list every day. Focus on the less important items and tasks later.

Every evening (after work) or first thing in the morning, take about fifteen minutes to create a daily to-do list for yourself. List all of your prescheduled appointments in your daily schedule, allowing ample time to get to and from the appointments, and if necessary, allocating time to prepare for them in advance. Along with your appointments, list all of those little tasks you have to get done and add those to your list. Finally, examine the major projects, goals, and objectives in your life and divide them into smaller, more manageable tasks. Incorporate these tasks into your to-do list as well. After listing all of the things that need to get done that day or the next day, determine approximately how long each task will take.

Now, set your priorities. On your to-do list, place an "A" next to the items or tasks that will produce the most valuable results. These are the items that must get done, no matter what. Then, go back to the top of your list and place a "B" next to important tasks that need to get done, but that aren't as critical or time-sensitive as your "A" items. Finally, place a "C" next to items or tasks that should get done, but that aren't too important. Make sure you attempt to complete your high-priority items and tasks early in the day, giving those items your full attention.

Keep in mind that urgent tasks have short-term consequences, but tasks that you determine will have long-term implications help you to reach your goals. Properly categorize your to-do list so that your focus is on achieving what's truly important as well as what's time-sensitive.

After you adopt this daily list, use it in every aspect of your life and keep all of your plans (personal and professional) in one place. Keeping a separate schedule for your personal and professional life can get confusing and may result in accidentally double-booking your time.

Throughout the day, especially when you're trying to focus on accomplishing a specific task, keep interruptions to a minimum. Each time you get interrupted, not only are you kept from completing the task you're working on, you're also distracted, causing you to spend time refocusing after the interruption.

Learn how to delegate responsibilities and tasks that can help you free up your time and reduce work that your particular skills, experience, and knowledge aren't required for. For example, subordinates at work can be assigned to gather facts, prepare rough drafts of letters and reports, make photocopies or handle printing and collating, sort through mail (e-mail), screen incoming calls and voicemail messages, handle data entry, run errands, and handle tasks that aren't part of your core responsibilities. Likewise, at home, your children can be taught to help with laundry, clean up, prepare meals, take care of pets, do lawn work, and complete other household tasks.

When delegating a task, make sure you assign the right person to the job. Focus on obtaining the desired results, but don't necessary dictate how something should get done (providing the desired result will ultimately be achieved). Trust the person you assign to handle the task without your having to look over his or her shoulder. Provide a deadline and seek out periodic updates or progress reports, as necessary. Be sure to provide frequent feedback and praise.

Purchasing Time-Management Tools

You can become a more organized person and better utilize your time by incorporating a new set of skills into your life and using them on an ongoing basis. To accomplish this, you'll want to immediately begin utilizing some type of time-management tool, such as a personal (paper-based) planner, personal digital assistant (PDA), or scheduling software on your computer. Simply buying one of these time-management tools, however, is not enough. You must learn how to use it, and then make a concerted effort to incorporate it into your life on an ongoing basis.

Printed Daily Planners

A traditional (printed) planner usually consists of a binder containing various specially designed pages that help you plan your time, manage to-do lists, keep track of expenses, and plan your goals. Two of the best known companies that manufacture traditional planners in a wide range of styles and formats are Franklin Covey and Day-Timer, Inc.

You can purchase the planners developed by these two companies from office-supply stores, by visiting their Web sites, or through mail order. Franklin Covey also has its own chain of retail stores located in upscale malls throughout America.

Personal Digital Assistants (PDAs)

Personal digital assistants (PDAs) take the paper out of planners. Palm Computing, Inc. (*www.palm.com*) is the manufacturer of the most popular handheld personal digital assistants in the world. The Palm OS (operating system) dominates almost 80 percent of the PDA market. Handspring, Inc. (*www.handspring.com*) is a manufacturer of Palm OS–compatible PDAs, called Visors. These models are designed with slightly different features than the Palm PDAs, but have the same primary built-in software (which includes a detailed scheduler and to-do list manager).

In addition to having a powerful built-in scheduling program, these units also contain a built-in contact-management program, calculator, memo pad, expense calculator/tracker, clock, and the ability to sync information with a desktop computer. The Palm product line consists of models ranging in price from around $100 to $400. While all of the Palm units have the same basic built-in applications, the more expensive units offer a smaller size, more internal memory, wireless communication capabilities, and/or better quality (in some cases, full-color) LCD screens. The Handspring Visor units are comparable in price, but offer slightly different hardware designs and functionality.

Choosing the right model for your needs is a matter of personal preference, but whichever you choose, you'll quickly discover that any of the Palm or Handspring units are extremely valuable tools to help you become more organized.

One of the best features of these powerful handheld units is that information between the Palm and any PC or Macintosh can be exchanged in seconds using one-button synchronization. Information can easily be transferred between popular time-management and contact-management programs, such as Act!, Outlook, Lotus Organizer, SideKick, and other programs. You can quickly transfer text documents, spreadsheet data, database entries, and e-mail messages, so a vast amount of information can be carried with you anytime, anywhere.

There are also over 5,000 optional programs that can be added to the Palm PDA units, making them even more powerful and versatile. One excellent resource for finding inexpensive (shareware) or totally free programs for your Palm OS–compatible PDA is available at the PalmSpot

Web site (✑www.palmspot.com/software). America Online also offers a large database of Palm OS applications (keyword: PDA).

In addition to thousands of add-on programs that allow you to customize your PDA to handle a wide range of tasks, a selection of optional accessories are also available. Wireless modems, traditional modems, GPS (global positioning system) receivers, portable digital cameras, MP3 players, full-size keyboards, and travel cases are available to enhance the power and capabilities of these units.

FACT

Franklin Covey's "What Matters Most" time-management program has been adapted into a software package designed specifically for the Palm PDAs. This program is designed to teach people how to become more organized, set goals and priorities, reduce stress in their lives, gain more confidence, and better organize critical information. For more information, call 800-236-5285 or visit the company's Web site at ✑www.franklincovey.com. Special workshops that teach the "What Matters Most" course are offered nationwide.

Time-Management Computer Software

These days, millions of people have access to desktop computers. Personal information managers (PIMs) are software packages designed to handle a wide range of time-management and organizational functions. Many of these programs offer powerful scheduling, electronic filing, and contact-management modules; integrate e-mail and fax technology; and offer the ability to link documents created in programs such as Microsoft Word or Excel. The following are some of the more popular PIMs available for personal (desktop) computers. These packages can be purchased wherever software is sold.

- **Act!** (Interact Commerce Corporation, ✑www.act.com): Available for PC, Macintosh, Palm OS, and the Internet, this is an incredibly powerful, versatile, and customizable time-management, organizational, and contact-management tool.

- **Microsoft Outlook** (Microsoft Corporation, ✍ *www.microsoft.com*):
  Available for PC-based computers running Windows 95 or higher, a
  version of this program comes with Microsoft Office as well as with
  the Microsoft Explorer Internet browser.
- **Day-Timer Organizer** (Day-Timer, Inc., ✍ *www.daytimer.com*):
  This software, available for PCs, takes the extremely popular
  Day-Timer planners and offers a digital version, which includes
  powerful time-management and contact-management applications.
- **Franklin Planner Software for Windows** (Franklin Covey,
  ✍ *www.franklincovey.com*): This software utilizes the time-management
  and organizational techniques used in the company's printed planners,
  but adds additional functionality and versatility, allowing you to easily
  synchronize with a Palm OS–compatible PDA. A free thirty-day trial
  version of the software is available from the company's Web site.

Online-Based Time-Management and Organizational Applications

A growing number of Internet-based time-management applications
can be used alone or in conjunction with a software package or PDA.
The benefit of using any of these applications is that your schedule and
data can be accessed from any device that connects to the Internet. The
majority of these online applications cost nothing to use.

- **Franklin Planner Online** (✍ *www.franklinplanner.com*): This free
  service gives you the following online applications: track personal and
  group schedules, store all of your personal and business contact
  information, view calendars, follow your financial portfolios, receive
  reminder and event notifications, receive weather forecasts and
  inspiring quotes for the day, and set up your own private discussion
  boards for your family, organization, or club. You can also use the
  Event Directory to track sports schedules, holidays, movie releases,
  and more. The information you add to the scheduling portion of this
  online application can be synchronized with a software package, such
  as Microsoft Outlook or Act! or with a PDA.

- **Interact.com** (*www.interact.com*): The power of ACT! has been added to this online-based application, which can be accessed by any computer, PDA, or cellular phone that can access the Web. This is a powerful scheduling and contact management tool that can be used alone or in conjunction with Act! or Microsoft Outlook. This application integrates scheduling, contact management, to-do list management, file management, and e-mail.
- **Day-Timer Digital** (*http://digital.daytimer.com*): Manage your scheduling, address book, to-do lists, and other information online using techniques and on-screen forms that are based on Day-Timer's proven time-management and organizational tools. View scheduling information in several different daily, weekly, and monthly formats. Data can be printed or transferred to any one of several popular PC-based software packages or to a PDA.
- **Yahoo! Calendar** (*http://calendar.yahoo.com*): This is a simple (and free) scheduling application that is part of the Yahoo! Internet search engine. You can enter, view, and store appointments and scheduling information in a variety of daily, weekly, monthly, or yearly formats.

By applying time-management and organization skills to everything you do, you'll find your life will become less stressful, as you become more productive. Taking advantage of the time-management and organization tools available to you will also help you better achieve your goals.

CHAPTER 14

Organizing Your Car

Y ou probably spend a considerable amount of time in your vehicle. This chapter offers tips and strategies for keeping everything associated with your vehicle organized, including its contents and its ongoing care and maintenance. Making a small investment of time and money every few weeks in your vehicle will greatly reduce your repair costs and keep your car running smoother.

Choosing the Right Car for Your Needs

To ensure that you get the most out of your vehicle, it's important that you choose the right car for your needs. The American Automobile Association's (AAA) Web site (✐ *http://aaa.carprices.com*) offers a free New Car Matchmaker service that is designed to help you select the right type of vehicle for you. This service divides up the primary uses of a vehicle into the following categories.

- **Family Taxi** Used for transporting kids, pets, and groceries, this type of vehicle is designed to be practical and safe, with plenty of cargo space.
- **Commuter Mobile** This type of car is affordable and reliable, because it's used primarily for the commute to and from work.
- **First Car** Inexpensive, reliable, and with few frills, this type of car is designed for first-time drivers, students, and people on a tight budget.
- **Recreational Vehicle** This type of four-wheel-drive vehicle is designed to take on a multitude of different terrains.
- **Mobile Office** If you're always on the go for work, your car should be comfortable, reliable, and perhaps luxurious (if you'll be using it to transport executives or important clients).

A wide range of automobile makes and models will easily fit each of these categories. The trick is choosing a vehicle that you can afford, one that offers safety, luxury, and cargo space, but gives decent gas mileage and is inexpensive to maintain.

After you purchase or lease a vehicle, the first thing you should do is learn how to properly care for your vehicle. Even if you don't plan to change your own oil or replace your own spark plugs, spend time reading the owner's manual for your car. You'll need to know things like how often to change the oil, what the tire pressure should be maintained at, how often you need to schedule service appointments, and how to ensure that you get the best performance out of your car.

Maintaining Your Car

In the glove compartment of your car, keep a maintenance log of all work that's done on your vehicle. Within a file (kept at home or in your car), keep copies of all maintenance and repair receipts, warrantee information, and other related records. Each time you have work done on your car, ask when the next scheduled maintenance should be done. Mark your calendar or make a notation in your planner or PDA to remind you what needs to be done and when.

Also, try to get all of your car work done at a single location, whether at your local dealership, gas station, Jiffy Lube, and so on. This will ensure that you don't overlap maintenance procedures or do maintenance that isn't necessary, such as replacing your car's air filter too often.

Use **TABLE 14-1** to track vehicle maintenance information.

TABLE 14-1

VEHICLE MAINTENANCE INFORMATION			
ITEM	CHECKED/SERVICED DATE	CHECKED/SERVICED MILEAGE	NEXT SCHEDULED CHECK/SERVICE
Air cleaner filter			
Air conditioning			
Airbags			
Alternator/generator			
Ball, joints, and steering			
Brake fluid			
Brake hoses			
Brake lights			
Catalytic converter			
Child safety seat			
Cooling system			
Distributor cap and rotor			
Drive shaft boots			
EGR valve			
Engine coolant			
Engine oil			
Engine oil filter			
Evaporative emission			

VEHICLE MAINTENANCE INFORMATION (continued)			
ITEM	CHECKED/SERVICED DATE	CHECKED/SERVICED MILEAGE	NEXT SCHEDULED CHECK/SERVICE
Exhaust system			
Fire extinguisher			
First-aid kit			
Front brake pads			
Front rotors/drums			
Fuel filter			
Fuel hoses			
Fuel system			
Headlights			
Ignition cables			
Interior light(s)			
Other drive belts			
PCV valve/breather filter			
Power steering			
Radiator hoses			
Rear brake pads			
Rear rotors/drums			
Roadside emergency supplies			
Running lights			
Seatbelts			
Spark plugs			
Timing belt			
Tire pressure			
Tire rotation			
Tire wear			
Transaxle fluid			
Transmission			
Transmission filter			
Transmission fluid			
Vehicle inspection sticker			
Water pump			
Wheels balanced			

While most cars manufactured today are capable of lasting well over 100,000 miles, to keep your car operating smoothly, you'll want to have the items in the following sections checked regularly. Visiting your car's dealership or a Jiffy Lube (✆ 800-344-6933, ✐ *www.jiffylube.com*) every 3,000 miles, for example, helps ensure that your car is maintained properly.

Air Filtration

Automobile engines draw air from outside the vehicle to assist in the burning of fuel. About 12,000 gallons of air are needed for every gallon of gasoline used. The vehicle's air filter removes dust, dirt, and other particles from the airflow before it reaches the engine. Air filters become dirty and wear out over time and should be replaced based on manufacturer's recommendations or based on inspection during a service. The positive crankcase ventilation (PCV) system draws gasoline fumes out of the engine crankcase and reburns them in the engine. This keeps the engine cleaner and reduces air pollution as well. These fumes pass through the PCV valve on their way to the engine intake manifold. PCV valves become restricted and sometimes clogged with dirt and should be inspected or replaced at regular intervals.

Battery

Don't let the battery stand in a discharged condition. Always keep the acid level between the lower and upper lines marked on the front side of the container. Keep battery tops clean, dry, and free of corrosive matter. Protect the battery from strong impacts or shocks. Clean battery terminals to prevent corrosion. Inspect the vent tube, ensuring that it's not bent, twisted, or clogged.

Brakes

The brakes should never be binding and the car should always be able to roll freely. The handbrake has a tendency to stick and cause a drag—make a special mention to have it checked at service.

Chassis Lubrication

A vehicle's suspension usually consists of numerous moving parts. Heavy grease is injected between the moving joints to prevent wear and metal-to-metal contact. Points that may need greasing include steering components, front and rear suspension parts, and drivelines.

Climate Control (Air Conditioning)

Much like your refrigerator at home, an automotive cooling system uses an evaporator, condenser, and compressor to remove heat from the air. Air from the passenger compartment is circulated past the refrigerant-filled evaporator, and then back into the passenger compartment. The refrigerant makes the hot air's moisture condense into drops of water, removing the heat from the air. Periodic service is required to keep the system running at its peak during the hot periods.

Clutch

The clutch should always be properly adjusted. A little unnoticeable slipping could be causing you to pay a few hundred dollars extra per year in fuel bills.

Engine Lubrication (Oil)

Motor oil is the lifeblood of your car. When the vehicle is running, motor oil circulates through the engine to lubricate the moving parts and reduce friction. It also cools the engine, allowing it to operate at safe temperatures. Quality motor oils contain additives that clean internal engine parts by breaking down contaminants. When the proper viscosity is used, motor oil promotes easy starting at all temperatures. Changing the oil is the best preventive maintenance for an engine. Clean motor oil will prolong the engine life and increase fuel economy. Oil should be replaced following manufacturer's recommendations, which is usually every 3,000 miles for most drivers.

Fuel Injection

With more efficiency than the older-style carburetor, fuel-injection systems control fuel use and actually spray gasoline into the engine when needed. Using fuel injection, the engine combines gas vapors and air to create a combustible air-fuel mixture. The spark plugs ignite the mixture, creating a series of small explosions that drive the wheels and make the car go. Fuel injection systems vary the richness of the mixture to suit different operating conditions. Most automotive experts recommend that fuel injection systems should be professionally cleaned once each year. When possible, use a fuel additive cleaner every three months.

Lights

Burned-out bulbs should be properly replaced to keep the vehicle operating in a safe manner. Halogen bulbs that are improperly replaced will have a shorter life and will not illuminate the road as effectively.

Radiator

The radiator system should be serviced according to the manufacturer's recommended mileage interval. This includes a system flush, fluid replacement, and a pressure test of the radiator cap.

Tire Pressure

Tires provide traction for moving a vehicle and assist the brakes in stopping. When properly inflated, they absorb bumps on the road and provide a smooth ride. To operate smoothly, it is essential that a tire and wheel be properly inflated and balanced. Tire imbalance will cause a poor ride, excessive tire wear, and steering and suspension unit wear (due to continual shaking). To compensate for variations in tire wear, most manufacturers recommend a tire rotation and balance every 6,000 miles.

Transmission

The automatic transmission assumes the task of shifting gears. Most automatic transmissions use a hydraulic system to monitor engine RPMs and select the appropriate gears. Like the engine, fluid circulates through the system to lubricate and cool the moving parts, and a replaceable filter removes impurities. Automatic transmissions fluid should be replaced following the manufacturer's recommended mileage interval. Under normal circumstances, the transmission pan gasket and filter should not need to be replaced prior to the 100,000 mile change (assuming that the transmission fluid has been changed following manufacturer's guidelines).

Windshield Wiper Blades

Wiper blades remove rain and snow from the windshield to improve visibility while driving. Over time, hot and cold temperatures and extreme weather conditions cause the wiper materials to break down. Replace them every six months or when visibility is diminished. Each time you get gas, take a moment to wipe off the blades using a rag or paper towel (and if possible, some rubbing alcohol).

Jiffy Lube spokesperson Lucille Treganowan suggests a great way to remember to check and change your coolant. "Most people change antifreeze in the fall. A good way to remember is to check and change your antifreeze when you change your clocks back from Daylight Savings Time."

Planning for Emergencies

Within your car, you should always keep a first-aid kit and roadside emergency kit. Jiffy Lube recommends that you keep the following items in your vehicle in order to deal with emergencies:

- Cat-box filler or rock salt (if you get stuck in snow or icy conditions)
- Fluorescent safety vest (to wear if you have to repair a car on the side of the road)
- Wrench

- An old scarf and an old belt for emergency hose repairs
- An old shower curtain for ground covering if you have to crawl under the car
- Battery jumper cables
- Cigarette lighter
- Blanket
- Emergency flares
- First-aid kit
- Flashlight and extra batteries
- Folding shovel or a short-handed shovel
- Funnel
- Mechanic's wire
- Pad and paper
- Plastic jug of water
- Pliers
- Rubber hammer
- Spray can of penetrating oil
- Standard screwdriver
- Wheel chock
- Work gloves

In case of an emergency, such as a car accident, flat tire, overheating, and so on, take the following precautions when dealing with the situation. First and foremost, try to remain calm. Move the car completely off the road and turn on the car's hazard lights to signal your need for help. Raise the hood and tie a white cloth on the antenna or door handle to signal to police that you're in need of assistance. Ignite emergency flares, if necessary. While waiting for help to arrive, stay inside your car with the windows up and the doors locked. Don't accept a ride home from a passing motorist. If you must repair your car at night (especially when on the side of a busy road), wear a fluorescent safety vest and never stand near the edge of the highway while checking your car. Use a cellular telephone to call the police and/or AAA (or another roadside assistance organization).

Organizing the Stuff in Your Car

You can find at least some storage space within any vehicle. How you utilize this space, whether it is the glove compartment, trunk, space under the seats, a roof rack or bike/ski rack, and so on, is up to you.

Depending on your needs, car manufacturers offer add-on accessories to make storing and transporting various items easier. Check with your car dealer for a list of genuine accessories available for the make and model of your vehicle.

Some of the most useful organization items you may consider adding to your vehicle include a coin sorter (for toll money and parking meters), a sunglass holder, cellular phone holder/hands-free kit, and CD holder. You may also want to purchase a plastic container (to be kept in your garage or in your trunk) to store car-cleaning products).

To keep your glove compartment organized, purchase a vinyl portfolio for storing maps and papers (such as your registration and vehicle owner's manual). At least once per month, sort through your glove compartment and throw away garbage and other useless items.

To avoid creating a mess in your car, invest a few dollars in a small garbage pouch that fits in between the two front seats of your car (or behind one of the seats) for easy access. Get in the habit of emptying this garbage bag daily or weekly.

CHAPTER 15

Coordinating a Move

This chapter offers detailed tips and strategies for making a move or relocation as easy as possible. You'll discover how to take a well-organized approach to packing and learn some of the secrets for making your move as stress-free as possible.

Preplanning Your Move

As soon as you decide a move or relocation is in your future, you'll quickly discover you're about to embark on a tremendous task that will take several weeks or months to properly plan and execute. There are many factors to consider when making a move. You have to find a new home, apartment, or condo; sell your old home or terminate your current lease; pack all of your belongings, arrange to move those belongings, and unpack in your new home; and inform others of your new address.

The Internet is filled with resources that can help as you research your new areas. For example, Monster.com (one of the Internet's most popular career-oriented Web sites) offers a special area that focuses on issues of interest to people who are moving or relocating. To utilize some of these free resources, point your Web browser to ✍ *www.monstermoving.com*. In addition to providing relocation information specific to more than 1,500 cities nationwide, Monstermoving.com enables users to research real estate or rental properties, check out mortgage and insurance rates, and compare quotes from moving companies or truck rental companies.

Keep in mind, however, that Monstermoving.com is just one of many online-based resources designed to help people plan their move. Another extremely comprehensive site of interest to people planning a move is Moving.com (✍ *www.moving.com*).

> As a free service to (potential) customers, U-Haul offers a video series called "Moving Made Easier." You can borrow these videos from any participating U-Haul location. Point your Web browser to ✍ *www.uhaul.com* or call ☎ 800-468-4285.

Choosing How You'll Actually Move

After you know where you're going to move and when, it's time to figure out how you'll transport your belongings from your old home to your new home. As with every other aspect of the whole moving process, here, too, you have many options. Some of the most common moving options include the following.

Full-Service Movers

These services handle just about every aspect of your physical move. This includes packing your furniture and belongings, supplying all packing materials (like boxes), loading/unloading the truck, and driving your belongings from one location to the other. For many people, this option is definitely the most appealing; however, it's also the most expensive. Many factors will contribute to determining the cost of using a full-service mover, such as the number of laborers (movers) required for the job, the size of the truck, the time of year, the distance of the move, and the amount of furniture/belongings you'll be moving.

If you'll be using the services of a full-service mover, be sure to shop around for the best price. Utilize the various online services (such as Monstermoving.com and Moving.com), plus call the various moving companies that advertise in the Yellow Pages. Ideally, you want to hire a mover that's experienced, ensured, has a top-notch reputation, and comes highly recommended by close friends or family members. Before actually hiring a mover, consider contacting the Better Business Bureau (✍ *www.bbb.org*) or Chamber of Commerce in your area to ensure the company you're about to hire is reputable. The American Moving and Storage Association (✍ *www.moving.org*) can also be contacted to find or check out a moving company. After all, you'll be trusting this company with the safety of all your personal belongings and furniture.

The biggest benefit to hiring a Full Service Mover is you'll save countless hours actually packing your belongings and furniture. In addition, assuming the people you hire are competent, you'll also be insuring that everything is packed properly (using the best possible packing materials). This will minimize the potential of something being damaged or destroyed in transit. Utilizing a full-service mover also ensures that you won't overexert yourself trying to carry your king-sized bed, a dresser, or a couch up and down stairs, for example.

A full-service mover will actually drive the moving truck from one location to the next. This means you won't have to make multiple trips, and you won't have to drive a rented truck that you're not comfortable operating. Additional services are also sometimes offered (for a fee), such as temporary storage and the moving of specialty items (such as a piano or vehicle).

While you'll want to oversee every aspect of your move if you hire a full-service mover, it'll be necessary for you to ultimately trust your belongings with total strangers. Some people consider this an invasion of their privacy; however, it's a decision you'll need to make on a personal level. By first carefully researching the moving company you hire, the majority of your concerns will likely be eliminated.

Prior to the actual move, the people hired to do the packing and loading/unloading will review every item and check it for preexisting damage. Make sure you're present for this inspection and that you agree with the assessment prior to the items being packed and moved. Be on the lookout for items that are bent, burned, broken, chipped, dented, gouged, rusted, covered in mildew, scratched, worn, torn, soiled, faded, or loose.

ALERT!

Full-service movers are registered and/or licensed by the state's department of transportation (DOT). One way to determine whether the moving company you're about to hire is legitimate is to contact the DOT in your state.

When you initially make contact with a full-service mover in order to obtain a quote or estimate, you'll be asked a series of questions. The company will want to know where you're moving from and where you are moving to. The exact number of miles between locations will need to be calculated. You'll also need to describe how much stuff will need to be packed up and moved. You may be asked how many furnished rooms are in your home, how much furniture is in each room, and how cluttered with stuff the various rooms are. From this information, the moving company will attempt to calculate the weight of your belongings and how many people will be required to pack everything up, load the truck, and execute the move.

A full-service mover will provide you with a free quote or estimate that falls into one of three categories. Make sure everything you agree to is in writing and is signed and dated by all parties. The type of quote you receive will be classified as one of the following:

- **Binding:** In this situation, the mover provides you with a guaranteed price, within a small percentage of deviation. This price is based on a complete list of items to be moved and the type of service performed. To obtain this type of quote, a representative from the moving company will have to do an in-person inspection of your home.
- **Non-binding or hourly rate:** Instead of providing an estimate relating directly to the cost of your move, in this situation, you'll be provided with little more than a detailed price list regarding what the moving company charges for each of its services. The rates should, however, be based on the movers' previous experience with jobs similar to yours. Until the move is actually complete, you won't be able to calculate exact cost of the move.
- **Not to exceed:** When a mover gives you a price, the actual final price for the move cannot exceed the estimate figure in this situation. From the mover's standpoint, the quote is binding. If the move comes in under the estimated amount, you'll pay that lesser price.

Be sure to contact several full-service movers and have them each provide you with a free estimate or quote prior to determining which company you'll hire. Keep in mind, however, that price should not be your deciding factor. The reputation of the moving company is just as important. Make sure the company you choose is insured and that the estimate you obtain is based on everything you need to be moved.

If you obtain multiple estimates and the price ranges vary greatly, make sure you ask plenty of questions to determine why one company is quoting a price that's so much higher or lower than the competition. Make sure you get all quotes and estimates in writing and that the document you receive outlines the exact services you will receive for the fee quoted.

Full-service movers use their own terminology and legalese. The American Moving and Storage Association (✎ *www.moving.org)* offers a free, seventeen-page guide called "Consumer Handbook: A Practical Guide to Interstate Moving" that explains what consumers should be aware of when hiring a mover.

In order to get the best possible quotes and ensure the availability of the moving company you choose, it's best to start making contact with moving companies at least six to eight weeks prior to your actual move date. During peak moving seasons (spring and summer), more advance notice may be required. Keep in mind that the very beginning and end of each month are also typically busy moving times, as are weekends. If you can move in the middle of a month and on a weekday, you may be able to obtain lower rates from a full-service mover.

Hiring a full-service mover to handle your packing will save you a lot of time and effort; however, pack up your own jewelry, memorabilia, family heirlooms, firearms, photo albums, items used in conjunction with your hobbies, medications, and anything else that's valuable or can't easily be replaced. You'll also want to transport these items yourself, in your own vehicle, as opposed to placing them on a moving truck.

Pick-up and Delivery Service/Self-Service Movers

If you can't afford a full service, yet you don't want to deal with all of the responsibility of a do-it-yourself move, consider hiring a pick-up and delivery service (PUD) or self-service moving company. After evaluating your needs, this type of service will determine exactly what size moving truck you need and deliver it to your home, typically at least two days prior to the actual move. It's then you're responsibility to pack up your belongings and load the truck.

After the truck is fully loaded, it's picked up by a professional driver and driven to your destination. You don't have to drive the truck, but you are responsible for your own packing and manual labor.

The price you pay for this service is based primarily on the amount of space you fill in the truck (based on the truck's weight) and the distance of your move.

For a separate and additional fee, you can also hire laborers who will help you move large pieces of furniture and heavy boxes from your home into the truck, and then assist you in unloading the truck at your destination. These laborers are typically paid by the hour. If you hire laborers who are professional movers, these people will know how to properly pack up your belongings and load them efficiently into the truck.

Do-It-Yourself Move

Hiring a full-service mover takes much of the work out of your actual move. If, however, you choose to handle the entire move yourself, it's critical that you take a well-organized approach to this process. This section offers information on how to plan your own move, efficiently and safely pack your belongings, and then execute the actual move using a truck you've rented and will be driving.

When you hire a full-service mover, for example, you'll be given one total estimate or quote for the entire move. Taking a do-it-yourself approach will mean having to price and pay for each aspect of the moving process separately. The following are some of the individual costs you'll need to consider: dollies, fuel charges, furniture pads, hotels, hourly laborers (if needed), insurance, packing materials (boxes, tape, bubble wrap, and so on), tolls, truck-mileage charges, truck-rental charge (including a deposit), and warehouse/storage fees (if necessary). Don't forget to also estimate the value of your time.

Managing and handling your own move has several pros and cons. While you'll save considerable money, you'll need to make a significantly larger investment of your time, plus have to put forth a tremendous physical effort to carry, load, and unload boxes and furniture. By handling your own move, you have total control over scheduling, but you're also taking sole responsibility for all of your belongings. If you pack something incorrectly and it breaks, it's your own fault.

Choosing Packing Materials

Handling your own move requires that you personally pack up all of your belongs. To do this, you'll need plenty of boxes, packing tape, bubble wrap, box labels, and other moving supplies. Don't cut corners when packing your personal belongings. Make sure that each item is packed in the right box size and surrounded by ample packing materials to avoid damage. When you purchase your moving supplies, be sure to stock up on boxes of various sizes. The following are additional supplies you'll probably want on-hand to make your packing easier: "fragile" labels, box labels, bubble wrap, dish dividers and boxes, markers, packing paper (not newspapers), packing tape (two inches wide), plastic mattress covers, stretch wrap, Styrofoam peanuts, and tape gun/dispenser.

Instead of having to purchase individual boxes, U-Haul offers special box kits that contain everything you need to pack up specific rooms of your home or specific types of belongings. These kits range from starter kits that include several boxes, roll of tape, bubble wrap, markers, and a utility box to a protection kit that includes a large variety of bubble wrap, foam cushion, and wraps for dishes and glasses.

The following are some other providers of moving/shipping supplies:

- AllBoxes Direct (✎ www.allboxes.com)
- Moving.com (✎ www.moving.com)
- LowCostBoxes.com (✎ www.lowcostboxes.com)
- BoxesNstuff.com (✆ 800-528-8218, ✎ www.boxesnstuff.com)
- Your local grocery store/supermarket, and your local office supply superstore (Staples, OfficeMax, and so on)

The following are basic guidelines, according to U-Haul, for choosing the best boxes for specific types of items. If you choose to purchase your boxes from another supplier, you can match up the box size with the item based on **TABLE 16-2**.

TABLE 16-2

BEST BOXES FOR HOUSEHOLD ITEMS

ITEM	BOX SIZE
Books, record albums, CDs, tools	Small box (16" × 12" × 12"/1.5 cubic feet)
Kitchen items, toys, stereo components	Medium box (18" × 18" × 16"/3.0 cubic feet)
Lamp shades, clothing, stereo speakers	Large box (18" × 18" × 24"/4.5 cubic feet)
Linens, pillows, towels, comforters	Extra-large box (24" × 18" × 24"/6.0 cubic feet)
China, dishes, antiques, fragile items	U-Haul dish pack box (18" × 18" × 28"/5.2 cubic feet)
Large plates, salad plates, saucers, bowls	U-Haul dish saver box (24" × 12" × 11"/1.85 cubic feet)
Glasses, cups, knickknacks	U-Haul glass pack box (24" × 12" × 11"/1.85 cubic feet)
TVs (up to 19"), microwave, stereo components	U-Haul TV/microwave box (24" × 24" × 20"/6.7 cubic feet)
VCRs, CD players, electronics components	U-Haul electronics box (20" × 20" × 12"/2.8 cubic feet)
Dining room chairs, large house plants, hanging cloths, draperies	U-Haul wardrobe box (24" × 21" × 48"/14.0 cubic feet)

Packing Your Items

Your home contains thousands of different items. This section helps you pack specific groups of items in the safest possible way. As you pack your belongings, select the right type of box for the right items and label every box. On the outside of the box, write its contents, what room they're from, and where the box should be unpacked in your new home. Also, number all of the boxes by room. If a box is fragile, be sure to clearly write "Handle with Care," "Glass," "Fragile," or "Heavy" on the cartons using large and bold letters. It's also an excellent strategy to keep the total weight of every box under fifty pounds. Use the following label as a guide.

```
ROOM NAME
Box ___ of ___
Destination Location
Contents
```

Don't mix and match items. When choosing what to put within each box, keep similar items together. For example, if one drawer of your dresser contains socks, underwear, and T-shirts, these should be kept together and not placed in a box with your CD collection. This strategy will save you a lot of time later when unpacking and having to locate items in your collection of boxes.

As you begin packing, do one room of your home at a time. After an entire room is packed up and all of the boxes are labeled, start working on the next room. Make sure you avoid packing essential items you'll need to use up until moving day. Pack those items separately.

When packing boxes, avoid using old newspaper to wrap your possessions and protect them against breakage. The ink from the newspaper will often rub off on the items wrapped in them. Instead, purchase plain white wrapping or packing paper from any moving-supply store. You can also use bubble wrap as a packing alternative.

Whenever possible, have a professional mover handle your packing or consult with the manufacturer of the item you're packing to ensure its safety when being transported. When moving electronics, for example, the safest transport method is always within the item's original packaging. The following are suggestions for packing common items.

Beds

Take apart the bed frames and mark the pieces. Tie or tape the bed rails together. Place all screws, bolts, nuts, and so on in a plastic bag and tape the bag to the rails. Tie large pads around the headboard and footboards. To protect the mattress, leave sheets on or cover it with a plastic mattress cover.

Books

Never pack more than thirty pounds of books in a box. Fill small spaces in each box with smaller paperbacks or other packing materials. Alternate bindings every few books to keep stacks level in each box. Seal the box and label it.

Chairs

Wrap arms of chairs with blank newsprint or bubble wrap and tape. Leave slipcovers on or cover with large sheets. Cover the entire chair with furniture pads.

Clothing

Hang clothes from closets in specially designed wardrobe boxes. Pack some clothes from bureaus in boxes or suitcases so the bureaus won't be too heavy to move. Consider using some clothes as packing material in between breakable items or to fill spaces in other boxes that contain items from bedrooms. Mark boxes "Clothing" or with the person's name. If you'll be transporting clothing by car, you can leave garments on hangers and place plastic bags over them.

Computers

First, back up all the files on your computer. Keep the back-up data separate from your computer. Your computer company may recommend that you park your hard drive, which involves using a special program (possibly called SHIP.EXE) that makes recording heads in the hard drive pull back from the data area into a safer area of the CPU. Pack your disks in a separate box, but not with or near anything magnetic. Bundle cables and wires and color-code or label them. Put each computer component (keyboard, monitor, CPU, and so on) in a plastic bag to keep dirt out during the move, and then place them inside their original boxes. Fit cables and other accessories in the sides of each box and fill with peanuts. (If you don't have the original boxes, use the double-box method: Fill the smaller of the two boxes with Styrofoam peanuts, put the bagged monitor or CPU in the middle, and fill the box the rest of the way so the component sits in the middle of the box without touching the sides. Fit in cables and accessories, close and seal that box, and then fill the bottom of the second box with peanuts, put the sealed box in, and fill all around the rest of the way with peanuts.) If you have a small printer, you can pack it with your CPU. Be sure to remove the printer cartridges. If your printer uses pins to form-feed paper, leave the paper in during the move to keep the pins in place. Mark each box "Computer" and "Fragile."

Cups, Glassware, and Knickknacks

For plates and bowls, layer bubble wrap in between each item and leave ample space at the top of the box to fill in with padding, bubble wrap, or paper. Place wadded paper or peanuts in the bottom of a box and put layers of plates or bowls on top. Then fill in the top and sides with peanuts or paper. Seal the box and mark it "Fragile." For glasses and teacups, wrap each glass or teacup in a piece of bubble wrap and tape it. Put a layer of peanuts or wadded-up paper on the bottom of the box. Place wrapped cups or glasses on top, setting them upright as if you were placing them on the table. Place a layer of cardboard and another layer of packing material on top and the sides. Keep layering in wrapped cups and peanuts until you've reached the top. Put a final layer of packing material on top. Seal the boxes and mark them "Fragile."

Dishes

Wrap each plate or dish in bubble wrap and tape shut. Also, put layers of bubble wrap in between plates. Fill the bottom of the box with peanuts or wadded paper. Fill in sides and top with peanuts and wadded paper. For larger breakable items (such as Pyrex dishes, china serving bowls, glass coffee pots, and so on) wrap these items in bubble wrap and tape shut. Put two or three smaller items or one larger item in the center of a small box filled with peanuts. Make sure you put a layer of peanuts or wadded paper between smaller items. Seal the boxes and mark them "Fragile."

Dressers and Desks

Remove all the contents from shelves. If you have drawers, you can keep some items inside if they're not too heavy. Wad up paper in the empty spaces and tape the drawers shut to keep items inside the drawers from moving or getting damaged. Fill in empty spaces with lightweight items, like pillows. Close and lock the drawers, doors, or openings. Tie the drawer handles together, if applicable. Tie large padding or old blankets around the outside.

Home Electronics

This category includes TVs, stereos, VCRs, DVD players, and so on. Make sure the electronic equipment is turned off. Check your manual to make sure there are no special moving preparations you need to make to stabilize internal components. Wrap up the cord for the TV and VCR, put the electronic equipment in the original boxes, and fill the box with peanuts. (Wrap your TV and VCR in plastic bags before immersing in peanuts so the peanuts don't get inside the machines). Put the TV and VCR in separate boxes. Seal the boxes and mark them "Fragile."

Household Plants

Place plants in large boxes, but first cover foliage in plastic bags punched with small holes for air. Don't expose the plants to excessive heat or cold.

Jewelry

Pack these items in your own suitcase that will be carried with you at all times. Each item should be individually wrapped in a jewelry pouch or protective box. Contact your local jeweler for details on how to care for specific items.

Kitchenware

Select a few pieces of essential cookware (a couple of pots, a frying pan, some cooking spoons, a spatula, and utensils) for everyone to use on the first day you're in your new home. Label this box "Kitchen—First Day" and put it near the door of the truck. Put blank newsprint (or ripped-open paper bags) between the items. Fill in spaces with wadded blank newsprint. Seal and mark the box "Kitchen."

Lamps

Take light bulbs, harps, and lampshades off each lamp. Wrap lampshades in bubble wrap and stack them in a large box with wadded paper. Wrap cords around each lamp and wrap each lamp completely in bubble wrap. An alternative is to place lamps in boxes with wadded paper.

Mirrors/Artwork

Put tape across the front of the mirror in the shape of an "X." This keeps the pieces in place if the glass breaks. Wrap the mirror in bubble wrap or blank newsprint, sealed with tape. Fill loose spaces with lightly wadded paper. Place mirror in a flat box and mark it "Fragile."

Gardening Supplies

Clean your lawnmower of all grass and debris (use a hose). Clean other lawn tools and equipment. Drain gas and oil out of the lawnmower into storage containers. Contact your local recycling company or Environmental Protection Agency office for information on disposing of the gas and oil. Tape or tie handles of rakes, shovels, and other garden tools. Pack smaller garden/lawn items in a box. Drain your garden hose down a hill, roll up, and put in a box.

Refrigerator/Freezer

Empty out the contents and defrost at least one or two days before the move. Empty the drainage pan underneath and disconnect and drain your automatic icemaker. Clean the walls, drawers, and shelves. Some refrigerators have leveling rollers, which are wheels that raise and lower each corner of the refrigerator so it is even. Check your manual to see whether you should raise or lower these rollers for the move. Wrap shelves (especially if they are glass) and tape them together. Tape down all other loose parts, including the drawers on the inside and the electrical cord and doors on the outside. Wrap the entire appliance in large pads.

Rugs and Curtains

Roll all rugs and carpets and tie the rolls closed. Fold the curtains carefully and pack them in boxes or furniture drawers where they won't be crushed.

Small Kitchen Appliances

Group kitchen appliances, like blenders and toasters, or other small household appliances, like handheld vacuums and telephones, two or three to a box. Make sure the bottom of the box is securely taped, and then pad the bottom of the box with blank newsprint (wadded up, not shredded) or with towels and sheets. Put the appliances in and pad them well all around with packing material. Place another layer of packing materials on top, seal the box, and mark it "Kitchen Appliances."

Tables

If possible, remove the legs and load the flat surface into the truck on its side edge after wrapping it in furniture pads or blankets. Otherwise, load into truck with legs facing up after wrapping the flat surface and legs in furniture pads for protection.

Washing Machines

Do all your laundry a couple of days before you're ready to move. When you're ready to pack the washer and dryer, drain all the water out of the washer. If possible, take the washer outside and tip it sideways to empty out remaining water from the water hose. Then dry the interior with a towel. Take out all accessories and fittings and put them in a plastic bag. Stuff towels between the washing machine sides and the tub to keep the tub from rotating. Fill the basket with clothes, linens, and stuffed animals (that's right, stuffed animals). Also include a box of baking soda (the kind that has air vents so you don't have to tear open the top of the box) to cut down on mildew. Tape the lid and electrical cord down, and then tie a large pad around the outside.

> If you come across furniture or clothing items that you no longer have a use for, consider donating these items to charity. Contact your local Goodwill or Salvation Army office—they may even be able to pick up the items! You may be entitled to a tax deduction for your donation, plus you'll have less stuff to carry when you move.

Choosing the Right Moving Vehicle

If you check the Yellow Pages or visit any truck rental location, you'll find a wide selection of vehicles you can rent in order to make your do-it-yourself move possible. The size of the vehicle (truck, van, or trailer) you choose should be based upon how much stuff you need to transport, how many trips between the two locations you plan to make, and the cost.

Typically, when you rent a truck or trailer, you'll pay a flat daily fee for the vehicle itself, plus mileage and insurance. You'll also be responsible for gas, tolls, and other related expenses. If you're moving a short distance, across town, for example, you may want to rent a van and make multiple trips over a period of several days. Your other option is to rent a large truck or trailer and make one trip with all of your furniture and belongings.

ALERT!

In addition to purchasing insurance on the vehicle you rent, make sure the contents you're transporting are properly insured. Most personal auto insurance policies don't cover insurance for rental trucks. Contact your insurance provider about obtaining damage-waiver protection on the rental truck in addition to cargo protection, medical costs, and life insurance.

According to U-Haul, if you'll be transporting the contents of a four-bedroom home (2,000 square feet or larger), you'll probably want to rent a truck with a 26-foot trailer. This size truck offers about 1,538 cubic feet of storage space (10' × 20' × 8'). To move the contents of a three to four bedroom home (1,600 to 2,000 square feet), you may consider a 24-foot trailer, which offers approximately 1,350 cubic feet of storage space (10' × 15' × 8'). The contents of a smaller two or three bedroom home (1,200 to 1,600 square feet) can most likely be moved using a 17-foot trailer which offers approximately 849 cubic feet of storage space (10' × 10' × 8'). To move the contents of a one bedroom home (up to 1,200 square feet), consider using a 14-foot trailer. This size truck offers up to 669 cubic feet of storage space (5' × 10' × 8').

Moving the contents of an apartment or condo will require a smaller vehicle, such as a 10-foot truck, offering up to 368 cubic feet of storage space (5' × 10' × 8'). Other options include renting a van or sport utility vehicle or a trailer that can be towed behind your existing vehicle. U-Haul, for example, rents four sizes of trailers that can be towed behind most cars, vans, trucks, or sport utility vehicles equipped with a temporary or permanent trailer hitch (also offered by U-Haul). To move the contents of three rooms, U-Haul recommends using a 6' × 12' trailer (offering 396 cubic feet of storage space). A smaller, 5' × 8' trailer (208 cubic feet of storage space) is suitable for moving two rooms worth of contents, while for smaller jobs, either a 4' × 8' or a 4' × 6' trailer may be suitable.

When renting any type of truck, van, or trailer, make sure your belongings can be locked up safely and that the storage area of the vehicle offers adequate space for everything you'll be transporting. As you pack the vehicle, remember you'll be dealing with boxes, oddly shaped furniture, and items wrapped in pads. To get these items in and out of the truck, make sure you rent or acquire some type of dolly.

After you've taken inventory of what you need to have moved and you've calculated approximately how many boxes (in addition to pieces of furniture) need to be transported, contact several truck or van rental companies to inquire about the cost of renting a vehicle. You need to be able to answer the following questions in order to obtain an accurate price quote:

- How much stuff needs to be moved
- For how long you'll need the vehicle
- The dates the vehicle is needed
- The distance (in miles) that will be traveled
- The vehicle size needed
- Whether you'll rent the vehicle one way (dropping it off at a different location than you picked it up from) or make a round trip (dropping it off at the same location)

Packing Your Truck

Hertz offers the following suggestions for organizing how you actually pack your rental truck:

- Park your truck with the loading door as close as possible to the entrance you will be loading from.

- Carefully check the instructions for operating power lift gates in the back of some trucks.
- Pull out the loading ramp of the trailer and secure it on a flat surface.
- Load one entire section of the trailer at a time, securing the contents of each section before moving on to the next one. Load the boxes or furniture in an organized fashion to maximize space and ensure the safety of what's being loaded.
- Load large items, like appliances, first. Load furniture next. Stack smaller items and boxes from floor to ceiling.
- Place the heavier boxes on bottom and lighter ones on top. Stack boxes of equal weight and size. Be sure to fill open spaces with small boxes to keep items from shifting during transit. Furniture pads, blankets, and rope can be used to fill spaces and secure items.
- The heaviest boxes, appliances, and other large items should be placed toward the front of the trailer. For example, place the refrigerator in the front right area of the trailer, and your washer and dryer in the front left.
- Slide long items, such as floor lamps, along the sides of the trailer.
- Place mattresses, sofas, and tables on their sides against the inside walls of the trailer and tie them down.
- Stand mirrors and picture frames on edge. Tie them to the truck walls or place them between mattresses. Be sure to wrap them carefully.
- Place odd-shaped items on top of the load or along the walls, if you have room.
- Be certain your load is secure, check latches, and make sure your rear or side cargo door is securely locked.
- If you've packed your dressers with the contents of the drawers intact, load the dressers against the wall (facing the outside), so the drawers don't open during transit. It's an excellent idea to tie the drawers shut.
- Pack a box containing important tools and items you'll need for unpacking, and then load this box into the truck last so it is readily accessible when you're ready to unpack.

Your Moving Schedule

One of the tricks to organizing anything is to approach it with a well-thought-out plan. This certainly holds true for planning a move. A move includes many time-consuming steps. To properly organize your move, begin the planning as far in advance as possible. Use a calendar or planner to determine what needs to be done, and then place each item into a schedule.

As you begin the planning process, answer questions like the following:

- How much time is left until moving day?
- How much time between today and moving day can you dedicate to the move?
- How much time, if any, can you take off from work?
- Which tasks must be completed on weekdays, during business hours?
- Which tasks can be completed on weekends, evenings, and/or holidays?
- Who will be able to assist you in your move?
- What is your overall moving budget?

The following sections give you a rough schedule of tasks you'll likely need to complete prior to your move to another town, along with a basic timetable for completing each task. This is a two-month plan. If you don't have two months' notice prior to your move, adjust the schedule accordingly. Keep in mind that if you hire a full-service moving company, many of these tasks will be handled for you; however, you'll need to give the moving company proper notice.

Eight Weeks Prior to Move

Contact multiple moving companies to obtain estimates and quotes. Obtain references from potential movers and do your research on these companies. (An alternative is to reserve a truck from a rental company, such as U-Haul or Hertz.) Calculate potential moving expenses—contact your employer and/or the IRS to find out about tax deductions and possible assistance with moving expenses. If necessary, apply for financial assistance to pay for the move. Create a detailed schedule for your move.

Seven Weeks Prior to Move

Create an inventory of everything you own (furniture, electronics, belongings, clothing, and so on). From this inventory, determine what will be packed by the movers and what you'll handle yourself. Donate or throw away items that you won't be moving to your new home. Consider holding a garage sale (see Chapter 1) right away. Contact your insurance company to obtain insurance for the move and for your new residence. Begin dealing with change-of-address issues with licenses, insurance companies, credit card companies, schools, and so on. Order packing and shipping supplies (boxes, packing materials, tape, and so on) based on what you calculate your needs to be. Contact the current and new schools your child attends and will be attending and arrange for the transfer of records. Cancel or change your health club, video store, and/or country club memberships.

Six Weeks Prior to Move

Begin packing nonessential items. Confirm moving dates with the moving company you hire and complete all related paperwork. Contact your current landlord to discuss your departure.

Five Weeks Prior to Move

Cancel local deliveries, such as newspapers, milk, and so on. Continue packing your personal and nonessential items. Get all of your financial records and personal paperwork in order. Register your pets in the city/town you'll be living in. Create a list of friends, relatives, businesses, and so on, you need to provide your new address to.

Four Weeks Prior to Move

Complete change-of-address forms with the post office and IRS. Close charge accounts with local merchants. Make airline and hotel reservations relating to your move. If necessary, reserve temporary storage space for your belongings. Notify your insurance companies of your move. Contact all utilities (gas, electric, telephone, water, trash removal, cable TV, propane, and so on) and inform them of your move.

Three Weeks Prior to Move

Arrange for a babysitter to watch your kids on moving day. Continue sorting and packing all belongings. Return library books and videos, pick up dry-cleaning, and so on.

Two Weeks Prior to Move

Contact utility companies for your new residence and arrange for service. Make final packing decisions and make sure you have all of the right packing materials. Clean your home. Transfer all of your finances and bank accounts to branches near your new residence. Empty your safety deposit box at the local bank. Transfer all prescriptions to a pharmacy near your new residence.

One Week Prior to Move

Finish packing. Reconfirm the date with your moving company. Pack personal belongings in suitcases that will travel with you. Make sure all cartons are properly labeled and inventoried. Empty and defrost your refrigerator. Pack up all appliances (washer, dryer, freezer, stove, dishwasher, and so on).

Moving Day

Pack up your bed and last-minute items. Finish packing your unload-first box of essentials you'll need right away in your new home. Confirm the delivery date/time with the movers. Oversee all of the movers' actions. Review all moving-related paperwork, including your inventory sheets. Pack your valuables in your car. Turn off lights and heating or air conditioning, and lock up your home. Confine your pets and keep them out of the mover's way. During the move, be considerate of your neighbors. Try to avoid making too much noise early in the morning or late at night.

Move-In Day

Arrive at your new home before the moving company. Prepare the house to be moved into. Unpack your unload-first boxes from the moving truck. Inventory all items, furniture, and boxes as they're unloaded from the truck and place them in the appropriate rooms. Make sure all appliances are working properly after they're reconnected in your new home. Have payment ready for the moving company after the unloading is complete (you may need a certified check). Have a tool kit on-hand to fix and/or put together pieces of furniture or appliances in your new home. Start unpacking and enjoying your new home!

Announcing Your Move

Before your actual move (about thirty days prior to moving day), after you know exactly when and where you'll be moving to, you'll want to start notifying people about your move. First, contact the U.S. post office and complete a change-of-address form. You can do this in person at any post office or via the Internet by pointing your Web browser to ✑ *www.usps.com/moversnet.* Until people know about your move, the post office will either hold your mail for you or forward it to your new address.

First-Class, Priority, and Express Mail will all be forwarded for twelve months at no charge. Periodicals (newspapers and magazines) will be forwarded for sixty days at no charge. Standard mail (circulars, books, catalogs, and advertising mail weighing less than sixteen ounces) will not be forwarded unless requested by the mailer. Packages will be forwarded locally for twelve months at no charge. Forwarding charges are paid by the recipient if you move outside the local area. (Forwarding charges apply to packages weighing sixteen ounces or more that were not mailed as Priority Mail.)

In addition to the post office, it's critical that you inform the IRS of your new address. To do this, call ☎ 800-829-3676 or visit the IRS's Web site at ✑ *www.irs.ustreas.gov/forms_pubs/forms.html* to obtain an official change-of-address form.

How can I quickly notify people of my new address?
To make the process of telling people you've moved easier, a company called ChangeAddress.com (☎ 212-785-9745, ✉ *www.changeaddress.com*) offers an inexpensive ($9.95), online-based service for people in the process of moving. This is the fastest, easiest, most convenient, and secure way to notify businesses and institutions of your new address when you move.

CHAPTER 16

Staying Organized

After you've begun to organize your home and life, you must maintain your organizational efforts or risk ending up right back where you started. The tips in this chapter, therefore, show you how to stay organized as you go forward. In order to keep your momentum going, adopt these strategies for keeping your home the way you want it.

Keep Getting Rid of Clutter

The chapters in this book show you how to identify and deal with clutter in various areas of your home. To continue your organizational efforts, periodically go through your entire home and distinguish between the belongings you need or want and items that can be thrown away, donated, filed, or put into storage. If an item hasn't been used in several months or years and has no importance or sentimental value, get rid of it!

Change Your Behavior

Figure out what's causing the clutter in your home and take steps to eliminate the mess. For example, when you get undressed at night, instead of throwing your dirty clothing on the floor (where they will pile up), place the clothes directly in a laundry hamper. Remember, clutter comes in many different forms. After you've identified the cluttered areas of your home, figure out the causes and address the underlying issues.

Make a Proper Place for Everything

After you decide where something belongs, you'll have little trouble finding it, so establish a home for everything in your house. As soon as you're done using the tool, piece of paper, or any other object, make sure you put it back in its proper place. Adopting this practice not only helps you stay organized, it also greatly reduces the amount of time you will spend cleaning your home in the future.

Keep Similar Items Together

When organizing a closet, storage bin, cabinet, dresser drawer, or medicine cabinet, empty out the contents of what you're organizing. Get rid of the clutter and anything that's no longer wanted or needed. Then group similar items together. Finally, put your items back in an organized manner, giving each item or group of items a proper place.

If you're reorganizing your dresser drawer, for example, consider using drawer dividers to keep items separated from each other. In a closet that's equipped with two hanging rods, use one rod for your everyday wardrobe and the other for formal wear or off-season clothing.

Take Advantage of Organizational Tools and Gadgets

If you look through mail-order catalogs (see Appendix 1), you'll find an abundance of organizational tools and useful gadgets on the market. These tools help you keep your belongings organized. When organizing your closet, for example, take advantage of specialty hangers, baskets, a shoe rack, a belt rack, and a jewelry organizer to maximize storage space. See Chapter 2 for more information on ways to clear out your closets.

Take Advantage of Every Possible Storage Space

You can, for example, store items under your bed. You can also install shelving above doorways and near the ceilings of a room and add hooks, racks, or compartments to the back of doorways (inside closets, for example). Areas such as your attic, garage, and basement also offer additional storage opportunities.

Utilize Technology to Stay Organized

A personal digital assistant (PDA), such as those from Palm and Handspring, are ideal for keeping track of your schedule and to-do lists. These handheld units can also store thousands of addresses and phone numbers and complete a wide range of other tasks. If you're someone who tends to write messages for yourself on many different pieces of scrap paper that wind up stuffed in your pockets or strewn around your home, a PDA allows you to keep this information in one place for easy reference.

Every Morning, Create a Detailed To-Do List

The list should include your personal and work-related objectives for the day. This list may include errands, meetings, appointments, phone calls to make, and e-mails to write. It should also include tasks that bring you closer to achieving your personal, professional, and financial long-term goals (see Chapter 13). After you create your to-do list, prioritize each task and input the appropriate information into your personal planner, PDA, or other scheduling tool. Ideally, you want to plan out as much of your day as possible, leaving time to deal with unexpected events.

Your to-do list can also keep your household organized and clean. For example, when you're about to embark on a massive clean-up or reorganization project, writing out a to-do list helps you clearly define your objectives, create a time frame, and take a well-thought-out approach to your efforts.

Create a Task List

For the day-to-day tasks that are necessary to run your home and keep it clean, follow these basic steps:

1. Create a list of what tasks you need to do (for example: cleaning the bathroom, doing laundry, changing bed linens, vacuuming, washing the kitchen floor, going to the dry cleaner, mowing the lawn, and so on).
2. Determine how often each of these tasks needs to be done.
3. Using a calendar, PDA, scheduler, or personal planner, create a schedule for accomplishing these tasks one at a time. For example, cleaning the bathroom may take thirty minutes after work on Mondays. Trips to the dry cleaner can be done on Tuesdays and Thursdays on the way to work or when dropping your kids off at soccer practice.

After you create a to-do list for keeping your home clean and organized, stick to it so that it becomes part of your ongoing routine.

Work Toward Achieving Your Goals

After you set long-term goals for yourself—whether they're personal, professional, or financial—determine exactly what it will take to achieve each goal. Divide up each long-term goal into a series of short-term or medium-term goals that are more easily achievable. After you create a series of smaller goals, develop a timeline and set specific deadlines. Each time you accomplish one of these smaller goals, you'll be that much closer to achieving one of your long-term goals.

In your mind, you want to know clearly what you're working toward, how much time you have to achieve your objectives, and what benefits achieving the goal brings. In your mind, you need to know why you're trying to achieve a specific objective and understand what positive benefits the outcome will have for you.

APPENDIX 1
Resources

Throughout this book, you'll find phone numbers and Web sites for a variety of organizational products, services, and information. All of that information is compiled here in a handy cheat sheet.

Organizational Consultants

California Closets   ✆ 888-336-9709   ✍ *www.calclosets.com*
Closet Factory   ✆ 800-692-5673   ✍ *www.closet-factory.com*
National Association of Professional Organizers   ✍ *www.napo.net*
Organization by Design   ✆ 800-578-3770   ✍ *www.dressingwell.com*
Storage by Design   ✆ 877-7720-2313   ✍ *www.customclosets.com*
Techline   ✆ 800-356-8400   ✍ *www.techlineusa.com*

Mail-Order and Internet Companies That Carry Organizational Products

A Better Hanger Company   ✍ *www.abetterhanger.com*
Container World, Inc.   ✍ *www.storagesources.com*
Everything 4 Baby   ✍ *http://everything4baby.freeyellow.com*
Frontgate   ✆ 800-626-6488   ✍ *www.frontgate.com*
HomeStore.com   ✍ *www.homestore.com*
Ikea   ✍ *www.ikea-usa.com*
Lillian Vernon   ✆ 800-505-2250   ✍ *www.lillianvernon.com*
Organize Everything   ✍ *www.organize-everything.com*
Stacks and Stacks   ✆ 877-278-2257   ✍ *www.stacksandstacks.com*
The Container Store   ✆ 800-733-3532   ✍ *www.containerstore.com*
The Hold Everything Catalog   ✆ 800-421-2264
The Sharper Image   ✆ 800-344-4444   ✍ *www.sharperimage.com*

Unique Organizational Products

AeroBed   ✍ *www.aerobed.com/beds.html*
APM Shelf Store   ✍ *www.shelvesonline.com*
Basis Design   ✍ *www.basisdesign.com*
Brookstone's Hard-to-Find Tools Catalog   ✆ 800-926-7000   ✍ *www.brookstone.com*
Clothes Hangers Online   ✆ 800-600-9817   ✍ *http://hangersonline.store.yahoo.com*
Diaper Genie from Playtex   ✆ 800-843-6430   ✍ *www.playtexbaby.com/diapergenie.htm*
Double Hang   ✍ *www.organize-everything.com*   ✍ *doublehang.html*

Dura ✍ *www.thefittedgarage.com/index.html*

Garage Storage Cabinets ✍ *www.gsc-cabinets.com*

Gladware ✍ *www.gladware.com*

Hangco ✍ *www.trendmarketing.net*

Hanger Handler ✆ 888-266-8246 ✍ *www.hangerhandler.com*

Hinge-It Valet ✍ *www.organize-everything.com/hinitinval1.html*

InterMetro ✍ *www.metro.com* ✍ *consumer/index.cfm*

Jam-It Natural Wood Valet ✍ *www.organize-everything.com/jamitslackrack.html*

Ladder Pros ✍ *www.ladderpros.com/attic.htm*

Organize-It ✍ *www.organizes-it.com/garage.htm*

Restoration Hardware ✍ *www.restorationhardware.com*

Round-A-Belt Organizer ✍ *www.netwurx.net/~organize*

Rubbermaid ✍ *www.rubbermaid.com*

Shelving Direct ✍ *www.shelving-direct.com*

Solutions ✆ 800-342-9988 ✍ *www.solutionscatalog.com*

Space Bag ✆ 800-469-9044 ✍ *www.spacebag.com*

Stack-On ✍ *www.stack-on.com/tool_and_hardware/garage*

Stacks and Stacks HomeWares ✍ *http://shop.yahoo.com/stacks/6123.html*

StorageBord ✍ *www.isobordenterprises.com/p_storagebord.htm*

StoreWall ✆ 414-224-0878 ✍ *www.storewall.com/residential/garage.htm*

The Closet Carousel System ✆ 800-896-0902 ✍ *http://closets.net//frm2.htm*

Tupperware ✍ *www.tupperware.com*

Wood Logic Storage Products ✆ 800-303-4393 ✍ *www.woodlogic.com/products.htm*

Woodstore ✍ *http://woodstore.woodmall.com/homplan.html*

Furniture

Amotek ✆ 800-242-4777 ✍ *www.amotek.com/product.html*

Armoires & More ✍ *www.armoirestore.com*

BackSaver Products Company ✆ 800-251-2225

Bhome.com ✆ 612-861-0102 ✍ *www.bhome.com*

Bunk Beds Plus ✆ 219-672-3491 ✍ *www.bunkbedsplus.com*

Bunks 'n' Stuff ✆ 800-355-1997 ✍ *www.bunksnstuff.com*

Ergomax Seating System ✆ 800-332-5635 ✍ *www.americanergonomics.com*

Ethan Allen ✍ *www.ethanallen.com*

Herman Miller for the Home ✆ 800-646-4400 🖫 *www.hmstore.com* or
🖫 *www.hermanmiller.com*

Home Office Furniture System 🖫 *www.hofs.com*

Lux Company, Inc. ✆ 800-334-7426 🖫 *www.luxcompany.com*

Relax the Back ✆ 800-596-2225

Reliable Home Office ✆ 800-869-6000

The Great American Bunk Bed Company ✆ 866-4US-BUNK
🖫 *www.greatamericanbunkbed.com*

Kitchen/Dining Products, Services, and Information

American Wine Essentials, Inc. 🖫 *www.amwe-store.com*

Artisans on Web 🖫 *www.aoweb.com*

Cocktail Wireless 🖫 *http://165.254.148.22/cocktails.htm*

CookBook 🖫 *www.dovcom.com/cookbook.html*

Factory Direct Table Pad Co. ✆ 800-737-4194 🖫 *www.tablepads.com*

Gourmet Spot 🖫 *www.gourmetspot.com/kitchendesign.htm*

International Association of Dinnerware Matchers 🖫 *www.iadm.com*

International Wine Accessories 🖫 *www.iwawine.com*

iWANTaNewKITCHEN.com 🖫 *www.iwantanewkitchen.com*

Kitchen & Bath Design News 🖫 *www.kbdn.net*

Kitchen Source 🖫 *www.kitchensource.com*

Kitchen, Etc. ✆ 800-232-4070 🖫 *www.kitchenetc.com*

Kitchen.net 🖫 *www.kitchen-bath.com*

Kitchens.com ✆ 312-857-1600 🖫 *www.kitchens.com*

KitchenWeb 🖫 *www.kitchenweb.com*

MyShoppingCart 🖫 *www.palmsoftnet.com/myshopc/index.htm*

Old China Patterns Limited ✆ 800-663-4533 🖫 *www.chinapatterns.com/pouches.html*

Oneida, Ltd. 🖫 *www.oneida.com*

Set Your Table: Discontinued Tableware Dealers Directory
🖫 *www.setyourtable.com*

Western Silver ☎800-850-3579 ✍*www.westernsilver.com/flatware_guide.html*
Williams-Sonoma ☎800-541-2233 ✍*www.williams-sonoma.com*
Wine Enthusiast ✍*www.wineenthusiast.com*
Wine Lover's Page ✍*www.wineloverspage.com/pocketwinelist* or
   www.PocketWineList.com
Wine Racks USA ✍*www.wineracksusa.com*

Coupons

Cents Off ✍*www.CentsOff.com*
eCoupons ✍*www.eCoupons.com*
Refund Sweepers ✍*www.refundsweepers.com/foodstores.shtml*
SmartSource ✍*www.smartsource.com*
ValuPage ✍*www.supermarkets.com*

Laundry Products and Information

Amana ✍*www.amana.com*
GE ✍*www.geappliances.com/shop/prdct/wsh_dry*
Kenmore ✍*www.kenmore.com/sr/homepages/sears_homepage.jsp*
KitchenAid ✍*www.kitchenaid.com*
Maytag ✍*www.maytag.com*
What's the Best, Inc. ✍*www.whatsthebest-washer.com*
Whirlpool ✍*www.whirlpool.com*

Cleaning Products

Cheer ☎800-63-CHEER ✍*www.cheer.com*
Febreze ☎800-308-3279 ✍*www.febreze.com*
OxiClean ☎800-781-7529 ✍*www.greatcleaners.com*
Tarn-X from Jelmar ☎800-323-5497 ✍*www.jelmar.com*
Tide ☎800-879-8433 ✍*www.tide.com*
Wisk ☎800-ASK-WISK ✍*www.wisk.com*

Lighting Products

American Environmental Products ☎ 800-339-9572 ✍ *www.sunalite.com*
eLights ✍ *www.elights.com/closet.html*
Full Spectrum Solutions ✍ *www.fullspectrumsolutions.com*
Lighting Superstore ✍ *www.elights.com*
The American Lighting Association ☎ 800-274-4484

Landscape and Garage Products and Information

Backyard America ☎ 703-392-5152 ✍ *www.backyardamerica.com/sheds.htm*
Cody Mercantile ☎ 800-443-4934 ✍ *www.codymercantile.com*
Decks USA ☎ 330-788-7882 ✍ *www.decksusa.com*
Fiskars ✍ *www.fiskars.com*
Gardener's Supply Company ☎ 800-427-3363 ✍ *www.gardeners.com*
Garrett Wade Tool Catalog ☎ 800-221-2942 ✍ *www.garrettwade.com*
Home & Garden Television ✍ *www.hgtv.com*
Outdoor Décor ✍ *www.outdoordecor.com*
Rubbermaid ✍ *www.rubbermaid.com*
THE Directory ✍ *www.gardenbuildings.com*
The Harriet Carter Garden Tool Organizer ☎ 800-377-7878 ✍ *www.hcgifts.com/gartoolor.html*
The Plant Factory ☎ 334-653-7043 ✍ *http://theplantfactory.com/accessories-index.html*
The Step2 Company ☎ 800-347-8372
Tidy Garage ☎ 888-4-GARAGE ✍ *www.tidygarage.com/surelock.html*

Safety Products and Information

FDA's Food Information and Seafood Hotline ☎ 800-332-4010
Fight Bac! ✍ *www.fightbac.org*
Juvenile Products Manufacturers' Association ✍ *www.jpma.org*
National Safe Kids Campaign ✍ *www.safekids.org*
Safety 1st Childcare Products ☎ 800-723-3065 ✍ *www.safety1st.com*

The International Association of Child Safety ☎ 888-677-IACS
U.S. Consumer Product Safety Commission ☎ 800-638-2772 🖳 *www.cpsc.gov*
USDA's Meat and Poultry Hotline ☎ 800-535-4555

Moving, Storage, and Change-of-Address Resources

AllBoxes Direct 🖳 *www.allboxes.com*
boxes N stuff.com ☎ 800-528-8218 🖳 *www.boxesnstuff.com*
ChangeAddress.com ☎ 212-785-9745 🖳 *www.changeaddress.com*
Hertz ☎ 888-999-5500 🖳 *www.hertztrucks.com*
IRS 🖳 *www.irs.ustreas.gov/forms_pubs/forms.html*
LowCostBoxes.com 🖳 *www.lowcostboxes.com*
Migson Public Storage ☎ 877-564-4766 🖳 *www.migsonstorage.com*
Moving.com 🖳 *www.moving.com*
Public Storage ☎ 800-44STORE 🖳 *www.publicstorage.com*
Ryder Truck Rental ☎ 800-GO-RYDER 🖳 *www.yellowtruck.com*
Self Storage Net 🖳 *www.selfstorage.net*
Storage USA ☎ 800-STOR-USA 🖳 *www.sus.com*
The American Moving and Storage Association 🖳 *www.moving.org*
U.S. Post Office 🖳 *www.usps.com/moversnet*
U-Haul ☎ 800-468-4285 🖳 *www.uhaul.com*

Travel Information

AAA Travel Services ☎ 800-222-7448
America Online Travel 🖳 Keyword: travel
American Express Travel ☎ 800-346-3607 🖳 *www.itn.net*
Expedia.com 🖳 *www.expedia.com*
MapQuest 🖳 *www.mapquest.com*
Preview Travel 🖳 *www.previewtravel.com*
Priceline.com 🖳 *www.priceline.com*
Travelocity.com 🖳 *www.travelocity.com*
Yahoo! Travel 🖳 *http://travel.yahoo.com*

Automotive Information

American Automobile Association (AAA) ✑ *http://aaa.carprices.com*
AutoAccessory.com ✆ 888-734-8734 ✑ *www.autoaccessory.com*
AutoAnything.com ✆ 800-874-8888 ✑ *www.autoanything.com*
AutoSport ✆ 800-726-1199 ✑ *www.autosportcatalog.com*
Car Toys ✆ 800-997-3644 ✑ *www.cartoys.com*
Cardogz eLogBook ✑ *www.cardogz.com/log/AutoMaintLog.mv*
Jiffy Lube ✆ 800-344-6933 ✑ *www.jiffylube.com*

Weather Information

Internet Weather Source ✑ *http://weather.noaa.gov*
The Weather Channel ✑ *www.weather.com*
USA Today Weather ✑ *www.usatoday.com/weather/wfront.htm*
Yahoo! Weather ✑ *http://weather.yahoo.com*

Computer and Internet-Based Programs

Act! ✑ *www.act.com*
Adobe Acrobat ✑ *www.adobe.com*
Interact.com ✑ *www.interact.com*
Microsoft Outlook ✑ *www.microsoft.com*
PalmSpot ✑ *www.palmspot.com/software*
SimplyPostage ✑ *www.SimplyPostage.com*
Yahoo! Calendar ✑ *http://calendar.yahoo.com*

Electronic Equipment

Brother P-Touch system ✑ *www.brother.com/usa/label/label_cntr.html*
Handspring ✑ *www.handspring.com*
Hello Direct ✑ *www.hello-direct.com*
Palm ✑ *www.palm.com*
Sprint PCS ✆ 800-480-4PCS ✑ *www.sprintpcs.com*
The Rise & Shine Natural Alarm Clock ✆ 800-786-6850

Time-Management Products

Day-Timer, Inc. ☏ 800-225-5005 ✎ *www.daytimer.com*
Franklin Covey ☏ 800-819-1812 ✎ *www.franklincovey.com*

Books on Tape

Audio-Tech Business Book Summaries ☏ 800-776-1910 ✎ *www.audiotech.com*
Nightingale-Conant ☏ 800-647-9198 ✎ *www.nightingale.com*
Simon & Schuster Audio ✎ *www.simonsays.com/audio*

Photo and Scrapbook Resources

AlbumSource.com ☏ 866-772-7200 ✎ *www.albumsource.com*
Graceful Bee NewBees ✎ *http://gracefulbee.com/newbees/organization.html*
Scrapbook Tips.com ✎ *www.scrapbook-tips.com/OurGurus.asp*
Scrapbooking.com ✎ *http://scrapbooking.com*

Charitable Organizations

Career Gear ☏ 212-273-1194 ✎ *www.careergear.com*
Dress for Success ☏ 212-545-DSNY ✎ *www.dressforsuccess.org*
Goodwill Industries ☏ 800-664-6577 ✎ *www.goodwill.org*
The Salvation Army ☏ 845-620-7200 ✎ *www.salvationarmy.org*
The Women's Alliance ☏ 305-642-7600 ✎ *www.thewomensalliance.org*
Volunteers of America ☏ 800-899-0089 ✎ *www.volunteersofamerica.org*

Feng Shui

American Feng Shui Institute ☏ 626-571-2757 ✎ *www.amfengshui.com*
Feng Shui Help.com ✎ *www.fengshuihelp.com*
The Practitioner Referral List ✎ *www.fengshuiguild.com/practitioners.htm*

APPENDIX 2
Feng Shui

Feng shui (pronounced "fung shway"), is the study of energy and how it affects people positively or negatively. By altering your surroundings using the principles of feng shui, you have the ability to make your living and work environments more attuned to the life forces that surround you.

Organizing with Feng Shui

One of the first steps in creating a living environment that's based on the principles of feng shui is to clear the clutter and debris from your home and personal life. Clutter is trapped energy that has far-reaching effects physically, mentally, emotionally, and spiritually. It's believed that all forms of household clutter can also work to keep you in the past, congest your body, and make you feel lethargic and fatigued. Thus simply by cleaning up and eliminating the clutter in your home, if you believe in what feng shui offers, you can begin the process of transforming your life by releasing negative emotions, generating positive energy, and allowing yourself to create space in your life for the things you most want to achieve.

In an effort to rid yourself of clutter and tap the positive energies around you that exist within your home, feng shui consultants and practitioners recommend that you make a concerted effort to fix and repair everything in your home and garden that's broken, and clean whatever is dirty. For example, windows are the eyes of the Chi (the life force energy) and affect your clarity. Broken or dirty windows in your home can create conflict with your inner child. Likewise, broken or blocked doors block the voice of the adult. Following this belief system, your home's plumbing represents your own body's digestive system, so it's a good feng shui strategy to repair leaky faucets and clogged drains. Likewise, the electrical system in your home corresponds to your neurological system.

When designing, decorating, and organizing your home based upon the principles of feng shui, the main entrance represents the home's mouth of the Chi. Symbolically, this is how the entire Chi enters your home, so you want to keep your home's main entrance clear, open, and clutter-free. The front door needs to be large and easily accessible. Ideally, you want your home to be level to or higher than the street or sidewalk. The path to the front door should also be kept clear and even, with well-trimmed hedges and good lighting. Placing a fountain in front of your home is an excellent way to attract flowing money energy and help conduct it into your home. The water element is the universal symbol for wealth and prosperity.

Your home, after all, should be your safe haven, where you can exist in a state of peace. When you're at home, you should be able to relax, open your mind, and bask in the life force and positive energy around you.

Hiring a Feng Shui Consultant or Practitioner

To obtain a full understanding of the principles and theories of feng shui takes years of training and study. If you believe in what feng shui offers and want to understand how to properly design and organize your home around these age-old ideas and beliefs, hire a feng shui consultant or practitioner and have this person visit your home to offer guidance.

Unless you're building a home from scratch, chances are the structure of your home can't be easily changed. For example, you probably can't relocate the master bedroom or change the direction your home actually faces. Thus, feng shui offers cures that involve the use of symbolic items, color, and the positioning of furniture, for example, to help make your home align properly with the beliefs and principles behind feng shui. An expert will help you pinpoint and implement the cures needed for your home.

The very best way to find a feng shui expert in your community is through a referral from someone you know and trust. You may want to consult with the store manager of a New Age bookstore in your community, for example. Another resource for referrals is the Practitioner Referral List (✐ *www.fengshuiguild.com/practitioners.htm*), a Web site that acts as is a clearinghouse for practitioner referrals. This list is compiled and maintained by the Feng Shui Guild, an organization formed to bring together and support the international feng shui community. This group's purpose is to promote the use, practice, and teaching of feng shui.

According to the Feng Shui Guild, when you hire a consultant or practitioner to come into your home, you can expect to receive guidance in the following areas:

- Furniture placement
- Methods to create or enhance specific areas of your life
- The best rooms in a home or office for certain practices
- Ideas for using colors for a desired effect
- Optimizing outdoor environmental designs
- Creating a sanctuary or a space for peace and meditation within your home

- Correct positioning of home office elements including employees, guests, furniture, and so on
- Specific ideas for improving the entrance to your home to optimize the flow of Chi
- The best places for feng shui cures, such as wind chimes, mirrors, lights, fountains, mobiles, and candles

The price of an in-home consultation varies, so when making your appointment, determine what the appointment will include and agree on a fee.

Finding Out More About Feng Shui

While an expert who visits your home for a consultation can answer your questions and offer guidance, first do your own research to develop a basic understanding of the principles behind feng shui.

The Feng Shui Help.com Web site (*www.fengshuihelp.com*) provides free advice to people who want to achieve balance and harmony in their lives using this ancient Chinese art of placement. This Web site offers detailed advice for designing and decorating each area of your home.

Countless books, videos, and courses can also teach you more about feng shui. One excellent book is *The Everything® Feng Shui Book* by Katina Z. Jones (Adams Media Corporation).

Another way to find out more about feng shui is to participate in online courses created and administered by the American Feng Shui Institute (626-571-2757, *www.amfengshui.com*). Founded in 1991, the American Feng Shui Institute is the only center in the West that's dedicated to teaching the practice of feng shui as a scientific discipline. The online classes offered by the institute are self-paced study modules. They are segmented into four one-week lessons that lead you at your own pace. Each online class offered is a combination of self-study and instructor-led discussions through an online bulletin board. Each weekly module includes a self-test, and each class is finished with a final exam.

FACT

When translated into English, feng shui means "the way of wind and water" or "the natural forces of the universe." The ancient Chinese believed in and lived their lives by these natural forces. Europeans call the study of these forces "geomancy," and Hawaiians and the Native Americans practice their own form of feng shui. Thus the fundamental concepts behind feng shui have been studied throughout history by people around the world.

Understanding Ten Basic Principles of Feng Shui

As you work through each room or area of your home, keep these ten guidelines in mind.

Clear the Clutter
Besides taking up physical space, clutter can block new opportunities coming into your life and keep you firmly anchored in the past. Clearing out your home will make space for your future.

Keep the Front Entrance of Your Home Well-Maintained
According to feng shui, your front door is the entry point of all energy flowing into your home. The entrance area needs to be well defined and clean.

Allow Energy to Flow Freely
Energy is supposed to flow throughout your home in order to usher in good health and harmony. Avoid inhibiting or blocking this flow with clutter or awkwardly positioned furniture.

Contain the Energy
Energy needs to be able to flow around the house in order to nourish you. Avoid situations that allow the energy to simply rush through the house and quickly escape. The back door should not be

directly aligned with the front door, for example. If this is the case, one cure is to hang wind chimes between the two doors in order to moderate and redirect the flow of positive energy.

Make Sure Everything Works
Stay on top of maintenance. Fix items quickly as they break and keep your surroundings clean. It's believed that every job left half done somehow reflects an aspect of your life that is incomplete and needs attention.

Check Out Your Home for Negative Energies
Distortions in the electro-magnetic fields of the earth can impact your health and mental clarity over a period of time. If this is the situation in your home, seek out expert help to rebalance the energy of your home.

Be Aware of the Images and Symbols in Your Home
Your choice of art, for example, is considered a message from your subconscious. Look around you to determine what you have been unwittingly projecting into your space. Consider changing your art to reflect what you want from your future.

Create a Quiet Sanctuary Within Your Bedroom
Your bedroom needs to be a haven of peace and calmness in order to promote restful sleep each and every night. Avoid using this room for any stressful purpose, such as working.

Make the Kitchen a Center of Calmness
The kitchen is often considered the hub of family life. Make this room of your home a contained area where you can prepare the food. The quality of calmness you create in this room will be imbued into the food you eat.

Love Your Home and It Will Love You
Think of your home as a living entity. If you care for it properly, it will care for you by making you feel supported, safe, and nourished. Using the principles of feng shui, you have the power to easily change your home. By making certain changes, you can transform your life for the better.

Index